OTHER HUMAN BEINGS

Other Human Beings

David Cockburn

Lecturer in Philosophy
Saint David's University College, University of Wales

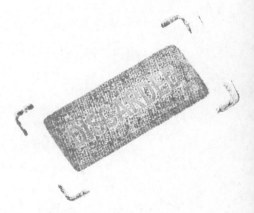

St. Martin's Press　　New York

First published in the United States of America in 1990

Printed in Singapore

ISBN 0–312–04846–7

Library of Congress Cataloging-in-Publication Data
Cockburn, David, 1949–
Other human beings/ David Cockburn.
p.   cm.
Includes bibliographical references.
ISBN 0–312–04846–7
1. Philosophical anthropology.   2. Interpersonal relations.
I. Title.
BD450.C585   1990
128 – dc20   90–33622
                                                              CIP

Contents

Acknowledgements

A limited amount of material in Chapter 9 appeared in my paper 'Commitment to Persons' which is included in D. Z. Phillips and Peter Winch (eds), *Wittgenstein: Attention to Particulars* (Macmillan, 1989). I am grateful to the editors for permission to use this material here.

I am extremely grateful to a number of people for help of various kinds. My debt to Peter Winch – both to his writings and to his personal help and encouragement – is very much greater than my explicit references to his work would suggest. Discussions with students and colleagues here at Lampeter over a number of years have played an important role in the development of my thought about these issues. Earlier versions of some of the material in Part III were read at University College of Swansea and at a meeting of the Society for the Philosophy of Education held at Gregynog in July 1988. I must thank all of those who contributed to the helpful discussions at those meetings. I owe special thanks to Michael McGhee and Prabodh Parikh who organised an international gathering of philosophers at Mahabaleshwar, India, in January 1987, and to the Mahesh Bhogilal Memorial Trust who sponsored the meeting; I must also acknowledge financial support from the Pantyfedwen Fund which enabled me to attend it. Discussions at this meeting played an important role in the development of my thinking about some of the central themes of the book. Lars Hertzberg, Michael McGhee and Bryn Browne read parts of an earlier draft and offered perceptive comments to which I am afraid that I have failed to do justice; I have also greatly benefited in a more general way from discussions with each of them. An earlier version of Chapter 7 was rewritten in the light of detailed comments by Owen Jones, Peter Smith and Bob Sharpe. Dewi Phillips read a complete draft of the book and offered many helpful comments. My greatest debt is to my wife Maureen. Without her help and influence this book would never have existed in anything like its present form.

Preface

This book revolves around three closely linked ideas: first, the suggestion that a view of what a person is cannot be separated from those attitudes which are expressive of a recognition that an individual is a person; second, the idea that much of what is distinctive of our thought about people has its fundamental place in our relations with *others*; and third, the insistence that much that is of value in our attitudes towards each other is quite compatible with, indeed actually requires, an identification of the person with the extended, tangible human being.

These ideas are linked through an argument which might be summarised in this way. It cannot be said that a metaphysical picture of what a person is grounds our understanding of the attitude towards others which is appropriate; rather, the metaphysics is an expression of the attitude – or, as I sometimes put it, of a particular ethical outlook – and the attitude itself has no ground. The special place which we are tempted to give to the first person point of view when discussing the notion of a person is, in part, an attempt to provide a grounding for the attitude. The futility of the attempt emerges in the fact that there are radical first/third person asymmetries in our thought about human beings. Thus the idea that what is of value in our relations with another must come from identifying with his point of view flows from philosophical confusion; it also leads to a distortion of important dimensions of our thought and, perhaps, to moral confusion. Once we free ourselves from the bias involved in that line of argument we can acknowledge that it is in our thought about *others* that the notion of a person has its primary place; and, with that, we can acknowledge the fundamental position of the extended, tangible human being in our thought. The emphasis on the first person point of view and the connected search for metaphysical grounding inevitably stand in the way of that acknowledgement; as does a more general bias which dictates that nothing *in* the world can be of value. The idea that utilitarianism represents a paradigm of rational concern and the closely linked idea that the categories of science are 'basic' are central to this general outlook. The outlook is reflected, in one way or another, in traditional dualism, in contemporary science led accounts of what a person is, and in the most

popular ways of understanding the notion of persons as individuals who persist through time. What links these is a failure to
acknowledge the tangible, persisting *human being* – a being with a
distinctive bodily form and having its own distinctive kind of value
– as a fundamental feature of our thought.

The book is divided into three parts. In Part I, I discuss the idea
that our attitudes towards others must be grounded in a picture of
what they are, my thought about myself playing a central role in
this grounding. Traditional forms of dualism along with sceptical
worries about the existence of others are fairly prominent here.
Part II focusses on various ways in which the extended, tangible
human being may, in philosophical discussions, be displaced from
its fundamental position in our thought. Themes which have been
important in two areas of recent philosophical work become central
here. In Chapter 7 I discuss the character of the relation between
our normal ('folk') understanding of people and an understanding
in terms of the categories of basic science; and in Chapter 8 I
consider familiar objections to the idea that the notion of a 'human
being' could, in itself, be an ethically significant category. In Part III
I am concerned with the idea of a person as a being that persists
through time; and I attempt to see what sense might be given to
talk of persons as irreplaceable individuals. In the final chapter of
Part III I bring together various strands of my discussion of the
relation between the first and third person points of view and, in
so doing, try to give what I hope is a fairly rich content to the idea
that the notion of a person has its primary position within the
context of a personal relationship.

The three parts of the book could, I think, be read as three
relatively independent essays. Having said that, I suspect that
many would find the discussions in the later parts thin and
unconvincing when read without the background of the discussion
in Part I. Despite the fact that the explicit focus of Part I is on ideas
which are not, perhaps, very central to the mainstream of contemporary philosophy of mind, the discussion here provides a framework without which the force of arguments in Parts II and III might
be quite unclear. For while Cartesian dualism is totally rejected by
the vast majority of contemporary philosophers I believe that the
considerations on which that rejection is based are often of quite
the wrong form; and, with that, that there is a clear sense in which
much that is central to philosophical dualism is still reflected in
many currently popular views in the philosophy of mind. Indeed,

it might be said that the title 'the philosophy of mind' embodies what I will suggest are serious misconceptions about the area of enquiry. In particular, first, the idea that our topic is 'the mind' is – in the most popular contemporary outlooks as clearly as in more traditional Cartesian approaches – strongly linked with a failure to appreciate the significance of the fact that our topic is *human beings*; and, second, it is assumed that the central philosophical questions about what people are can be discussed quite independently of any considerations of a, broadly speaking, ethical character. My rejection of the second of these ideas structures my discussion throughout the book; and in so far as that rejection is formally defended with arguments those arguments are to be found in Part I.

Analytical Table of Contents

1 (i) I do not think of other human beings as simply to be *used* in my attempts to attain my own ends; I have a distinctive range of responses to them. This special attitude which we have towards others must be given a central place in any attempt to say what it is to think of another as a person. (ii) Wittgenstein seems to reject the idea that the attitude is *grounded in* a recognition that the other is a being of a certain kind. We are inclined to resist the idea that the attitude is, in this sense, fundamental. The distinction between 'ethics' and 'the philosophy of mind' in part reflects this resistance.

2 (i) The idea that I need a special justification for thinking of another as a person – the idea that there is a problem of other minds – may reflect the curious assumption that things in the world are to be *used* in our attempts to achieve our ends unless reason is given for thinking otherwise. (ii) If we start with that paradigm of rationality in action it is quite obscure how placing the person outside the world with which we are confronted in experience – as the dualist does – can help us to escape its apparent implications for our treatment of others. Illustrated with reference to the claim that moving one's hand is a 'mental activity'.

3 (i) It might be argued that to give to our attitude towards others the place that Wittgenstein does is to ignore the fact/value distinction: we can imagine someone who clearly recognises those around him as people and yet whose attitude towards others is utterly different from that normal in our society; but what is right in this objection does not, properly understood, threaten Wittgenstein's approach. (ii) A very different objection would suggest that to deny that the 'recognition' is prior to the 'attitude' is to leave the attitude ungrounded, and so arbitrary, in a sense that is clearly unacceptable.

4 Would some other account of the relation between the 'recognition' and the 'attitude' remove the threat of arbitrariness? It might be thought that the attitude which I characteristically have towards others can be shown to be appropriate in terms of the fact that they are beings of the same kind as I am. There are, however, radical asymmetries in the attitudes which we take to be appropriate

towards ourselves and towards others. We cannot, then, escape the conclusion that our attitude towards others is underpinned by nothing by giving a fundamental position to the first person point of view.

5 (i) On Wittgenstein's view the connection between, for example, ascribing pain to another and thinking of them as one who is to be treated in a certain way is there from the start. (ii) The place that Wittgenstein gives to the attitude *does* leave room for the judgements that we normally want to make about the acceptability of an individual's thought about others. It is important to remember here that where we want to criticise a person's thought about others this is, characteristically, a *moral* criticism. (iii) There is still room for the claim that the reason it would be wrong for me to eliminate most of the human race from my picture of the world is the fact that 'they are *people*'.

6 (i) The *philosophical* mind/body contrast is closely linked with a number of serious confusions. (ii) The 'problem of other minds' springs, in part, from the way in which a range of states of very different kinds are grouped together as 'mental states'. The idea that sensations are 'in the mind' may flow from the thought that they are not in the hand in the sense in which a bullet is; and this is linked with a refusal to accept the significance of the fact that the hand is part of a human being. (iii) If one thinks of what is important in my attitude towards another as being a matter of 'seeing things from his point of view' – if one views relations between people exclusively in terms of the egoism/altruism distinction – one is bound to miss, or devalue, the role which the human bodily form plays in our relations with each other. To recognise this role is to recognise the fundamental position of the *human being* in our thought; and so to recognise another serious distortion introduced by the philosophical mind/body contrast. (iv) This is not to deny that various considerations of a, broadly speaking, ethical character could push us towards something closely akin to that contrast.

7 (i) The character of the relationship between our human ontology and the ontology of basic science is the currently dominant version of the 'mind–body' problem. (ii) The idea that beliefs, desires, sensations and so on must be related to neurophysiological states in one of certain familiar ways appears to rest on the assumption that the former states feature in our thought exclusively as explanations of the movements of human bodies; but our normal characterisations

of what we *observe* of each other are not in terms of the ontology of the physical sciences. (iii) Characterisations of human behaviour in physical terms would be basic in the relevant sense if an interest in predicting and controlling the non-human world was the basic form of our interest in each other. There are grounds for thinking that this assumption is at work in much materialist thinking. (iv) The assumption that there is a single form of interest which is basic to our thought about each other may be tempting in part because of the way in which it will provide a standard in terms of which different forms of description can be assessed. (v) This test for an acceptable ontology will, in the end, leave no significant place for the individual human being.

8 (i) The philosophical question 'What is a person?' is often a request for necessary and sufficient conditions of being a person. To insist that it must be possible to provide these is to insist that 'It is a person/human being' cannot be the most direct statement of my reasons for treating another as I do. (ii) Many philosophers are inclined to resist this: it is felt that it must be possible to say in virtue of which feature another is not, for example, to be killed or eaten. This feeling may be a reflection of a philosophically confused picture of the 'grounding' of our thought. (iii) Worries about giving a fundamental position to the notion of a 'human being' may also spring from the idea that a being's 'physiological characteristics' cannot possibly be of moral significance. This idea, and the terminology in which it is formulated, is another example of the 'devaluing' of the extended and tangible which finds its purest expression in the philosophical mind/body contrast. (iv) The ethical counterpart of the philosophical notion of 'the mind' is the idea that all that is important in our relations with another is of a single form. This idea is found in a number of contemporary discussions of our relations with animals; and does, on the face of it, contain serious moral dangers.

9 (i) My understanding of who this is – that this is an individual with a particular history – can have an important bearing on my thought about her. (ii) It is sometimes argued that the kind of importance which we attach to the question of who this is shows that what is crucial to its being a particular person – the same individual as one previously encountered – is quite distinct from what is involved in its being a particular *human being*. Thus, it is suggested that it is 'psychological continuity' that is crucial to personal identity; but there is at least room for the view that to give

this place to 'the mind' is to undermine what is of most value in our relations with others. (iii) Others suggest that the idea of a non-conditional commitment requires the idea of an 'unchanging core' behind the observable surface of the human being. This suggestion reflects either the familiar devaluing of the tangible or else a failure to accept that the *past* could matter to us.

10 (i) My thought of this as a particular individual may involve an idea of this person as being irreplaceable. That idea has a force which cannot be captured in terms of the thought that it is extra-ordinarily unlikely that anyone else should have just the set of characteristics which the loved one has. (ii) To capture this sense in which the other is irreplaceable we must acknowledge the role which her past plays in my conception of her. (iii) It might be objected that the suggestion underestimates the extent to which grief on the death of a loved one involves thoughts of the *future*. This objection involves a failure to appreciate how the gap in the future can only be characterised in terms of the past: it is a future without *her*.

11 (i) It is sometimes suggested that an adequate treatment of these issues must give the fundamental position to the first person point of view. Thus, it is argued that the kind of knowledge that I have of who I myself am shows that the question of which *person* I am is quite distinct from that of which *human being* I am. This seems to be simply a confusion. (ii) Alternatively, it might be argued that the first person point of view is fundamental in that the way in which my recognition of another as *this* individual ought to matter to me runs through my conception of how it matters to *her*; but there is an important sense in which a concern about who this is is characteristically absent from the first person point of view.

12 (i) We can, perhaps, understand denials of the reality of 'the self' in terms of the idea that there is no deep sense in which we are particular individuals: individuals with a particular history. How might that claim be defended? (ii) There are two strong stands in Modern Western Philosophy which *ought* to push us towards this conclusion: first, a certain picture of the way in which our thought should be grounded in the world (a picture of the relation between ethics and metaphysics) and, second, the fundamental position given to the first person point of view.

13 (i) To hold that persons are irreplaceable beings who persist through radical change is to hold that the form of concern which we perhaps see most clearly in the parent's thought about her child

is the model on which my attitude towards every human being is to be based. A philosophical use of the egoism/altruism contrast can obscure the possibility of this idea. Traces of what it might be to think of all mankind in this way can be seen in our normal thought. (ii) The objection that the parent's special form of concern for her child is the product of 'feeling' not 'recognition' rests either on philosophical confusion or on a commitment to some other ideal. (iii) To regard the way in which we may think of another in a personal relationship as the ideal is to think that part of the task facing each of us is that of coming to think of oneself as a person. It is not absurd to suggest that most do not attach the importance that they should to themselves. (iv) There is no reason to suppose that coming to 'see oneself as one among others' should exclusively involve movement in one direction; and there is some obscurity in my talk of 'directions of movement' since there is some obscurity about what is a 'pure form of first person thought'. (v) The first/third person asymmetries I have stressed have not been strongly tied to asymmetries in *action*. It might be argued that that casts serious doubt on the importance of my discussion.

Postscript (i) My use of the term 'ethics' has been very broad, in a way which is characteristic of empiricism. Given a more normal use of the term we may be able to give sense to the idea that 'ethics is grounded in metaphysics'. (ii) Central to the book has been the rejection of the possibility of a certain form of grounding of our thought. It is not obvious that the desire for grounding of that form need involve philosophical confusion.

Part I
The Reality of Others

1

'An Attitude towards a Soul'

(i) What is it to recognise the reality of another human being – to recognise them *as* a human being? We might say that it is to recognise them as a being that thinks, acts, sees, gets depressed and angry, feels pain, and so on. While nothing along these lines can, I think, be the whole story we can begin with this. Now, what is it to recognise another as a being with these features? There is no simple answer to this question. I want, however, to try to indicate in a general way a central aspect of the kind of answer that I think must be given.

'Pity, one may say, is a form of conviction that someone else is in pain.'[1] It is, of course, only a *form* of the conviction. My recognition of another's pain can come out in a variety of ways. I turn away in horror from the sight of the man lying by the road in obvious agony. The sadist thrills at the cries of his victim. The doctor coolly and efficiently attempts to relieve the suffering of the patient. As I look for the news that interests me I note with indifference that a rugby player was badly injured. There are, no doubt, interesting things to be said about the connections between these cases. What concerns me here, however, is simply the fact that we are, in many cases, moved by another's pain in one way or another. While indifference is very common if we try to imagine someone who is always indifferent to the sufferings of others, or who always regards them simply as a practical inconvenience – something, say, which prevents the other from working efficiently – we will be imagining someone who is so different from us that we might hesitate to ascribe to him any real understanding of our talk about pains. Of course, there will be *some* grounds for saying that he understands our talk if he is able, reasonably consistently, to give 'correct answers' to the question 'Is this person in pain?' If someone insists, for whatever reason, that this is sufficient to ascribe to him a full understanding of our talk I am not inclined to argue. Such a man would be very different from us and it is this difference which concerns me.

If someone is very angry with me I have reason to keep out of their way since I might get hit. If I do not recognise that this man who is glaring at me and clenching his fists is to be feared in this kind of way then there is something that I have failed to recognise about the situation with which I am confronted. This, however, is not the only way in which the anger of another can be fearful. For most of us another's intense anger can be disturbing in a way which is quite different from that in which a landslide is generally thought of as disturbing. We can, perhaps, imagine someone for whom this is not so. He 'recognises anger' where we recognise it; but for him, as we might put it, it is just a phenomenon of nature with potentially unpleasant consequences. For most of us, at least much of the time, another's anger is something quite different from this. It is a thing which can be fearful in a way which is quite independent of any expectation of unpleasant consequences. (If a landslide can be fearful in that way too this does not affect the point that concerns me.)

Strawson asks us to remember 'how much we actually mind, how much it matters to us, whether the actions of other people – and particularly of *some* other people – reflect attitudes towards us of goodwill, affection, or esteem on the one hand or contempt, indifference, or malevolence on the other.'[2] While there are many different forms of concern which could be mentioned here we can focus, for the moment, on the very general ways in which another's kindness can warm us or their cruelty or indifference hurt us. The warmth or hurt that I am speaking of here must be distinguished from the pleasure or displeasure which I feel on account of any benefit or injury to me – where 'benefit' and 'injury' are understood as effects which *could* have been brought about by something other than an agent. When I am moved by another's kind smile or deliberate rudeness there *is* no benefit or injury in that sense. It is distinct also from any hopes or fears for the future which the other's action may induce. The warmth or hostility of a stranger can move me without its having any effect on my expectations for the future. With this goes the fact that if I express my gratitude to another this is, in so far as it is a genuine expression, not simply an attempt to bring about more behaviour of this kind in the future. I should stress that I am not suggesting that it is a purely contingent truth that, for example, hostile action often brings injury in the restricted sense explained above. My point is just that the hurt that I suffer cannot be understood exclusively in terms of the hurt of the injury.

Such forms of concern about how another treats us are, I take it, characteristic of most of our relations with others. There are, no doubt, cases in which, say, my contempt for another is so total that I am, in these terms, quite indifferent to his treatment of me. To the extent to which this is true we might say that his actions are, for me, simply natural phenomena – on the same level as the branch which falls and hits me. We might also, perhaps, criticise my thought in terms of its involving a failure to recognise the reality of the other. If, however, these ways of speaking seem too 'metaphorical' to do serious philosophical work we can at least say that my thought about this individual lacks a dimension which is of central importance in the thought of most of us about most others. It is what it lacks that concerns me.

Simone Weil writes:

The human beings around us exert just by their presence a power which belongs uniquely to themselves to stop, to diminish, or modify, each movement which our bodies design. A person who crosses our path does not turn aside our steps in the same manner as a street sign, no one stands up, or moves about, or sits down again in quite the same fashion when he is alone in a room as when he has a visitor.[3]

For the moment I am concerned only with one of the strands of thought in this passage: 'no one stands up, or moves about, or sits down again in quite the same fashion' when another's eyes are on him. We can add: there are things that we would hesitate to do at all in front of others – or at least most others. Connected with this is the fact that eye contact with another is, for most of us, something of significance. The significance varies but it is rarely a matter of indifference whether, when, and how much we make eye contact with another. Now all of this connects in some way with the thought of others as having sight. We might say: 'Shame of a certain kind is a form of the conviction that someone else can see one';[4] but I do not want to insist on this way of putting the matter at this point. It is sufficient to note that the range of attitudes of which I have spoken is one of the ways in which our thought of others as having sight is manifested.

This very limited range of examples will suffice for my immediate purposes. A central feature of what I want to bring out could be put in this way: we do not think of others as simply things to be *used*. What I mean by this could be explained in this way. I have certain aims in life which can be specified without any reference to others. My own physical well-being and avoidance of physical pain are the most obvious examples. These aims are, on the face of it, to be sharply contrasted with the desire for, for example, friendship. Unless one thinks that what is really desired here is a certain state of oneself, which might have been caused by eating tomatoes but is in fact most efficiently caused by other people, the desire for friendship must be acknowledged to involve a non-functional concern for others: the other is not *simply* a means to my own ends. We need not, however, go into the details of this case. I do have ends which involve no essential reference to others, and my point is that I do not think of other human beings as simply means or impediments to those ends. A tree swaying dangerously in the wind may[5] present itself to me as simply a threat to my physical well-being. A human being writhing in pain or striking out in anger does not present himself to me simply in *that* way.

(ii) Wittgenstein writes: 'My attitude towards him is an attitude towards a soul. I am not of the *opinion* that he has a soul'.[6] It is, perhaps, not clear to what extent Wittgenstein's use of the term 'attitude' here conforms to normal usage. Further, its use within philosophy has been largely conditioned by just that range of assumptions which Wittgenstein wishes to undermine. There are, then, dangers here and it is important to be clear about the kind of work to which Wittgenstein is putting the word 'attitude'. Wittgenstein was writing against the background of a tradition in which it was customary to mark off my thought about other people from my thought about, say, stones by saying that I believe that the former, but not the latter, 'have minds'. His introduction of the term 'attitude' here represents a revolt against this way of speaking which has a number of dimensions. Part of what he wishes to highlight with this term is the fact that we *feel about* and *act towards* other human beings in ways that are utterly different from those in which we feel about and act towards, for example, stones. I have a certain 'practical orientation' towards another human being with whom I am confronted. This consists in part in the fact that there are things that I simply would not do, or would only do under extreme pressure, to him; in part in the fact that certain emotions and actions would come naturally to me in response to certain behaviour on his part. Now in speaking in terms of us as having a certain 'attitude towards' others, rather than in terms of us having a certain 'belief about' them, Wittgenstein is, in part, suggesting that this – what I called my 'practical orientation' – should be placed at the centre of the picture.

There are a number of distinctions which should, perhaps, be noted at this point. First, the fact that I have certain characteristic responses towards other human beings needs to be distinguished from the fact that I think of other human beings as beings towards which certain responses are *appropriate*: I think of the other as a being who is to be pitied and helped in certain circumstances, a being towards whom gratitude is to be felt in certain circumstances, and so on. We might express the point by saying that I think of the other as a being towards which there can be reason to respond in certain ways. Thus, I accept that the fact that another is in pain is, in itself, a *reason* for feeling pity – as his having brown hair, or an IQ of 135 is not. I accept that the fact that the huddled mass in the corner is a person is a reason for not doing certain things, such as kicking it. Now, as I suggested, to be moved to pity by another's pain is not the same thing as thinking that the other's pain is a reason for pity. Thus, the young child has, in a restricted form, the characteristic reactions towards others with whom it is confronted. However, the possibility of saying, in any rich sense, that it thinks of others as beings who are to be treated in certain ways only emerges gradually as the child develops. It cannot be said that the very young child thinks of the situation as presenting him with *reasons* for feeling and doing certain things. A clear foothold for that way of speaking of the child only emerges when he begins to give and accept reasons for feeling and action. The other side of this point is the fact that I may fail to respond in a particular way to another and yet recognise that there is reason to respond in that way. This, perhaps, is the state of most of us most of the time in our thought about most other human beings. I know that there are millions of people in the world living lives that are filled with awful suffering. I do virtually nothing for them and, for most of the time at any rate, their suffering barely touches me. I do, however, recognise that they *are* to be pitied and helped: that there is reason to feel and do certain things.

A further distinction here is this. I said that 'I think of other human beings as beings towards which certain responses are appropriate'. Now this formulation contains an ambiguity. It might be that I myself employ the notion of a 'human being' in the articulation of my thought. We might, however, also describe in these terms a case in which someone's thought is not consciously articulated in this way. The notion of a 'human being' might, that is, be introduced by a third party who, observing the way in which I reason about particular instances, concludes that another's being human is, in practice, a relevant consideration for me.[7] Thus, such a characterisation of my thinking could be correct even if I had no understanding of any expression corresponding to the term 'human being'.

Another ambiguity in the observation that 'I think of other human beings as beings towards which certain responses are appropriate' is bound up with the precise form which is attached to the word 'appropriate'. Thus, it might be said that if another has deliberately hurt me in some way I have reason to hurt them; in that sense my hurting the other would be 'appropriate'. To say that, however, is not to say that there is any sense at all in which it is *morally required* of me that I hurt the other. We can accept that a certain kind of situation provides a reason for a certain kind of response while thinking, in all cases, that it is completely admirable that a person in such a situation does not respond in this way. There is, then, a distinction between the acknowledgement of a reason in this, perhaps minimal, sense and the endorsement of the form of response which is in question.

A final possible distinction that I will note here is this. To accept that another's state is a reason to respond to him in a certain way is not simply to accept that it can intelligibly *be given* as a reason for responding in that way. Thus, I might, it seems, *understand* someone who suggests that the fact that this man has murdered is reason for him to be killed without agreeing with him: without, that is, accepting that it *is* a reason. Now there are limits to what we can make sense of here: that another has brown hair or an IQ of 135 cannot, without further explanation, be given as a reason for feeling pity. My point, however, is that the limits to sense do not coincide with the limits to what I accept as reasons. There is a distinction between understanding someone who suggests that something is a reason for a certain response and myself accepting that it is.

Which of these notions which I have distinguished should we see as fundamental to 'recognising the reality of another' or 'recognising that another is a person'? We are, perhaps, pulled in more than one direction here. The young child's reactions to others, it might be said, clearly create a place for saying that he thinks of what he sees around him as people. Equally, however, must it not be agreed that I recognise to be people those millions whose fate barely touches me? Well, it would be needlessly artificial to pick out one of these notions as *the* crucial one: the artificiality stemming in part from the fact that the way in which I have spoken of 'recognising the reality of another' is some way removed from ways of speaking which are normal in non-philosophical contexts; in part from the fact that there are intimate connections between these notions. Indeed, it would, I am sure, be impossible to classify our normal thought in any precise way in terms of the distinctions I have made. For the moment, then, all that is crucial for my purposes is Wittgenstein's suggestion that emotions and ways of acting of the kind of which I have spoken must, in one way or another, be given a central place in any philosophical discussion of our thought about human beings.

Expressing the matter in that way does not, however, bring clearly into focus what is, perhaps, most distinctive of Wittgenstein's discussion of these issues. For in giving a central place to our attitude towards another Wittgenstein explicitly rejects the idea that we are 'of the *opinion* that he has a soul'. He seems, that is, to reject the view that the attitude which we have towards another rests on something else: our grasp of the kind of being that the other is. This was reflected in my suggestion in section (i) that in speaking of various responses which we have to others we are speaking of what it *is* to recognise another as a person. It is suggested, then, that the attitude is what is *fundamental* in our thought about each other.

We might introduce a partial defence of Wittgenstein's move here by asking: is not what he speaks of the *important* thing? The idea that there is something distinct from all of this which we should speak of as the core of 'recognising another as a person' has the appearance of a philosophical invention. Further, even if that is unfair, even if there is such a thing, we should not place it at the centre of the picture. For what really matters in one person's thought about another is that he treats her in the way which we regard as appropriate: pities and helps her when she falls, feels gratitude towards her when she acts in certain ways, and so on; or, at least, recognises that the other *is* to be treated in these ways.

It will be replied, however, that there is a dangerous ambiguity here. In a purely practical sense, no doubt, it must be agreed that in the end the 'attitude' is the important thing. To say this, however, is not to say that the attitude is what is *fundamental*. 'For surely', it will be said, 'I have the attitude towards another *because* I recognise her reality. That is to say, my conviction that this is a person is distinct from the attitude towards the other in which that conviction is manifested. Thus, the attitude, however important it is from one point of view, should not be mentioned in an answer to the philosophical question "What is it to recognise the reality of another human being?"'

I have formulated both Wittgenstein's view and the protest against it in terms of the notion of recognising another individual as a person. It will help, I think, to place beside this a slightly different formulation of these ideas. A person, we might say, is a being that is to be treated in certain ways. That a certain attitude is appropriate towards a person is central to our understanding of what a person *is*. Similarly, another's pain, we might say, is something to be relieved, another's anger something to be feared, another's act of kindness something to feel gratitude for, another's gaze something to be avoided in certain circumstances, and so on. The appropriateness of these responses is central to our understanding of what pain, anger and so on *are*; perhaps in a way which is akin to that in which the fact that a chair is something to be sat on is central to our understanding of what a chair is.

Now the worry that I tried to articulate a moment ago might be expressed in this way: 'This characterisation of what a person is cannot be the most fundamental one. There must be a more basic characterisation of what a person is which makes no mention of our *responses* to other people. It must, that is, be possible to offer a characterisation which refers only to features intrinsic to a person. This must be so since it must be in virtue of such features that a being *is* to be treated in these ways.'

This protest might be backed up with arguments of two apparently totally different forms. The first would involve an appeal to the once much discussed idea that there is a 'gap between facts and values'. 'Wittgenstein's approach', it might be said, 'simply obliterates crucially important distinctions here in that it builds certain value judgements – views about how we ought to treat the things we encounter in the world – into our understanding of what those things *are*. This can only lead to confusion. For it is clear that my recognition of what the facts are, my recognition, for example, that this is a person, leaves completely open the question of what my attitude towards the facts ought to be. To speak, as Wittgenstein does, as if this is not so is to attempt to smuggle in one's personal moral views under the guise of a piece of neutral, philosophical definition.'

This first objection, then, is that getting straight about the facts leaves con pletely open the question of what my attitude towards the facts ought to be. A quite different line of attack would insist that it is getting straight about the facts that *determines* what my attitude should be. Far from appealing to the idea that what attitude I adopt is entirely up to me this objection appeals to the suggestion that what attitude I adopt is obviously *not* arbitrary in that sense. Now my attitude towards the other can, it is argued, only fail to be arbitrary if it is grounded in something else: namely, my recognition of his reality. Thus, the latter must be independent of, and prior to the former.

This use of the distinction between 'recognising the reality of another' and 'having a certain attitude towards another' might, then, be defended in two almost diametrically opposed ways. No doubt this has much to do with the strong hold which it has within philosophy. The distinction, understood in this way, runs, I think, pretty deep in contemporary thought and is, indeed, reflected in a standard demarcation within philosophy: that between 'the philosophy of mind' and 'ethics'. It has been thought that the central issues in the 'philosophy of mind' can be discussed quite independently of any connection which they may have with questions concerning what could be described as our 'ethical' relations with others. Thus, a great deal of work in the 'philosophy of mind' contains no, or extremely limited, reference to this dimension of our thought about each other. Further, when the links between our conception of a person and our ethical thought are stressed, as, for example, in Parfit's work,[8] it is still characteristically assumed that the latter is *grounded in* the former: that the 'philosophy of mind' is logically prior, and so can be discussed quite independently of the implications which it has for our ethical thought.

One of my central aims in this book is to cast doubt on this way of representing the relation between an individual's *understanding* of what he is confronted with when he is confronted with another human being and his *attitude towards* that with which he is confronted. Inseparably connected with this is the doubt that I hope to cast on the associated picture of the relation between 'the philosophy of mind' – or, more generally, 'metaphysics' – and 'ethics'. My immediate aim in Chapter 2, however, will be the more modest one of suggesting that helpful light may be thrown on central issues within the philosophy of mind when these are placed in an explicitly ethical context. At this stage, then, I need only assume agreement on two weak claims: first, that what Wittgenstein speaks of as our 'attitude' towards others is an important feature of our lives, and, second, that the attitude which we characteristically[9] have is in some fairly direct way connected with our recognition of them as people.

2

Scepticism, Dualism and Action

(i) The 'problem of other minds', as it is traditionally understood, is a problem about my right to take certain of the things that I see around me as beings that, for example, feel pain, get angry, act and see. The problem might be presented in the form of the question: what justification do I have for taking these beings that I see around me to be people? The question, in its traditional form, assumes that there is a crucial contrast with regard to the need for justification between my thought of you as a person and my thought of this as a stone; it assumes that the former stands in need of justification in a way in which the latter does not. It is assumed, that is, that it is consistent with everything that I can actually observe of the other that he is not a being of the kind that feels pain and so on. What is crucial for *that* is something which, in some sense, lies behind the human being that I can observe.[1] Thus, there is *room* for a sceptical doubt which needs to be removed, if possible, by some justification for thinking that what I observe points to the presence of that which is crucial.

The enormous intuitive appeal of philosophical views which, in this sense, leave room for 'scepticism about other minds', is, from one point of view, rather mysterious. After all, the suggestion that it is at least *possible* that my wife is not a person does not, prior to all the philosophy, seem very tempting. Despite what some have claimed, the same must be said of the view that if, for example, my one-year-old child hits his finger with a hammer and collapses to the ground screaming there is always room for the suggestion that perhaps he is not really in pain.[2] Yet it takes only the slightest of promptings of the right kind to lead the unprepared to a view within which there is room for scepticism about other minds. Leading someone to scepticism itself is, of course, another matter; we only get *there* when we conclude that the argument from analogy cannot do the work that is asked of it. What concerns me now, however, is the attraction of views within which there is a sceptical doubt to be answered.

13

It might be said that any mystery about the appeal of a dualism which, in this sense, leaves room for scepticism disappears when one bears in mind the special place which we are inclined to give to the first person point of view in discussions of these issues. My conception of *others* as beings that feel pain, see, and so on is, we feel, derivative from my conception of *myself* as such a being; and that is bound to leave us with a problem about my justification for taking others to be beings like myself. That, however, leaves us with the need to explain why we are tempted to give *that* place to the first person point of view. After all, nobody, on reflection, will, I take it, suggest that this is the way things develop in practice: that the child goes through such a process of analogical reasoning before he responds to his mother's smile or looks into her eyes.

It was once quite widely felt that the structure of our language was responsible for the pictures which grip us when we think philosophically about these issues: 'We say "He has a pain in his leg" just as we say "He has a splinter in his leg"'. Thus we come to think of pain as a kind of "inner object". Yet clearly pains are not "inner" in just the sense in which splinters or bones are: we do not find a pain if we open him up, and he can report his pains without examining his body at all. Pains, we conclude, must be "inner" and "hidden from others" in a more radical sense than bones'. Yet while the structure of our language may place no obstacles to our temptation to slide into these images any explanation along these lines clearly needs supplementing. For one thing, we need an account of why it is that we are inclined to model pains on splinters and bones rather than the other way round. So far as the *language* goes we could, it seems, go equally happily either way; yet there appears to be *no* pull in the other direction. Further, we say 'He has a pain in his leg', but also 'He is in great pain'. Now just think of the trouble that we could get ourselves into with the latter locution if we really set our minds on it! Yet we don't. There is, then, more explaining to be done here.

Well, the story here is, presumably, a complex one. The more general Cartesian epistemological project plays a role. Relevant in a rather different way are the difficulties that *can* be involved in getting to know about certain features of another's 'mental life', and the difficulties that can be involved in getting close to another, even though one may know a lot *about* them.[3] Perhaps, too, a touch of wishful thinking is playing a part here. I believe, however, that some of the important influences on our thought can only be appreciated when a central place is given to those reactions to others which are highlighted in Wittgenstein's approach to these issues.

I stressed in Chapter 1 that another person is, for me, something which is in certain circumstances, to be pitied, feared in a quite distinctive way, thanked, hidden from, and so on. The thought of the other as a being that feels pain, gets angry, acts and sees is closely, perhaps inseparably, linked with responses of these kinds. Now, if one supposed that the beings that we directly encounter in the world are obviously not, in themselves, appropriate objects of these responses then one would conclude that it is only in so far as the real person 'lies behind the surface' that such responses could possibly be in place. One would conclude, that is, that our normal thought commits us to the idea that the being that feels pain, gets angry, acts and sees is not to be found in the world of extended, tangible entities.

The idea, then, would be this. Some *other* attitude towards the things that we encounter in the world is the norm: in the absence of special justification the things that we encounter are to be treated in some other way. Being a deviation from a norm our attitude towards other human beings stands in need of special justification.

What, then, is the norm? Are we to say that things in the world are to be *used* in our attempts to achieve our ends unless reason is given, in particular cases, for thinking otherwise? It is an odd assumption but one which has a strong hold both within and outside philosophy. Indeed, it is, in part, the strength of that hold which leads me to suspect that something along these lines may play a significant role in our thought here. The unyielding attraction of utilitarianism is one manifestation of this hold. The attraction lies in the idea that the possibility of bringing about desirable states in the future, or avoiding undesirable ones, is the only thing that can move a rational being to action. Thus, everything with which we are confronted is, for the rational being, simply a means to this end.

Utilitarianism insists that the end is the welfare of *everyone*; that others are not to be regarded as simply means to my own ends. Its analogue at the level of the individual – egoism – is what primarily concerns me here. What links these doctrines, when they are presented in a certain spirit, is a picture of where an onus of proof lies. As I expressed it, the crucial thought is this: things in the world are to be *used* in our attempts to achieve our ends unless reason is given, in particular cases, for thinking otherwise. Since I do not think of other human beings as simply things to be used in my attempts to achieve my ends a special justification is needed for my having towards them the attitude that I do.

I have no argument against this assumption. If it is deeply held it will, I think, be no use pointing to the fact that, for example, the very young child responds spontaneously to its mother's smile: without justification it has an attitude towards its mother which is not purely functional. For it will be said that, in so far as we are rational, *we* will demand a justification for that for which the child does not. (Quite a few other things, about 'survival value' for example, are likely to be said too.) Some will hold that the assumption is a grotesque reversal of the truth; that *nothing* in the world is simply a thing to be used in our attempts to achieve our ends (with or without the addition: 'unless reason is given, in particular cases, for thinking otherwise'). I doubt if philosphy can do much to help resolve the issue. My hope is that by bringing the assumption clearly into focus we can loosen the hold of the idea that my attitude towards others would be out of place unless the other 'lies behind what I can observe of him'.

In addition to this there is, perhaps, one other thing that can be done. This is to argue that if such a special justification were needed it could not be had. In the remainder of this chapter I will pursue this by considering further the suggestion that our attitude towards each other could only be appropriate if the real person is distinct from the human being which is encountered in the world. I will focus here on an aspect of our thought about human beings in connection with which this idea is particularly tempting: our thought of each other as beings that *act*. (In Chapter 4 I will consider in more general terms attempts to provide philosophical justifications for the character of thought about others.)

(ii) We draw a distinction between what a person *does* and other happenings in the world: between, for example, the sense in which a person can be said to have killed someone and the sense in which a tree can. The distinction has application within the class of things which, in a broad sense, a person can be said to have done. If I am pushed out of a window and my head crushes the skull of someone below there is a sense in which I can be said to have injured them; but this is not the sense in which we are interested when discussing human actions. Connected with this is the fact that we distinguish between a person's actions and 'mere movements' of his body: between, for example, the case in which someone shakes his head and that in which his head shakes as a result of some physiological disorder.

We distinguish, then, between what a person does (in the relevant sense) and what happens to him or to parts of his body. The distinction is an important one in that it is closely tied up with a range of ways of thinking about human actions which are absolutely fundamental to our lives.

Consider first my thought about my own future actions. I think of it as being in some sense up to me what I will do. I do not think of my own future behaviour as being simply something to be predicted on the basis of my knowledge of the laws of nature – as I think of the weather as simply something to be predicted. I ask myself 'What shall I do?' In asking this I am not asking: what, given the present causal set-up, is it most likely that I will end up doing? I am asking rather: what would it be best for me to do? The question calls for a decision, not a prediction. In this respect my thought about my own future behaviour is quite different from my thought about other future happenings.

This point has an analogue in our thought about others. Other human beings are to be reasoned with. I do not simply try to bring you to do what I think would be for the best, as I try to bring it about that my car functions properly. I try to persuade you that it would be for the best; I present what I take to be reasons for doing one thing rather than another. Of course, reasoning with another is, at least given our present knowledge, often the most effective way of bringing them to do something. The thought that others are to be reasoned with does, however, clearly go beyond this. Even if a more effective technique was available in a particular case – say hypnosis – I might think it quite inappropriate to use it. That, in a particular case, a certain bad argument is likely to be more effective than a good one does not automatically mean that I will prefer it. That I believe that I could persuade another by what I take to be a good argument does not automatically mean that I will try to do so; I might think it important that he should reach his own decision.

Another aspect of our notion of agency is seen in our thought about the past actions of ourselves and others. We praise and blame, reward and punish, feel gratitude and resentment towards others on account of actions they have performed. We are hurt or

warmed by another's cruelty or kindness. We feel pride, shame
and guilt about our own past actions. We apologise for what we
have done and ask to be forgiven. These ways of thinking mark off
our thought about past actions from our thought about other past
happenings.

Consider now the following remark:-

When, eg, we think of ourselves as having moved our hand, we
are thinking of ourselves as having performed an activity of a
certain kind, and, it almost goes without saying, a *mental* activity
of a certain kind.[4]

I am not quite sure why Prichard feels this 'almost goes without
saying', nor, indeed, what he means by it. One possibility,
however, is that he reasoned in the following way: 'Nothing that
we *see* when we look at another human being could, in itself, be
grounds for responding to him any differently from the way in
which we respond to a physical object. What we see is, in itself,
just another event in nature and so is to be regarded in the ways
which are appropriate to this. That is to say, nothing in what we
see does, in itself, provide any foothold for the notion of an *agent* or
of what he *does*. It must, then, be something that lies behind and
causes the movements that we observe that provides a foothold for
talk of agency, as opposed to mere happening: that creates a place
for those responses to others which are distinctive of our thought
of them as agents. Sometimes, for example, we resent or are hurt
by what another has done. We ask questions about his *reasons* for
doing it. We do not think of it as simply a natural event whose
causes are to be sought in order that we might prevent its
recurrence. This way of thinking requires for its ground the belief
that the movements of the body were caused by an event in a mind
– by an act of willing.'

Our aim was to characterise the distinction between what a
person *does* and *what happens to him*. It is suggested that a person
can be held responsible for happenings in the world which can be
traced back in a certain way to his performance of an act of will; but
now surely we can ask: is willing something that a person does, or
is it something that happens to him? If it is said that the question is
in some way illegitimate a reason must be given. If, on the other
hand, the question can be asked, our original problem has simply
been shifted. We must now ask: what is the force of the claim that

willing (or a particular act of willing) is something that a person *does*?

We can put the same point in a slightly different way. It is said that nothing in what we see when we look at another could be grounds for responding to him in the distinctive ways in which we do. What grounds these responses must, then, be an occurrence in a non-extended entity without mass, solidity or spatial location which lies behind what we actually observe. It is only because 'A man, considered as a moral being, . . . is not really *in* the world at all: the world, that is, in which actions in the ordinary sense and their consequences occur'[5] that we can have reason for responding to him in these ways. Now, however, we face the question: just how does what happens in this other realm ground – provide reason for – such responses? Without some attempt to answer this question the postulation of this other realm achieves nothing at all. We have simply replaced one mystery – that concerning the relation between what we observe and our responses – by another – that concerning the relation between something that we do not observe and our responses. Now it might be said: 'Mental events are very different in character from events of any other kind. It is an intrinsic part of their nature that they can have kinds of significance which no other events can have.' To say this is not, however, to remove the mystery. It is simply to tell us that we must live with it. In which case we can reply: some things in the normal world with which we are confronted in experience just do have kinds of significance which others do not.

I asked: what is the force of the claim that willing is something that a person *does*? Why should it be assumed that this question must have an answer? Is it not a request that 'willing' should have 'its nature expressed in terms of the nature of other things'?[6] It might be argued that the request would be reasonable if there were beings who understood what it was to act but who had never had direct experience of acting. Such beings could only come by their understanding by having the nature of 'willing' 'expressed in terms of the nature of other things'. In fact, however, since willing is a *mental* activity all of us *have* had direct experience of acting. Thus, I know from my own experience what is the force of the claim that willing is something that a person *does*. I know because I have experienced the difference between myself raising my arm and someone else taking hold of my arm and raising it.

This suggestion is not, I think, as attractive as the parallel move in the case of pain: the idea that I learn what it is to act through my own experience of acting is not as tempting as the idea that I learn what kind of thing pain is through my own experience of pains. While this is certainly connected with doubts about whether there is a characteristic experience of acting, I will put the emphasis somewhere else. The thought of myself or another as *doing* something is closely connected with the thought of that person as being an appropriate object of certain attitudes. To have grasped the force of the claim that 'willing is something that a person *does*' is, at least in part, to have grasped that certain attitudes towards oneself or another are in place. It is to have grasped that it is appropriate to *reason* with another rather than simply to try to causally influence their 'behaviour', that resentment, remorse and gratitude can be appropriate, and so on. Now the question is: how is an experience that I have when acting supposed to show me this? Will careful reflection on what goes on in me when I act with cruelty or kindness inevitably make transparent to me the appropriateness of certain responses to such actions?

The difficulty that I am trying to bring out here has two aspects. We can ask first: how is an experience that I have when acting supposed to show me that certain ways of feeling and thinking about *myself* are appropriate? *Perhaps* when the child focuses carefully on what goes on within him next time he is cruel to his little sister he will come to feel, or acknowledge the appropriateness of, shame; but then again, perhaps he won't. The second question here is this: even if the appropriateness of certain ways of thinking about myself could, in some sense, be 'drawn from' my own experience of acting how would that help to show me how it is appropriate to think of the actions of others? How, for example, is the way in which I may feel about myself when I have acted well towards another supposed to show me that gratitude is in place when another acts well towards me? Are there self-directed feelings which must inevitably transform into gratitude, resentment or forgiveness when directed towards another? Again, think of the way in which I might be hurt by another's hostility or indifference. Is there something which is revealed when we adopt the agent's perspective and which shows a response of this form to be appropriate? (One might think in particular here of ill treatment which I suffer at the hands of a stranger.) When attention is paid to the details of our responses, the idea that the first person point of view might provide the grounding that we are seeking for our responses to the actions of others does, I believe, begin to evaporate. I will not develop this point in any detail but simply mention one, particularly striking, asymmetry in our thought about the actions of ourselves and others which raises further problems of the same form. There are circumstances in which we would be astonished if an individual did not blame himself on account of what he had done and yet in which we would think it quite out of place for us to blame him, or, at least, to blame him in anything like the same way. Think, for example, of a woman whose momentary reckless driving results in a child's death, or of a man of deep pacifist convictions who, under enormous pressure, deliberately kills another human being. While *our* recognition of what has been done might be primarily expressed in our pity for the individual we might regard self-blame as the surest mark of *his* acknowledgement of what he has done.[7] (I am aware that some will feel that my blunt appeal to this asymmetry – as if it was a basic and inescapable fact of life – is a good bit *too* blunt. There is a powerful temptation to say that this feature of our normal thought *must* embody a confusion; as there is a temptation to say that it *must* be irrational to be distressed about a stranger's treatment of oneself since the fact that it was *you* he was treating in this way played no role at all in his thinking. I hope that later discussion of other first/third person asymetries, in particular in Chapters 4 and 11, will, by bringing out how pervasive asymmetries of this general form are in this area, help to cast doubt on the conception of rationality presupposed in this objection.)

It is, then, quite obscure in what sense my own experience of acting reveals to me how it is appropriate to respond to the actions of others; and, with that, quite obscure in what sense the notion of action can be 'drawn from' my own experience of acting. Now I should stress that I am not suggesting that the notion of action can be 'drawn from' somewhere else: that, for example, what we see when we look at another acting shows us the appropriateness of these reactions. My point, as before, is simply that the idea that the real action lies behind what we actually see does not *remove* any difficulty.

If we start with the idea that the things that happen around us are, other things being equal, to be thought of in terms of their usefulness in serving our purposes we cannot escape it. While in the grip of this paradigm of rationality in action we try to escape its implications by placing the agent outside the world with which we are confronted in experience. Corresponding to the 'deep' (non-functional) significance which we attach to actions we need a 'deep' (outside the world of extended and observable things) truth. Prichard's suggestion that 'it almost goes without saying' that when we move our hand we perform a 'mental' activity is, I believe, in part an expression of this idea.[8] We do not stop to ask how this 'deep' truth would help us to escape the implications of that paradigm of rationality in action. (As Wittgenstein puts the thought in a rather different context: 'Mental processes just are queer.'[9]) To leave a place for the special kinds of significance which we attach to what people do we must then, at the beginning, reject the paradigm of rationality in action which led us to think that 'a man, considered as a moral being, is not really *in* the world at all'.

The traditional dualist characteristically suggests that the denial of dualism is fundamentally degrading: is a denial of everything that is of value in our relations with others. Now the particular form of dualism which I have been considering is not popular among professional philosophers today and is, indeed, rapidly losing its hold in a more general way. What motivates this widespread rejection of dualism is, however, often considerations of a very different character from those presented here. This comes out in the fact that many of those who reject dualism *share*, in some form, the assumption that unless dualism is true the special kinds of significance which we attach to other human beings must be out of place. The 'functional' paradigm of rationality in action has lost none of its power. I will return to this in Chapter 7.

3

Facts and Values

(i) I suggested in Chapter 2 that our inclination to say that the real person 'lies behind the surface' that we observe – where that phrase is understood in a way that creates a place for philosophical scepticism – may be partially explained in the following way. We feel that it is only in so far as this is so – only in so far as the real person is not to be found in *this* world – that our distinctive responses to each other could possibly be in place. Now in so far as we are influenced by that idea the proposal that these responses should be given a central place in philosophical discussions of the notion of a person will be vindicated: if we want to understand why people are tempted by certain views within the philosophy of mind we will need to keep these reactions in mind. It will be clear from my discussion in Chapter 1, however, that I take Wittgenstein's suggestion here to be considerably richer than this would indicate. For Wittgenstein is not simply reminding us that there is a very close connection between these responses and our understanding of those around us as people. He is, in addition, offering us a picture of the kind of connection that is. In speaking in terms of 'an attitude towards a soul' he is rejecting the idea that these responses are based on something more basic: 'a recognition that these others around me are people'. The attitude is what is basic in our relations with each other; it does not have, or need, any underpinning in the form of a 'belief' about the character of what we are confronted with. To 'recognise these as people', we might say, just *is* to have the attitude.

I suggested in Chapter 1 that there are two, apparently quite different, ways in which doubts might be raised about Wittgenstein's approach here. The first would appeal to the idea that there is 'a gap between facts and values'. The second would suggest that Wittgenstein's approach, denying as it does that our attitude towards others is grounded in our recognition of features that they possess, implies that that attitude is completely arbitrary. In this chapter I want first to try to do something to undermine the first of these objections and, second, to develop the second objection in greater detail.

The first objection, then, is that it is one thing to recognise another as a person and quite another to hold any particular views about how he is to be treated. Thus, we can imagine cases in which someone clearly recognises those around him as people and yet whose value judgements – judgements about how people are to be treated – are *utterly* different from our own; and, with this, whose responses to other people are utterly different from those which are normal in our society.

Confronted with a fossilised philosophical distinction, such as the 'fact'/'value' distinction or the 'mental'/'physical' distinction, one has a number of options. What is clear in many such cases is that the use to which a distinction has been put has depended on the fact that the range of examples borne in mind has been significantly restricted. Thus, we might, as I will, grant that there is a gap between 'fact' and 'value' but add that, given the understanding of the terms 'fact' and 'value' on which that can be said, these terms do not offer an exhaustive categorisation of our thought.

One aspect of this can be brought out in this way. Suppose that I am confronted with a young child who is obviously in great pain and I have to hand a harmless means of easing his suffering. I am not certain whether those philosophers who spoke of a gap between facts and values would have said that the claim that I have reason to help the child is a 'value (or moral) judgement'. It would not, I suppose, normally be described in those terms; and, with that, most of those who do, in practice, insist that our moral views are entirely a matter of personal decision would not, I suppose, speak in this way of the claim that I have reason to help this child. Of course, the situation might be such that there are also reasons not to help the child; it might, indeed, be such that any claim about *what is to be done* could be said to be a matter of 'personal judgement': the situation is complex and, recognising that there is room for different views about what ought to be done, I would not be inclined to say that someone who saw things differently from me must be wrong. It would, however, be a very different matter if someone questioned whether there was any reason to help the child. Now even here there may be important distinctions to be drawn. Consider someone whose acknowledgement that this is a young child in great pain is followed by 'but he is one of *them*', where these words serve to completely cancel the appearance of a reason to help. Horrific as we might find such a man he would be quite different from the one who does not acknowledge that there is an appearance that needs to be cancelled. In imagining an individual of the latter kind we would be imagining a figure who was foreign to us in a significantly more radical sense.

Now my point here is this. It might be said that in grasping what a pain is I am not committed to any particular set of moral views; and, more generally, it might be argued that no particular moral outlook must be built into an account of what it is to recognise another as a person since such recognition is compatible with utterly different moral outlooks. The acceptability of such claims is, however, dependent on the fact that certain basic features of our thought – such as that a person in pain is, 'other things being equal', to be helped – are taken to be more fundamental than anything which is properly spoken of as a 'moral view'. At any rate, it is, I think, not *obvious* that we can imagine an individual whose thought lacks features such as this and yet who would share enough with us that we would, without hesitation, want to ascribe to him an understanding of all our talk about persons and their states.

We might further ease the way for this view of the matter by considering another dimension of our thought which may be obscured by common ways of speaking of a 'fact'/'value' distinction – another way in which that way of speaking can create a lopsided picture. The notion of 'value', tied, as it is here, to the notion of 'morality', focuses attention on a certain limited range of our reactions, to the exclusion of others. The terminology focuses our attention on the way in which we *act* towards others as opposed to the emotions that we feel on account of them; and, perhaps, on a restricted class of actions. We think, for example, of the action taken to relieve the other's pain. We do not think of the pity that is felt for the other, of the horror at the sight of the other's contorted face and the urge to turn away. We overlook, perhaps, the response of sympathy which finds expression in the ways I try to comfort the other, the way in which my thoughts may keep returning, with horror, to the incident, and so on. Similarly with other examples. For example, philosophical discussion of our responses to the actions of others has tended to focus on praise and blame, reward and punishment. The range of reactions which Strawson places at the centre of the picture – resentment, gratitude, hurt feelings, and so on[1] – tend to be excluded from the picture when the emphasis is on our 'moral thought'. Again, philosophical discussion of a certain style has a tendency to focus on our obligation, for example, not to kill, betray or enslave others; the ways in which the presence of another can be a comfort to us, the sight of another can be a joy, or physical contact with another can be of enormous importance to us, tend to be regarded as, at best, fringe phenomena.

Common philosophical terminology and standard demarcations within philosophy – for example, that between 'moral philosophy' and 'the philosophy of mind' – have a tendency, then, to focus our thought on certain phenomena of human life to the exclusion of others. This focusing of attention, in turn, re-enforces the terminology and the demarcations for it makes it easier for us to suppose that we can, and indeed must, get clear about what it is to think of another as a person quite independently of considering those responses to others which most of us take to be appropriate. This comes about because it will seem clear to us, as indeed it is, that two individuals can be widely separated in their 'moral' outlook and yet have a common understanding of what it is they are confronted with when they are confronted with another human being. Now while, as I have suggested, there is nothing wrong with that thought there is a danger that we will forget the rich shared background of responses which characteristically lies behind such differences in moral outlook. Thus, we come to think that we have a clear picture of an individual who shares enough with us for us to be able to say that we have a common understanding of that with which we are confronted with yet whose 'attitude' towards this is utterly different from ours; and so that an account of what it is to think of another as a person can, and must, be given quite independently of any discussion of those responses to others in which our recognition of them is characteristically expressed. That is the assumption on which I am trying to cast some doubt.

It may, however, still seem clear to some that there are, in practice, obvious cases of individuals whose attitude is, at least in particular instances, utterly different from the kind of norm which I have set up and yet who unambiguously recognise that what they are confronted with is a person, a person in pain, or whatever it may be. I am not thinking now of cases in which an individual is untouched by the other. I am thinking rather of cases in which there is a decisive response to the other which is quite different from any 'norm' which might be suggested, and yet which equally expresses an understanding that it is a *person* with which he is dealing. For example, the pleasure which some take in inflicting pain expresses their understanding of what the other is undergoing as unambiguously as does the pity of which I have spoken. Is it not clear, then, that we must distinguish sharply between the understanding and the attitude: that it must be possible to give an account of what the understanding consists in while making no mention of the various attitudes in which the understanding may be expressed?

Any characterisation of the 'normal' attitude towards another person in pain is clearly going to involve some complexity. There is not only the pity but also the horror: the urge to help and comfort which is connected with the former lies beside the urge to turn away which is connected with the latter. I do not know whether the fascination which we may have for another in pain should be counted as part of the 'normal' attitude. At any rate, the urge to look, which may itself be a form that our horror can take but also merges into something more sinister, is a familiar enough feature of our experience. Likewise, the place which the urge to hurt another has in human life would almost certainly be misrepresented if it was set in too sharp a contrast with our 'normal' reaction. In particular, the tendency to pass on to others the evil that is done to us may be as basic as any human reaction.

The range of, more or less, normal reactions may, then, be rather wider than my discussion in Chapter 1 suggested. In making this point I do not mean to deny that there are reactions to another's suffering which could hardly be described as 'normal' and yet which are clearly reactions to the *suffering*. Certainly the urge to hurt may cross normal boundaries and take abnormal forms without thereby ceasing to be an 'urge to hurt'. When we remember the wide spectrum of 'normal' reactions, however, it becomes clear, I believe, that the seeds of such responses are to be found in more familiar settings. Further, the seeds may not only be there in the sense that responses of this *kind* are widespread. The 'abnormal' response may be *parasitic on* quite central aspects of the normal response. For example, the urge to humiliate or physically injure another is, at least in many cases, expressive of the recognition that the other is not to be treated in these ways. What he sees in the action is crucially dependent on his acceptance that in treating the other in these ways he is violating a demand which she makes on him. Now this relation of dependence, I am suggesting, may play a vital part in creating the possibility of our seeing such a response as expressive of an understanding that this is a person in pain. (I should stress that I am not suggesting that all reactions which most would find clearly morally objectionable are parasitic on ones which we take to be admirable. My point is simply that what we find here is not simply a collection of reactions which are linked by no more than our decision to call them all 'reactions to suffering' or 'reactions to human beings'; there are strong internal relations between the reactions. While in my example an unsympathetic response is dependent on a more primitive sympathetic response I take it that examples could be produced in which the relation runs in the opposite direction. Closely connected with this is the fact that for a reaction to be 'primitive' is not for it to be justified. I suspect that quite a bit of thinking in this area – including, I'm afraid, my own – suffers from a failure to keep absolutely clear about this point.)

The objection to the suggestion that it is our attitude towards another which is basic in our thought about them was this: it is one thing to recognise another as a person and quite another to hold any particular moral views about how he is to be treated. I have been suggesting that we can grant that, provided that we keep this point sharply separated from the philosophical 'recognition'/ 'attitude' contrast. Thus, it must be granted that we can imagine an individual who clearly recognises those around him as people yet does not share our own moral outlook. What we produce when we do this, however, is, I think, something that falls short of the picture of a radical alien that forms the background to much philosophical thought about these issues. Our feeling that the recognition is clearly present is dependent on the way in which we take for granted a background of reactions shared with us. Now this background of shared reactions can fall short of a shared 'moral outlook' in a variety of ways. It may fail to be that since the individual – a young child say – may *have* the reactions yet not have *endorsed* them in the way necessary for us to be able to say that he has a moral outlook. Again, the shared reactions may (will) include some – for example, the urge to hurt – which *we* would not endorse; and also some – for example, the idea that pain is, 'other things being equal', to be relieved – that have a too fundamental position in our thought to be said to be features of our 'moral outlook'. Provided, then, that we are working with a broad under-standing of what is part of an individual's 'attitude' towards others, and that we keep in mind the richness of what we might speak of as our 'normal attitude', we will not, I think, find it obvious that we can imagine an individual who clearly recognises those around him as people yet totally lacks our normal attitude towards them.[2]

I am not sure how one might prove decisively that there is a mistake in the way of presenting these matters which I am rejecting. Indeed, if someone who was clearly not under the influence of the confusions which I have been discussing continued to present matters in terms of the philosophical 'recognition'/'attitude' contrast I am not sure that I would want to speak of a 'mistake' in his thought. People who are wholly lacking in the relevant attitude towards other human beings (or wholly lacking in the relevant responses to a *particular* feature of the lives of others, such as their pains) and yet whose thought and talk about others is in other respects completely normal are not a common feature of our experience.[3] A consequence of this is that there is no well established way of describing such people. While, then, one might be suspicious of a philosopher's firm insistence that we and such an individual could not be said to differ in our understanding of the world and of our language there may be little room for the claim that he is actually mistaken in his suggestion.

At this point, then, I could only repeat my earlier insistence that to the extent that an individual's 'recognition of the reality of another' is divorced in some such way as this from our normal attitude towards others it ceases to be a notion in which I have much interest. What is important in our thought about others – at any rate, what interests me – is what Wittgenstein speaks of as our attitude towards them. Any suggestion that there is something distinct from this, namely 'recognising that the other is a person', which also needs to be considered is only relevant to my concerns in so far as it is argued that this is linked in a pretty direct way with the attitude. Thus, suppose that we can imagine someone who in connection with, say, a particular race uses the language of 'pain', 'anger' and so on and yet whose use of these words in this context is disconnected in a *radical* way from our normal attitudes: when we give the fact that one of these people 'is in pain' as a reason for our pity he is at sea in just the way that we would be if, without explanation, someone offered 'He has an IQ of 135' as a reason for pity; he is quite mystified by our tendency to turn away from the sight of suffering; and so on. Despite his use of the language of 'pain', and so on, I would, depending on just how radical the difference is, say that such a person was not ascribing pain and anger to these people; and, in an extreme case, that he does not recognise them as people. I need not, however, insist on this description. What is undeniable is that this individual is different from us in a crucial way. It is the difference that interests me.

(ii) The first objection to Wittgenstein's approach appeals to the idea that my understanding of what a person is leaves completely open the question of what my attitude towards persons should be. The second objection appeals to the apparently diametrically opposed idea that it is my understanding of what a person is which *closes* the question of what my attitude towards persons should be. According to this view, my acceptance that anything that is a person is an appropriate object of this range of reactions is *grounded in* my understanding of what a person is; my acceptance of another's pain as something to be relieved is *grounded in* my understanding of what pain is; and so on. My grasp of what people, pains, anger, and so on *are* is prior to and independent of my acceptance of them as providing me with reasons for actions and feelings of various kinds. This, it is argued, must be so since otherwise my understanding of what I have reason to do and feel would be arbitrary, a matter of personal idiosyncrasy, in a way which is in conflict in a pretty fundamental way with crucial features of our normal thought.

These claims might be further defended in the following way.

'Most of us take all the members of the species homo sapiens to be people in this sense – beings who are to be treated in these ways. Beyond that, we take members of other species to be appropriate objects of these responses in more limited ways; and there are many significant distinctions that we draw here: flies, most of us feel, are not to be treated just as dogs are. Now while there is rough agreement over most of this, disputes about just what forms of treatment are appropriate are a reasonably familiar feature of our experience. Consider, for example, disputes about our treatment of the foetus, or about our right to raise and kill animals for food. Behind some of these disputes there may lie complete agreement about the *kind* of creature with which we are dealing; it is, we might say, purely in our value judgements that we differ. Other cases are, however, different. Some, for example, say that we need feel no concern for the fish caught on the hook since fish do not feel pain. Remarks of a similar form are familiar in defences of factory farming; and have, indeed, arisen in connection with the treatment of other races. ("They do not feel pain as intensely as we do.") A deviation in a different direction from the norm in our society is found in the suggestion that flowers feel pain and are to be treated accordingly. Now in all these cases it is clear that claims about how a certain group is to be treated do not lie at the most fundamental level. These claims are defended or attacked by means of appeals to features of the group in question; appeals, that is, to their *intrinsic* characteristics, such as that they are creatures of a kind which do or do not feel pain.'

'This, as I say, is the way that such disputes do in practice appear to go. That a group is to be treated in a certain way is taken to be a *consequence* of the fact that members of it are, in themselves, creatures of a certain kind. "Creature of a kind which is to be treated in these ways" is not, then, the most fundamental characterisation of the kind of creature with which we are dealing. Now this feature of our normal way of understanding these issues must not be taken lightly. For what it brings out is the centrality of the idea that how beings with which I am confronted are to be treated is not a purely arbitrary matter. What attitude is appropriate towards another, for example towards another human being, is not a matter of mere personal preference, nor of the way in which I happen to be disposed to treat them. No doubt certain of our attitudes towards certain of the things around us could be understood as arbitrary in that sense: taste in colours for example. There are, perhaps, other cases in which we feel that there is some, but more limited, room for the influence of personal idiosyncrasies: whether it is acceptable to eat meat is not purely a matter of personal preference, but there is, it might be said, room for more than one defensible view on this. Such cases, however, have as a background another range of cases in which our attitudes are firmly anchored in the world. That I think of cows as creatures of a kind which are not to be treated in certain – inhumane – ways is not simply a reflection of my own reactions to cows; so that if this way of thinking became inconvenient a quite acceptable solution would be to simply try to change my reactions. My thinking of cows in that way is a reflection of my recognition of something about cows; in particular, it is a reflection of my recognition that they can suffer. It is this fact which stops my thought of how they are to be treated from being purely arbitrary in the objectionable sense.'

The same point can arise at another level. I spoke of another's pain as being 'something to be relieved', of another's anger as being 'something to be feared', and so on. Now again it will be said that while this way of speaking does highlight something which is central to our thought it does not capture what is *fundamental* in our thought. A pain, after all, is to be relieved because of what it is *in itself* – because, we might put it, of what it *feels* like. It is in virtue of this that it is to be relieved, just as it is in virtue of its shape and size that a chair is to be sat on. That a pain is to be relieved – that it is a thing of that kind – is not, then, the most primitive characterisation of it. Similarly with another's anger, gaze, and so on: these present themselves to me as things to be feared or hidden from because of my understanding of what, in some more fundamental sense, they *are*. The consequence of denying this will, it seems, again be arbitrariness of a quite extraordinary kind. For it will leave open the possibility that another might 'find' in the world things utterly different from what I find: where I find 'pains', things to be relieved, he finds things to be nurtured; and there will be no room for the idea that one of us is right and the other wrong because of the character of what we are speaking of. To avoid the conclusion that my attitude towards what I encounter in the world is, in this sense, totally arbitrary we must acknowledge that, as we might put it, metaphysics is prior to ethics.

This, I think, is the best, and most common, ground for feeling that questions about what a person is, or what it is to think of another as a person, must be prior to and independent of questions concerning what attitude towards persons is appropriate. It is, however, clear that some further work is needed if it is to be shown that anything along these lines can remove the supposed threat of 'arbitrariness'. In particular, it will need to be shown in what way the connection between, on the one hand, this prior 'understanding of what a person is' and, on the other, our acceptance that a person is to be treated in certain ways is not an 'arbitrary' one. For, of course, unless this form of treatment can in some way be shown to be *justified* by 'the fact that a person is a being of this kind' the supposed benefits of this way of viewing the matter will have been lost completely. It is to the question of how this connection might be made that I will now turn.

4

Justification and the First Person

The young child unreflectively has a certain attitude towards the human beings that it encounters. It has a pattern of reactions to others out of which develops the more complex range of reactions of adult human beings to each other. It responds to another's smile, looks into another's eyes, seeks the comfort of physical contact and so on. What the child observes of the other is, by itself, enough to bring forth the response. Further, responses of this kind are (at least) as 'basic' in the child's life as are its responses to anything else in its environment. As soon as we can see in the child's life any recognisable responses to things around it, beyond the most primitive biological reflexes, we can see such distinctive reactions to other human beings.

At least I rather suspect that all of that is so. In any case, let us assume for the moment that it is, for the assumption will help to highlight the philosophical issue. It is clear, I think, that the philosopher who is worried about 'arbitrariness' need not question these claims provided they are understood as purely empirical claims about child development. Such a philosopher will, however, insist that the truth of all that leaves completely open the question: is there anything in what the child, or we, observe which shows these reactions to be appropriate?

In one sense it might be said that there is. We might say that what we observe is, for example, a man writhing in agony; and the fact that that is what we are observing shows certain reactions to be appropriate. This, however, may not get us to the heart of the matter. For we need to be absolutely clear that in speaking in this way we are not taking for granted reactions to such situations which all of us happen to have in a strong form but which are 'arbitrary' in the sense which has been argued to be objectionable. We need to imagine, then, that we are confronted with somebody to whom these reactions are quite foreign; who has, for example, never thought of anything with which he is confronted as anything

33

other than an object to be *used* by him. Our question will then be: could we, by carefully pointing out to this man observable features of that with which he is confronted, bring him to see, at least, how these reactions could be thought to be appropriate? Well, perhaps he has never looked properly at a human face before; and when we somehow manage to get him to focus his attention in the right way he responds to the other's expression in the way we judge to be appropriate. Again, however, we are, it seems, completely dependent on the fact that a particular situation happens to call forth the same response in him as it does in us. We are no nearer to taking a step beyond the way human beings *happen* to respond to each other and it is quite obscure how any development along these lines could do anything to remove this form of 'arbitrariness'.

In Chapter 2 I discussed one kind of consideration which I suggested might push us towards the view that the real person 'lies behind' the human being that others can observe (where this phrase is understood in a way which leaves room for philosophical scepticism.) The idea there was that if the person was the extended, tangible human being then the attitude which we have towards others would clearly *not* be appropriate. A different kind of pressure in the same direction might arise from the considerations of my last paragraph. The idea now would be that if the person was the extended, tangible human being then the attitude which we have towards others could not be *shown to be* appropriate. Thus, suppose that we think that our attitude towards others would be arbitrary in an objectionable sense if it could not be shown to be appropriate by a consideration of its object; and that the force of 'shown to be appropriate' here is such that this will only have been achieved if the demonstration does not in any way presuppose reactions that we happen to have to others but could conceivably lack. It is, I have suggested, quite obscure how anything in what we observe of others could provide the basis for such a demonstration: there is nothing in what we observe which would inevitably reveal to a total alien the appropriateness of our attitude. Thus, what is crucial to our thought of others as people, we will conclude, must be something which, in the relevant sense, lies behind what we observe.

Even if taking that step was progress, however, it could hardly be the end of the matter. To say that the real person 'lies behind the surface' is not in itself to meet the worry about arbitrariness. For we still need to see how what 'lies behind the surface' might do the work which what 'is on the surface' could not do. We are, that is, still left with the question: what could a *justification* for our having towards others the particular attitude that we do possibly look like? Now, a dogmatic answer to this question might just reveal the paucity of my own imagination so perhaps I should speak instead of the form which it is widely assumed such a justification must take. We must start with a case in which the appropriateness of the attitude is not, at least for our present purposes, in question. This position is filled by the attitude that I have towards *myself*. That I ought to have this attitude towards others will then be demonstrated, or at least made probable, by showing, as conclusively as this can be done, that others are in the relevant respect like me.

The argument from analogy is of this form. As it is normally presented it starts with the idea that: 'When I believe that someone else is in pain I am believing that he is feeling the same thing as I feel when I am in pain.' Now that much should, perhaps, be quite uncontroversial. We are, however, tempted to think (and one who believes that we need an argument from analogy does think) that this is in some way an *explanation* of what I believe: that it elucidates what it is that I believe. We think that my experience of my own pains is the primary fact and that to judge that another is in pain is to project what I learn from my own case onto the other. My own pain serves as a model by means of which I am to understand what it is for another to be in pain. Thus, I need a justification for thinking of others as beings of a kind that feel pain. The justification is provided by the fact that there are great similarities in appearance and behaviour between myself and others. These give me good reason to believe that those ways of thinking which are clearly in place in my own case are also in place in the case of others; that is to say, for thinking that others feel pain.

I will not pursue directly the question of whether the argument from analogy could justify what it is supposed to justify; for my interest in the argument stems from the special place which it takes the first person point of view to have in our thought about human beings. It is assumed that the individual's thought about himself serves as a model on which his thought about others can be based. The 'arbitrariness' of my attitude towards others is removed by showing that it is the analogue in relations with others of the attitude which is clearly securely grounded in the case of my thought about myself. Now my question will be: even if the argument from analogy was, in its own terms, successful, would what it justified remotely resemble those ways of thinking about others, of responding to them, which we take to be appropriate?

I touched on this question as it arises in connection with our thought about another's actions in Chapter 2. I want now to consider in the same light our thought about physical pain. Consider, then, my thought about my own physical pain. My own pain is, other things being equal, something to be relieved if at all possible; and it is something to be feared. If you ask why I am taking some aspirin the answer 'I have a headache' gives a reason for what I am doing. If you ask why I am afraid the answer 'I have to undergo a painful operation' gives a reason for my fear. The argument from analogy can, then, be construed as an attempt to show that such attitudes, which are appropriate in my thought about myself, are also appropriate in my thought about others; and so to show that the attitude which I have towards others is not totally arbitrary.

There are, however, difficulties here. Another's pain is something to be relieved. It is not, however, something to be feared – at least in the way that my own pain is. So if I transfer this, that pain is something to be feared, to my thought about another's pain I will be going badly wrong. Now it might be said in reply that in understanding what is involved in the move from the first to the third person I understand that this component, the appropriateness of fear, drops out. This suggestion cannot, however, be taken seriously until we are told why the same point does not apply to the thought of another's pain as something to be relieved. Alternatively, it might be said that the argument from analogy has the conclusion that another's pain is something to be feared, and it *is – by the other*; but now if this is said it must also be said that what the argument establishes is that another's pain is something to be relieved by the other. While there is nothing wrong with that conclusion we have now lost something of central importance to what the argument was supposed to achieve. It was supposed to justify the way in which *I* think of the *other*: to show me, for example, that I have reason to help the other in certain circumstances. As we are now being asked to take the argument the idea that it might show me anything about what my attitude towards the other should be has been completely abandoned.

To say that another's pain is not something to be feared in the sense in which my own pain is is not to say that we care less about the pains of others than about our own. It is to make a point about the form which our concern takes. I might be as much, or more, horrified at the prospect of a loved one's suffering as at the prospect of my own, but the form which my horror takes is not fear.[1] One way in which we might approach this is this. We might say that another person in pain is to be pitied. Now, while there is such a thing as 'self-pity' to which people are, to various degrees, prone, it is hardly *the* characteristic form taken by one's concern about one's own pain. If my thought of others as appropriate objects of pity were dependent on my pitying myself when in pain the less self-absorbed among us would be mystified by the thought.

The language of 'pity' and 'self-pity' may, however, not be too helpful here. One problem lies in the fact that the relation between pity and self-pity may be less clear than the terms would suggest. Another problem is that the terminology is simply too crude to do justice to our thought. Is, for example, 'pity' really the word for what I may feel in the face of my young child's prolonged and intense suffering? In any case, what is needed here is a considera-tion of a kind of detail which no terminology of this kind can, by itself, highlight sufficiently.

Consider, for example, our thought about the *past* pains of ourselves and others. That I suffered severe pain yesterday is not, in itself, something to be distressed about. I look back at yester-day's pain with relief that it is over, not horror that I suffered so badly. This *radical* asymmetry in my thought about my own past and future pains is not reflected in my thought about the pains of others. Certainly I may be relieved that a loved one's suffering is over. Nevertheless, the news that a loved one suffered terribly yesterday can fill me with horror in a way which is not radically different from that in which the news that he will suffer terribly tomorrow fills me with horror.[2] With that, most, I take it, would regard as absurd the suggestion that 'Distress about the sufferings undergone in the First World War is wholly misplaced since it is all in the past.'

Another important asymmetry here is to be seen in the role which the human form plays in my response to the pain of another. Consider, for example, the kind of concern about another's pain which is expressed in my watching him closely for changes for better or worse. Again, consider the way in which my horror at another's pain may be tied up with a difficulty in looking at him, and, in particular, at his face. Consider also the ways in

which my expressions of sympathy for the other may be inseparable from the fact that he is of the human form: I might, for
example, look into his eyes. Now, it is, perhaps, imaginable that
my bodily form should enter into my thought about my own pain
in some, though not all, of these ways. It is clear, however, that it
does not characteristically do so. It seems, then, that we have here
another way in which the kind of horror that I might feel in the face
of another's pain is quite different from anything that most of us
feel about our own. (I will develop this point in greater detail in
Chapter 6.)

It is, perhaps, with the case of physical pain that it is most
tempting to think that our responses to others could be *justified* by
appeal to the supposedly more basic ways in which I am concerned
about my own states. I will return to this case at later points in this
book as I believe that there are other deep and important asymmetries here which I have not yet touched on. For the moment,
however, I will turn to some cases in which this model of justification has far less plausibility. Take the significance that we attach to
another's look. How is my own experience of seeing supposed to
show me that the fact that another's eyes are on me is something of
significance; or that eye contact with another is something of
significance? It will not do to answer that my own experience of
seeing shows me that the eyes are connected with knowledge and
that the significance which the other's look has for me lies in the
recognition that when his eyes are on me he learns about me. For
one thing, this still leaves us with the question: what in my own
experience of knowing something about another shows me that a
significance of the relevant kind is to be attached to *another*
knowing something about *me*? For another, this understanding of
the significance which another's look can have for me is seriously
impoverished. When I hide from another's gaze it may not be at all
through fear of what they will learn about me. There are aspects of
our lives – most obviously, perhaps, aspects with a strong 'biological' dimension – which we do not suppose others to be
ignorant of yet which we would be loath to have observed by
them. Similarly, the significance of eye contact with another – for
example the difficulty that we may have in meeting their gaze –
need have nothing to do with thoughts concerning what they may
learn about us.

Again, consider the way in which another's anger can be fearful.
There is the fear which is tied up with thoughts about what might

happen: with, for example, my worry that I might get hit. That, however, is not what concerns us here since there is, I take it, little temptation to think that my recognition of the other as fearful in *that* sense is dependent on my own experience of anger. What is at issue is the other way in which most of us find another's intense anger, especially if it is directed at us, disturbing. Now consider someone who is never disturbed in this way by another's anger and is mystified by the way in which others are disturbed. Is there any reason to suppose that a careful consideration of 'what it feel like to be angry', that close reflection on his own state next time he is angry, will help to make things clear to him? oes my own anger present itself to me as something dreadful in *that* sense?

It might be replied that I may think of my own anger as some- thing dreadful in the relevant sense; for example, I acknowledge it as something to be feared by the one I am angry with. Similarly, I may recognise my own gaze as something of significance in the sense I have discussed. In certain circumstances I do not look at another: not because I do not enjoy the sight but because a person is not to be looked at when in such a condition. Thus, it might be said, there is not, as I have suggested, a radical asymmetry between my thought about myself – my anger, my look – and my thought about others. Where, then, is the difficulty in the idea that these ways of thinking about others could be shown to be appro- priate in the way suggested by the argument from analogy?

The fact that asymmetries in our thought may be less marked than I have suggested does not itself show that our thought about others might be justified by an appeal to our thought about ourselves. *That* could only be said if there was a clear sense in which the relevant feature of my thought about myself was more basic, more firmly rooted, than its analogue in my thought about others. Now there *is* some temptation to think that the ways in which I characteristically care about my own physical pain are quite transparently appropriate and so that they can serve as a suitable ground for justifying my concern about the pains of others. Here, however, the strong asymmetries in our thought stand in the way of the justifying step. In other cases the asymmetries are less marked; but, with that, the temptation to think that my thought about myself is more transparently in place than its analogue in my thought about others is weakened. For example, is the idea that *my* gaze is something to be avoided by others when in a certain state (for instance, when naked) in any relevant sense more basic than the idea that the *other's* gaze has that significance – that is, is to be avoided by me when I am in that state? If not, the idea that the former can serve as the basis for an analogical justification of the latter collapses.

My last paragraph is connected with a further point. I have constantly appealed to the idea of what is 'basic' in our thought. The idea that we might justify our thought about others by an appeal to our thought about ourselves turns on the view that the latter is more 'basic', more 'firmly grounded', than the former. Now what sense of 'basic' is relevant here? We are not, I take it, concerned with what is psychologically basic. One who sees a place for the argument from analogy can, as I remarked earlier, acknowledge that the young child has a powerful natural response to the eyes and facial expression of others as soon as he is capable of discerning these at all. He can allow this since what he is concerned with is the *justification* of our thought, not its genesis. The idea, then, is that our thought about others stands in need of justification in a way in which our thought about ourselves does not; but in what sense does my thought about myself not stand in need of justification? Consider, for example, the case in which the idea behind the argument from analogy is most appealing: the case of physical pain. Can my own experience of pain be said to *show* me that pain is something to be relieved and something to be feared? Can my proneness to these ways of caring be understood as a reflection of my recognition of a truth: the truth that pains are a kind of thing to be concerned about in these ways? Only if something of this form can be said can the ways I think of my own pains serve, by way of an analogical argument, to remove the threat of 'arbitrariness' in my attitude towards the pains of others.

Now there are, I believe, tempting illusions here. We are inclined to think, first, that what is logically basic is my concern about a pain I am feeling *now*. My concern about future pain can, it is thought, be shown to be appropriate by an appeal to the more basic form of concern that I feel about a present pain. Concern about my own present pain, it is then thought, is logically inescapable and so constitutes a suitable basis on which justifications can be built.

It is the second stage of this line of thought which concerns me now.[3] *Is* there a sense in which concern about my own present pains is 'logically inescapable'? Well, yes, there is. We could not ascribe pain at all to a being that did not characteristically 'respond to its own pain' in certain ways. That a person is, for example, inclined to nurse the painful spot, to relieve the pain by, say, changing position, and so on is crucial to the possibility of our thinking of him as a being that does feel pain. In this sense, being susceptible to pains and being disposed to have a certain attitude towards one's pains are inseparable. [4] To say that the attitude is, in this sense, inescapable is, however, not at all the same as saying that it can be seen to be appropriate by reflection on the nature of pains. What we have here is not a *justification* of the attitude; the connection is of a kind which *pre-empts* any questions about justification. My attitude towards my own present pains does not stand in need of justification; but the reason for this is *not* that that attitude is transparently appropriate given the nature of pains.

I formulated a possible protest against Wittgenstein's approach to 'the reality of others' in terms of the insistence that 'metaphysics is prior to ethics'. The idea was that the appropriateness of our attitude towards and treatment of others turns on something that is more basic: on, that is, the truth or falsity of our thought that the other is a being of a kind that feels pain, anger, and so on. It is then supposed that this thought can be shown to be justified by means of the argument from analogy. One way in which my argument in this chapter might be characterised is this. Even if the argument from analogy could justify my thought of the other as a being that feels pain, and so on, it still would not have justified the attitude which I have towards the other; and it would have failed in this task at two stages. First, there is no sense in which the attitude which I have towards others could be said to be derived by analogy from the attitude which I have towards myself: if the argument from analogy was capable of justifying something here the ways of thinking of others which it would justify would be wildly different from what we take to be appropriate. Now one might think that the correct conclusion to draw from this is that our present ways of thinking of others stand in need of revision. If this is said some careful work will need to be done to see just what revisions will be called for. For example, what form will my concern for another's pain take if I transfer all that can be transferred from the concern that I characteristically have about my own pain? We need not pursue that question however, since the search for a 'logical grounding' for our attitude towards others collapses at another point. The foundation on which the justification is built, namely, my attitude towards myself, is no more firmly grounded, in the relevant sense, than that which it is supposed to underpin. If there is *any* sense in which it can be said to be 'more firmly grounded', which I rather doubt, that sense is quite irrelevant to the worry about 'arbitrariness'.

Should we conclude that no argument of this form can establish, or give me good reason to believe, that these beings that I see are people; should we, that is, conclude that the argument from analogy fails? Or should we conclude that while the argument might, so far as what I have said goes, still establish *that*, it does not establish that they are to be treated any differently from, say, a stone? These are not questions that I will pursue. What I have wanted to bring out is that *if* we construe the relation between the 'metaphysics' and the 'ethics' in this way we are going to face serious difficulties in connecting the two together.[5] We are going to face serious difficulties in showing how the metaphysics supports particular claims about what our attitude towards, and treatment of, others should be. It is, then, quite unclear how anything along the familiar lines considered in this chapter – anything of even roughly the form of the argument from analogy – could remove the supposed threat of arbitrariness in my attitude towards others.

5

Arbitrariness

(i) Our problem was that of explaining the connection between the notion of a person and that attitude which we think to be appropriate towards persons: between my thought of these beings that I see around me as people and my having towards them the attitude which I characteristically do. Now the situation for the approach discussed in my previous chapter is, in fact, rather worse than the closing remarks of that chapter might suggest. It is not simply that the approach which attempts to ground all our responses in the first person point of view fails to provide the justification that it seeks for our attitude towards others. For one might think (as I do) that the notion of 'justification' invoked here is seriously misconceived and yet hold that there is an important connection between the recognition of another as a person and the having of a certain attitude towards the other. Now on the approach I have been considering it is insisted that it ought to be possible to bring someone to have the normal attitude towards the beings around him *by* bringing him to recognise that they are people; that is what is required by the thought that this characteristic attitude stands in need of justification. My recognition of these beings as people is, then, on this view, quite independent of my having towards them the relevant attitude; for if it were not it could not serve to justify the attitude. This, I have argued, appears to leave us with no answer to the question: just what is the connection between my 'recognition of these beings as people' and my having this attitude towards them? In failing to substantiate its favoured account of this relation that approach leaves us with no answer of any kind to this question.

Wittgenstein suggests an answer to this question; but it is an answer which requires us to abandon this whole way of looking at the matter. Consider the following passage from *Zettel*:

540. It is a help here to remember that it is a primitive reaction to tend, to treat, the part that hurts when someone else is in pain; and not merely when oneself is – and so to pay attention to other

people's pain-behaviour, as one does *not* pay attention to one's own pain behaviour.

541. But what is the word 'primitive' meant to say here? Presumably that this sort of behaviour is *pre-linguistic*: that a language-game is based *on it*, that it is the prototype of a way of thinking and not the result of thought.

A 'language-game is based on' the reaction; it is 'the prototype of a way of thinking'. Wittgenstein rejects the idea that my thought of others as, for example, beings that feel pain is completely separable from my readiness to respond to them in these ways. With this must go the idea that the thought could underpin the reaction: the idea that we could show the reaction to be appropriate *by* showing that these are beings of the kind that feel pain.

I take it that considered simply as an account of the development of a child's picture of the world Wittgenstein's suggestion has great plausibility. As I remarked before, the child does, from a very early age, have towards others many of those distinctive reactions which I have mentioned. There is no reason to suppose that there is any sense in which these reactions are dependent on something that is more basic in the child's life: namely, the thought that these beings he sees around him are people who feel pain, get upset, and so on. As the child develops we teach him to ascribe pain to others, to say 'Daddy is in pain', in just those circumstances in which he is already responding in an instinctive way to one who is in pain. Just how much in the child's responses to others is innate and how much is the product of imitation, explicit training, and so on is not important here. Nor is it important to be clear what in his responses can be said to be *pre*-linguistic and what is picked up as he learns the language. ('Be nice to Daddy; he's got a bad headache.') What is crucial, at least for my purposes, is that the connection between ascribing pain to another and thinking of them as one who is to be treated in a certain way is there from the start. Or, to move to a different level, a person is from the start a being towards which a certain attitude is appropriate.

As I said, as an account of the development of the child's thought, something along these lines appears to be very plausible. The idea that 'understanding what a person is' is prior to and quite independent of 'acknowledging that a person is a being towards which a certain attitude is appropriate' does not derive from a detached examination of human life. It derives, as I suggested

earlier, from the idea that if this is denied we will be committed to
the conclusion that what attitude we take to be appropriate
towards others is not grounded in anything, and so is completely
arbitrary. Thus, certain forms of criticism of the thought of myself
and others – forms of criticism which we feel *must* be possible –
would not be possible. Now I have argued that if that was a real
worry it would be a worry that would not be removed by the
suggestion that there is something that we can call 'understanding
what a person is' which is prior to and independent of the attitude;
for it would still need to be shown how *the connection between the
understanding and the attitude* was not an arbitrary one. Given that
this is so we have here no reason for moving towards that way of
viewing the matter. I want, however, to suggest now that the
worry may not have quite the force which it initially appears to.

(ii) There are, perhaps, two broad categories of relevant cases in
which we feel that there must be room for criticism of someone's
attitude towards others. There are cases in which a person fails to
have towards a certain group of beings the attitude which we hold
to be appropriate; and there are cases in which a person has
towards certain things, say plants, features of the attitude which
we have towards other human beings but which we hold to be
clearly inappropriate here. The two kinds of case raise rather
different issues. In this section I will focus on the first.[1] Now I have
characterised this group of cases in very general terms. It would, as
it stands, cover cases in which it is held that some, or most, of us
fail to have a proper attitude towards animals, those who are
suffering sufficiently out of our sight to go unnoticed, members of
other races or of the opposite sex, the mentally handicapped, and
so on. I suspect, however, that the differences between these cases
are not of great importance from the point of view that concerns
me at the moment.

Consider, then, a case in which we want to criticise someone's
attitude towards members of other races. There is a range of cases
we can imagine here. An extreme case would be that suggested by
Wittgenstein in which a slave owner regards his slaves as automata.[2] Closer to what we might find in practice would be cases in
which concern about the well-being of members of other races is
severely limited, certain forms of respect for the other – for
example, that involved in stepping aside when on a collision
course with them – are entirely absent or dramatically truncated,

and so on. We can imagine that the lack of concern is accompanied by the insistence that 'They do not feel pain as intensely as we do'.

We want to say that there is something wrong in this individual's attitude; that the attitude is wrong because of the character of its object: because these are *people*. Have I not argued, however, that we cannot say this: that we cannot say that the appropriateness or inappropriateness of an individual's attitude towards others is dependent on the kind of being that the other is? That would be a simplification (which I have, no doubt, fallen into at times.) What should, I think, be said is this. We *can* say that there is a lack of 'fit' between an individual's attitude and its object, but only on the assumption that he shares a good deal with us. When I have spoken of there being no need of, and no possibility of, a justification of our attitude towards others my remarks were made within the context of a particular philosophical tradition. Within that tradition a central image is that of a man who gazes in a slightly bemused way at others not sure whether to say 'Hello' or to use them as a doorstop.[3] With such a being there would be no reason to think that he had missed something: no reason to think that more careful consideration of what he is confronted with would bring him round to our way of regarding others. With that, the suggestion that he has 'got something wrong' is emptied of content. Now it is rarely, I think, at all like this in the cases with which we are confronted in practice.

It may be a help to remember that in most cases which arise in practice we do not *just* want to say that the individual has got something wrong. Or rather, we characteristically take this criticism to be a criticism *of the person*. It is not simply that he has slipped up in his inferences from the evidence. (As I might fail to be afraid because I have not noticed the danger). We, at any rate often, feel that there is a place for moral criticism of him. Now what is it that creates a place for criticism of this form? There may be a variety of cases here but one is surely this. We feel that he is to be criticised because we suspect that he is only able to sustain his attitude towards these people by refusing, or failing, to look at them properly.

We want to say that his failure to have an appropriate attitude shows that he has got something wrong. He is not just different from us; he is to be corrected. Those who say that members of another race 'do not feel pain as intensely as we do' have got their facts wrong and, accordingly, their concern *ought* not to be limited in the way in which it is. Now the importance of remembering that we generally feel that *moral* criticism is possible here lies in what that reveals about the *kind* of 'mistake about the facts' which is involved here. The 'mistake' (if that is the right word) is one that would be corrected if his attention to the individuals in question was what we hold it should be. We suspect that if he really looked at the other he would not say that they 'do not feel pain as intensely as we do'; that if he lived closely with them he would ascribe to them the depth of feeling which he has, up till now, only associated with members of his own race. If he looked properly the full range of 'reactions to persons' would become engaged. It is this that allows us to say: 'There is something wrong in this individual's attitude. And the attitude is wrong because of the character of its object; because these are *people*.'⁴

One, though not the only, case in which moral criticism is in place is that in which the lack of attention to the other is motivated: he does not look because, in some sense, he knows what he will see. I will not pursue the further intriguing questions which arise here since my aim has only been to dissociate the kind of judgement we want to make in such cases from certain philosophical pictures. In particular, I am suggesting, the judgement that such a person has got something wrong is in no way dependent on the philosophical picture of the relation between understanding on the one hand and emotion and action on the other which has dominated Modern English-speaking philosophy. With that point goes another. We are, for reasons outlined at the beginning of Chapter 4, inclined to think that such a judgement is dependent on the thought that the real person 'lies behind the human being that we encounter' – where these words are understood in a way which leaves room for scepticism. 'For', we might reason, 'these people see what we see yet they react differently. Thus, if their thought is in conflict with the facts *what* it is in conflict with must lie behind the observable surface.' I am suggesting that the criticism that we want to make in these cases is not only consistent with but indeed *requires* that it is what is there, to be seen, in front of him which shows his judgements about, and associated attitude towards, these people to be inappropriate. It is only because what is there to be seen shows him to be wrong that our criticism of his thought can be *moral* criticism.

Suppose that the following question is raised: 'Is it not just *true* that people of other races feel pain as intensely as we do? Were not

those who denied this just wrong? Their words simply did not
match the facts and their attitude towards and treatment of other
races was unacceptable because of what the facts were.' I am
suggesting that all of this almost certainly can be said. 'Almost
certainly' because the possibility of saying this is dependent on
further features of the lives of those whose thought we are
criticising. The words which we address to them – 'Other races feel
pain as intensely as we do' – can serve as a reminder, or a
correction, only if they share enough with us that they have within
them the possibility of being 'reminded' or 'corrected'. In the vast
majority of cases we can safely assume that this is so. Thus, there is
no question of us here arbitrarily, that is to say, without justification, trying to bring the others round to our way of viewing the
matter.

Consider now Wittgenstein's slave-owners who regard their
slaves as automatons:

> In lectures Wittgenstein imagined a tribe of people who had the
> idea that their slaves had no feelings, no souls – that they were
> automatons – despite the fact that the slaves had human bodies,
> behaved like their masters, and even spoke the same language.
> Wittgenstein undertook to try to give sense to that idea. When a
> slave injured himself or fell ill or complained of pains, his master
> would try to heal him. The master would let him rest when he
> was fatigued, feed him when he was hungry and thirsty, and so
> on. Furthermore, the masters would apply to the slaves our
> usual distinctions between genuine complaints and malingering.
> So what could it mean to say that they had the idea that the
> slaves were automatons? Well, they would *look* at the slaves in a
> peculiar way. They would observe and comment on their move-
> ments *as if* they were machines. ('Notice how smoothly his limbs
> move.') They would discard them when they were worn and
> useless, like machines. If a slave received a mortal injury and
> twisted and screamed in agony, no master would avert his gaze
> in horror or prevent his children from observing the scene, any
> more than he would if the ceiling fell on a printing press. Here is
> difference in 'attitude' that is not a matter of believing or expecting
> different facts.[5]

This, of course, is only the beginning of a story and I suspect that
an attempt to really fill in the details would prove a tricky business.

Be that as it may, let us suppose that this attitude survives unscathed through constant confrontation with the details of the lives of their slaves. We must suppose further that, with the significant exception of the fact that their attitude is what it is, we have no grounds for claiming that they are not looking properly at their slaves – not attending properly to what is in front of them. Now we will only be able to say that these slave-owners have 'got something wrong', that there is a dispute between us to be settled by confrontation with the relevant facts, if we think of the 'relevant facts' as 'lying behind the observable surface of the human being'; and the sense of this phrase which is involved here is not the familiar one in which the surface which another presents to us can be penetrated by patient interaction with him. For we are assuming that no amount of interaction with their slaves makes any difference to the attitude of these slave-owners. The sense of 'lies behind the surface' which will be required is that involved in the idea that it is consistent with everything that we can actually observe of another that he is not a person at all.

If we are to say that these slave-owners have 'got something wrong' then there will be strong pressure on us to view the matter in this way. Is it obvious, however, that this *is* what should be said? To put the same question in another way: would the suggestion that there was simply no such thing as resolving this difference between us and the slave-owners have the implication that our thought is 'arbitrary' in a sense that is obviously unacceptable? Do our normal ways of thinking commit us to the idea that it must be possible to justify our way of looking at things in the face of *this* kind of deviation?

We do not say that the tree has 'got something wrong' if it drops a branch on someone. If a tree regularly dropped branches on passers-by but only on members of one particular race we would, after a certain point, be astonished, but still would not, I think, speak of it as having 'got something wrong'. That point, I suppose, would apply also to the dog who showed strong discriminations along racial lines in its reactions to people. There is some sense in which neither the tree nor the dog shares enough with us for that way of speaking to find a foothold. Now is it clear that these slave-owners share what is needed with us for us to be able to say that they have got something wrong? It might be said that it is clear that they judge their slaves to be automatons and that is all that is needed for there to be room for the idea that they have got something wrong; but why should it be thought that *that* is any clearer than it was in the case of the dog? My suspicion is that we only think that these suggestions are clear because we fail to appreciate just how extraordinary the imagined case is. These slave-owners would be so alien to us, we would have so little grasp of what was going on, that it is quite unclear why we should be tempted to describe the situation in terms of a judgement that they make about their slaves, rather than in terms closer to those that we might employ in attempting to explain the dog's behaviour.

It is crucial to my suggestion here that these slave-owners *would* be utterly alien. If they could be represented as just a few more steps down the road of callousness and self-deception with which we are familiar my point would lose whatever force it has; but then, for reasons which I tried to establish earlier, the case would, in a different way, cease to be philosophically troubling.

(iii) I want very briefly to consider the way in which the points I have been making emerge within the context of the individual's thought about his own attitude to others. One might reason in the following way: 'To insist that the attitude is basic, beyond justification, in the way that Wittgenstein does is to insist that it is up to me to *choose* what attitude to adopt towards others. Thus, I can, for example, eliminate ninety-nine per cent of the human race from my picture of the world without being in any conflict with the facts. Now one should be suspicious of any philosophical view which has results which are as convenient as this.' One response to this would be to argue that we are, in fact, quite incapable of abandoning this attitude at will in the way suggested. 'Nature' as Hume might put it 'has not left this to (our) choice, and has doubtless esteemed it an affair of too great importance to be trusted to our uncertain reasonings and speculations'.[6] It might be replied, however, that this is simply not true: 'For one thing, most of us in fact lack the attitude in question towards ninety-nine per cent of the human race; newspaper reports of distant suffering produce no more than a ripple in our lives. Connected with this is the fact that we *do* have some control over our attitudes here. It is a control that we exercise every time we turn off the television reports which we cannot watch without being moved. In that sense we *can* think of others in a way which involves substantially less than what you have spoken of as "an attitude towards a person". Further, even if it was true that, given our nature, we could not have this impoverished attitude the sense of "could not" involved would not be the relevant one: we are being offered a psychological sense of "could not" where what is needed is an acknowledgement that to think differently from the way we do would be to be in conflict with the facts.'

The suggestion that most of us lack the attitude in question towards most of the human race needs to be treated with some care. I am not, in saying that, suggesting that perhaps most of us think pretty much as we should about the rest of mankind. My point is, rather, that it is important to be clear about the kind of deficiency there is in our thought. For example, we perhaps have the relevant attitude in the sense that we accept that we have good reason to do and feel certain things for others. Further, and connected with that, we perhaps would, and perhaps know that we would, respond in something closer to an 'appropriate' way if we were directly confronted with the sufferings of those in distant countries. In so far as this is so, I can view my own thought as subject to criticism in just the way in which I can view the thought of others as subject to criticism.

But does not all of this simply distort the crucial thing? 'For it suggests', it will be said, 'that the fundamental reason why it would be wrong for me to try to eliminate most of the human race from my picture of the world is to be found in certain features of my nature: in the fact, for example, that I would respond in a certain way if I looked more closely. Surely, however, it is in the nature of the *others*, not in *my* nature, that the fundamental reason is to be found: it is because these are people that it would be wrong for me to move in that direction.'

While I accept these claims about where 'the fundamental reason is to be found', I do not believe that anything that I have said is in conflict with them. Suppose that I had to hand the means to completely eliminate from my life the relevant attitude towards a large section of mankind. Once I had succeeded in doing this there would be no room for the suggestion that my thought was mistaken. What possible objection could there be then to my inducing this change in myself? There is, I think, nothing in what I have said which stands in the way of the claim that the most direct formulation of the objection will be in terms of the fact that 'These are people'. Of course, that is not something that I will acknowledge, at least in any significant sense, after I have induced the change; but what is the relevance of that? I can, and do, acknowledge it now; and it is reflection on the others, not reflection on myself, that will show me, if anything does, that the step is not one that I can take.

In Chapter 1 I presented a very rough indication of the form which I think an answer to the question 'What is it to recognise another as a person?' should take. I suggested that what Wittgenstein calls the 'attitude' which we have towards the other is fundamental here; and briefly discussed certain aspects of that attitude. Now the objection that we may feel to this is that in speaking of the attitude – rather than a judgement about what we are confronted with – as basic, our thought is represented as 'arbitrary' in a sense which is clearly disturbing. Besides suggesting, in Chapter 4, that if there is a worry of this form here no other picture can do anything to ease it, I have, in this chapter, tried to do something to defuse the worry. In conclusion, I should add that I do not believe that anything that I have said can, or should, remove all possible worries that one might have about what Wittgenstein speaks of as 'the arbitrariness of grammar'. For I do not think that finding Wittgenstein's thought disturbing at this point need involve any *mistake*. Indeed, I am inclined to say that there is something here which *ought*, at least now and then, to strike us as an astonishing discovery. I will return to this point in the Postscript.

Part II
The Mind, the Body
and the Human Being

6

The Mind and the Body

(i) 'My attitude towards him is an attitude towards a soul. I am not of the *opinion* that he has a soul.' Wittgenstein's remark must, I suggested, be viewed in the light of the familiar idea that we should mark my thought about other people off from my thought about, say, stones by saying that I believe that the former, but not the latter, 'have minds'. In Part I my emphasis was on the suggestion that we should think of what is basic in our thought about others as being a certain 'attitude' towards them rather than a certain 'belief' about them. Central to Part II will be the way in which the notion of a 'mind' which arises here, and its correlate the philosophical notion of a 'body', may introduce serious distortion into our thought; they do this in so far as they displace the notion of the *human being* from its fundamental place in our ontology.

It is important to be clear that the notions of 'mind' and 'body' which commonly arise here *are*, as I put it, philosophical ones. Certainly there is a mind/body contrast which plays a significant role in non-philosophical thought. That familiar contrast is, however, very different from the one which sometimes appears in philosophy. Thus, philosophers often speak as if physical sensations are 'mental states'. Yet our normal terminology involves an explicit *contrast* between 'physical' and 'mental' suffering: a pain in the knee falls on the 'bodily' side of the mind/body dichotomy. Closely linked with this is the fact that when we speak of 'the power of mind over matter' that *includes* cases in which a person controls his experience of pain by an effort of concentration and *excludes* normal cases of arm-raising or talking. (So if there is something to be wondered at in 'the power of mind over matter', as I am inclined to think there is, *what* is to be wondered at is not at all what the Cartesian dualist would have us believe; and it may take a bit of work to say just what it is that we should find remarkable.) Finally, for the moment, we can note that a common version of the philosophical contrast implies that the only alternative to its being her body that I am interested in is that it is her

55

mind that captivates me. In our normal thought, however, being interested in *her* is to be contrasted with both of those.

Now it might be said that none of this matters: that normal usage is not sacrosanct and that, in any case, the line between 'normal' and 'philosophical' usage is not easy to draw. Well, I accept some of that. First, I am not suggesting that most of us are completely free of what I am calling the 'philosophical' picture. My point is rather that in so far as we are in the grip of it it lies beside another picture with which it is quite inconsistent. Now, second, that might not have mattered. I believe, however, that it does matter. The way we are tempted to use the term 'mind' when thinking philosophically, the use, indeed, which is reflected in the label 'philosophy of mind', both reflects and fuels a number of *serious* confusions. The use of the term is, I believe, characteristically tied up with most or all of the following ways of thinking. (1) The idea that there is a clear thread which runs through all those states and activities which we ascribe to people but not to sticks and stones. (We pick out the thread with the term 'mental'.) In some sense all of those states have a single 'location' within the person; or, perhaps better, are states of a particular *part* of the person ('the mind'). (2) The idea that in saying what is special about people – marks them off in our thought from other, or most other, things – we must give *the* fundamental position to the first person point of view. (3) The idea that there is a single divide in nature which can be said to be *the* divide of fundamental moral significance. (A being either has a 'mind' or it does not.) (4) The tendency to view the human being, the extended, tangible being that we encounter in the world, as being, at most, of secondary importance in our relations with each other; the philosophical notion of a 'body' is a direct expression of this tendency. (5) The tendency to align the 'mind'/'body' contrast, in one way or another, with the contrast between the first and third person points of view; and, with that, to identify the third person point of view with the point of view of the physical sciences. That identification is, again, strongly reflected in the philosophical notion of a 'body'.

Of course, it is not the case that all of these ideas feature in the same way in the thought of everyone who employs the philosophical mind/body contrast. My aim in Part II will, however, be to look closely at what I take to be some of the most significant strands in this group of connected ideas. The main emphasis in the present chapter will be on certain ways in which the philosophical notions of 'the mind' and 'the body' are closely tied up with a focusing of attention away from the extended, tangible human being and a devaluing of its importance in our relations with each other. One central thread running through my discussion of this point will be the suggestion that, in certain frames of mind, we give to the first person point of view a priority which is seriously misplaced.

(ii) We can begin by considering two distortions which the philosophical notions of 'the mind' and 'the mental' may introduce into our thought. The first of these is linked with the way in which these notions, and the related philosophical notion of 'experience', may lead us to overlook the *variety* in the states and activities which we ascribe to people. This, I believe, is a source, additional to those discussed in Part I, of philosophical scepticism: an additional source of the idea that the extended, tangible being that we encounter is merely a 'surface', behind which lies everything of importance.

It is important to remember that we ascribe *many* kinds of things to people which we do not ascribe to trees or stones: sensations, emotions, thoughts, character traits, actions, and so on. Indeed, even to put the matter in this way is misleading for what I have picked out as 'kinds' of thing which we ascribe are, in reality, only rough classifications which are useful for certain purposes. *Any* attempt to impose some order here will, from some point of view or another, appear as a, potentially dangerous, distortion. For example, both within and outside philosophy 'love' is often classified along with anger and fear as an 'emotion'. Now, for certain purposes certain of those states which we speak of as 'love' might, without serious distortion, be grouped with certain of those states which we speak of as 'anger'. The terms 'love' and 'anger' are, however, themselves used in a widely diverse range of contexts. To group the love that may bind two adults together with the young child's ten-second flash of rage is asking for trouble; and the trouble is not only of a 'philosophical' kind if that means that it will have no serious ramifications in *life*. A crudeness in one's classifications here may be closely connected with a flattening of one's conception of the possibilities in life.

Now the terms 'mind' or 'mental' as they are widely used within philosophy introduce a crudeness of an altogether different order. The crudeness I am thinking of here lies in the thought that, in some sense or another, all of the items on my list are fundamentally of the same kind. Descartes' use of the term *'pensée'*[1] to cover, in effect, the whole of this range, is well known. The same viewpoint is reflected in uses of the words 'mind' and 'mental' in which sensations, emotions, thoughts, actions, and so on are all spoken of as episodes in an individual's 'mental' life. This is linked with the way in which when we are considering our knowledge of others we tend to lump together our knowledge of their abilities, character traits, emotions, thoughts, sensations, and so on under the general heading 'our knowledge of other minds'. One result of this is that we tend to overlook the fact that the *kind* of difficulty which may be involved in getting to know another may be very different in these different areas. The 'problem of other minds' is, in part, the result of our running together different kinds of problem which, if they were kept separate, would not lead us so readily to the problem in its distinctively philosophical form.

To see this, consider first the way in which we may want to insist that people are not transparent. Others, or at least some others, are, for various reasons, difficult to get to know well; and we are inclined to feel that any philosophical picture of a person which does not do justice to this difficulty is, in some way, degrading. Now when we think in this way we are, I suspect, thinking of certain relatively long-lasting feelings, concerns and character traits of the other. We are thinking, for example, of the fact that love or deep grief can, even when openly expressed, come out in very different ways, and of the fact that, for various reasons, people are often not open with each other about these things. Whether we think of this lack of openness as a tragedy or as admirable restraint it is a crucially significant feature of our relations with others which must not be obscured within our philosophy. A denial of the difficulty is felt to be degrading in so far as it can only be taken as a denial of the reality of these features of people's lives – a denial of everything that is of depth. We could also consider here the way in which, even when in one sense we know another well, we can have enormous difficulty in getting close to them – either because of something in them or because of something in us.[2]

Now this kind of thing, by itself, would, I think, never lead us to the idea that we need an argument from analogy with its suggestion that our knowledge of others is like our knowledge of the dark side of the moon before space travel. It would never lead us there since that picture totally misrepresents the kind of difficulty that I have been talking about. The distance between people which the argument from analogy presupposes has, for example, nothing to do with the idea that work, patience and sensitivity may be needed to get to know, or to get close to, another.

The argument from analogy thrives on physical sensations. This is, in a way, curious. Pains, as I have noted, are not features of our 'mental life'. We do not, in the normal course of things, think of them as part of our 'inner life', nor does the notion of 'depth' characteristically have application in connection with them; and we would generally think it both correct, and not in the least degrading, to acknowledge that, in this respect, people are, at least a good deal of the time, completely transparent. In a great many cases we simply 'see the pain in his features'.[3] Nevertheless, it is, of course, no accident that physical sensations tend to have a central place in philosophical discussions of 'the problem of other minds'. We are tempted to give a foundational place to the first person here, to *my* experience of feeling pain, in a way in which we are not in connection with, say, ascriptions of intelligence or generosity; and so to feel that ascribing pain to others when they behave in certain ways stands in need of some special justification.

I have discussed this idea of justification in Part I. My point now is that 'the problem of other minds' in its peculiarly philosophical form may gain much of its mesmerising power from our failure to distinguish clearly between the many quite different kinds of judgement which we make about others. In particular, the notion of 'the mind' leads us to combine, in a way which is both illegitimate and dangerous, the idea that it is a deep and important truth that others are not transparent with the idea that self-ascription is somehow more basic than other ascription. In this way, the crudity in the classification contributes to the traditional mind/body contrast which represents everything of significance, everything which is distinctive of persons, as lying behind the surface that we encounter.[4]

I want to turn now to another, connected, source of the idea that what we encounter of the other – the tangible human being – is a 'mere surface'. In a defence of the mind-brain identity thesis Armstrong makes the following remark: 'We say that we have a pain in the hand. The SENSATION of pain can hardly be in the hand, for sensations are in minds and the hand is not part of the mind';[5] and so the way is opened for locating the sensation in the brain and identifying it with a brain state. In that sense the effect of this startling argument is, again, a focusing of attention away from the human being. I will come back to that effect of the argument in section (iii). First I would like to say something about its source.

The idea that 'sensations are in minds', and so not in hands, that, indeed, this is so transparently clear as to need no elucidation or defence, can be traced in part to the lingering power of Cartesianism and the domination of philosophical thinking about people by the first person point of view. There is, however, another dimension to this which I want to consider briefly.[6] While in the normal course of things we say, without any feeling of oddity, that we have a tingling sensation in our hand, a certain philosophical frame of mind puts this way of speaking in a strange light. We ask 'How could a pain be in a hand?' While innocent in itself, this question has the effect of getting our attention firmly focused on the hand; and once our attention is focused in this way our normal ways of speaking begin to seem decidedly funny. For there is nothing in what we see when we look at the hand which shows us that we are right to say that there is a pain there; as, it seems, there is something in what we see when we look at the hand which shows us that we are right to say that there is a bullet there. Thus, we are forced to seek another location for the sensation. It might be added that neurophysiology points fairly clearly to the brain as the true location of the pain since there *is*, it seems, something in what we see when we look there which shows us that he is in pain.

While there *is* a contrast between the case of the pain and that of the bullet there are also dangers here: dangers which flow, in part, from a failure to reflect properly on the latter case. Thus, while what we see when we look at the hand does show us that there is a bullet there, the truth of our claim that there is a bullet there is not independent of a wider context. Most obviously it is dependent on the fact that this thing in my hand was made for a certain purpose; less obviously, the claim that it is a bullet, involving as it does the implication that it is a solid object, is dependent for its truth on the fact that this thing interacts with other things in various specific ways.[7] Similarly, but again more obviously, we can say that a peace treaty was signed in a particular city even though the truth of our claim that that is what happened is dependent on what happened in other places. Finally, an example which may in one respect bring us closer to the case of pain is to be found in the fact that we can say that the Equator passes through the Gilbert Islands even though there is nothing to be seen *there* which gives any indication that this is so.

We can say that the sensation is in the hand even though there is nothing to be seen there that guarantees, or perhaps even suggests, that this is so. If one is surprised at the way in which we speak here one should remind oneself of the circumstances in which we locate a sensation at a particular point. The hand is the hand of a person, and it is of the person that we say 'He feels a pain in his hand.' It is what we see in the person, and above all in his face, which allows us to ascribe pain to him; and it is his difficulties in using his hand, the way his attention is focused on it, and so on, which leads us to say that the pain is in the hand. A reminder of these points, a focusing of attention on the human being whose hand this is, should remove the mystery that we may feel when we ask 'How could a pain be in a hand?'; and, with that, should remove our temptation to identify somewhere else, 'the mind', as the *true* location of the pain.

Our observation of the human being might also play a role in leading us to think that he has a bullet in his hand. The role in that case is, however, quite different: what we see in the person having, in that case, very little connection with the *sense* of our judgement. If we set that case up as our paradigm we may feel that a consideration of the behaviour of the *person* could not possibly help to remove the mystery that we felt in the pain case. I have suggested, however, that our 'paradigm' is not quite as pure as we are tempted to think, and, with that, there are no grounds for setting it up *as* a paradigm. There is perhaps no harm in saying that the sense in which the pain can be said to be in the hand is different from that in which the bullet can be said to be there, provided one does not hope for any very systematic way of counting senses. If one does say this, however, one must not assume that this opens up the possibility of identifying somewhere else as the pain's location in a 'more literal sense'.

We need, then, to remember that the hand is the hand of a human being if we are to see the kind of sense which our talk of the pain as being in the hand has. The philosophical notion of 'the mind' springs in part from a picture which dictates that that *cannot* be right: that the sense of talk of what is going on in the hand could not possibly be dependent on anything external to the hand. Now my emphasis here has been on the notion of being 'located', but it could equally well be placed on the notion of 'something'. The thought, the same thought, would then be that if this is the only sense in which a pain can be said to be located somewhere then a pain is not 'something' – pains are not 'real things' – in the rich sense in which bullets and bones are. I suspect that my rejection of such ideas is the expression of a pretty fundamental opposition to a strong strand of contemporary philosphy of mind. An idea which runs very deep is the idea that only things that have location in the sense that bullets and bones do, and so that only things that have the kind of reality that bullets and bones have, are 'real' in some crucial sense. Thus, to be a 'realist' about pains is to hold that pains have location in *that* sense. But how are we to characterise this sense? I will return to this question in Chapter 7.

(iii) The philosophical mind/body contrast is a *rich* contrast. It draws sustenance from a diverse range of considerations only a few of which will be even touched on in this chapter. The sources considered in the previous section lie, perhaps, particularly near the surface of many philosophical discussions of these issues. In my attempt, in this section, to bring out the way in which the contrast involves a devaluing of the role played by the extended, tangible human being in our relations with each other another familiar source of the contrast will come into prominence: namely, the emphasis commonly given to the first person point of view in discussions of these issues.

It will, of course, be acknowledged by anyone that the extended, tangible being plays an ineliminable role in certain relationships between human beings. Most obviously perhaps, it is not as though the body is a tiresome, but in practice inescapable, intermediary in sexual relations between people. (Though we should not forget the thought that sex is a tiresome, but in practice inescapable, aspect of certain kinds of relation between people – a thought which is, I suspect, in some cases closely tied up with the issues that concern me here, and to which I will return in the next section.) What is not always acknowledged is the richness of the role which the human bodily form plays in a much wider range of relationships between people.

Now the features of our lives which concern me here are bound to be missed, or played down, within a tradition in which the first person point of view is given *the* fundamental position since first/ third person asymmetries are crucial here. They are crucial because there are various ways in which the human bodily form plays a role in my thought about others which it does not characteristically play in my thought about myself. One who does give this primacy to the first person point of view will, then, be inclined to view this involvement of the human form as a superficial feature of our relations with others.

I argued in Chapter 4 that giving *the* fundamental position to the first person point of view seriously distorts even that area of our thought where this emphasis is most naturally at home. It is in the case of physical sensations that it is most tempting to give an exclusive primacy to the first person point of view. Yet even here what it is to recognise that another is in a certain state, say pain, cannot illuminatingly be explained in terms of 'recognising that he is in the same state as I am in when I am in that state'. I defended that claim by arguing that what it is to *care* for another in pain cannot illuminatingly be explained in terms of 'caring for him as I spontaneously care about myself when in pain'. The idea that I was criticising there does, however, run quite deep in several areas of philosophy. To escape from egoism, we think, is to come to treat another's concerns as if they were my own; it is, for example, to come to care about the other's pains as I would care about them if they were my own. (Or should it be 'as *she* cares about them'? The most comfortable cases for this whole approach are, of course, those in which these coincide.) This is connected with a use which we are inclined to make of the egoism/altruism distinction both within and outside philosophy. Thus, we are, in certain frames of mind, inclined to view an individual's thought about another in terms of the following contrast: he is either concerned about how it is with *her* or he is concerned about the effect which she has on *him*. Now if we view our relations with others exclusively in terms of this contrast there is, I believe, much of importance that we will miss all together; or which, if we see it, will appear in a very dubious light. We will inevitably have a very thin picture of what is significant in our thought about others since we will only see as genuine thought about the other, as opposed to self-indulgence of some kind, that which can, in some way, be seen as a reflection of the other's thought about himself: to use the central example of Chapter 4, pain becomes 'something to be relieved'. The force of the kind of argument which I presented in that chapter is, however, in part dependent on a graphic presentation of a rich variety of illustrations. For the recognition that, in principle, the first person point of view *might* not have occupied that kind of position in our thought about each other is quite compatible with the insistence that it *does* or *ought to* occupy it. One whose picture of personal relations is firmly coloured by the egoism/altruism contrast will simply not acknowledge as such what I am claiming to be a distortion in his vision. With some, only an accumulation of examples which are not readily fitted into this mould will have any impact. (It is a crucial dimension of all this that some will find my argument in this area *morally* suspect.)

The examples which will be central in this section are ones in which the extended, tangible, human being plays in the concern I may feel for another a role that it does not characteristically play in the other's thought about himself. We can consider first the kind of importance which the physical presence of another can have for us: and, in particular, the way in which it can be a comfort to us. In a distressing or dangerous situation the presence of someone I know well can be an enormous help; and in a way that cannot be reduced to any confidence I may feel that they will find a way out of the difficulty: I might rather have her with me even though she might, in *that* sense, be more likely to be able to help if she were somewhere else. In a sufficiently alien environment the presence of *any* other human being can be a help in a comparable way. Again, the *contact* with another involved in saying 'Hello', or in the exchange of a smile or of some remarks about the weather, is important to virtually everyone in one way or another. The importance of contact of these forms is not unrelated to the variety of ways in which *physical* contact with others is enormously important to most of us. The young child's need for physical contact with his mother is perhaps, in a certain way, as basic as his need for food. The mother's need for contact with her child is of a related, though different, form. Different again, though on a spectrum with these, are the various ways in which physical contact between adults can be of importance. While contact which has an explicitly sexual dimension is, of course, pretty central here it is not sharply demarcated from other forms of physical contact which matter to most of us.

A person who was completely indifferent to any of the forms of contact with others which I have mentioned would be a person in whose life there was nothing remotely akin to at least some of the things which most have in mind when they speak of love or friendship. It is characteristic of caring for another that one wants to *be with* them. In most cases, if one cares for another one wants to *see* them: I am thinking here of, for example, the pleasure that a parent takes in watching her child absorbed in some activity. In many cases, one's caring for another takes a form in which a desire for physical contact with them, a desire to hug them for example, is of central importance. Physical contact, except in its most ritualised or functional forms, is generally a form of close personal contact. (It is true that in this society many, perhaps the majority, of our relationships with others involve little physical *contact*; but to say that is not, by any means, to say that within those relationships it is a matter of *indifference* whether or not we make physical contact.)

Any attempt to fit what matters to us here into the egoism/ altruism contrast is bound to lead to what, I hope, most will agree is serious distortion. It is, for example, not, or not exclusively, for one's child's or wife's sake that one wants to be with him or her; and the fact that it is not for their sake does not suggest that one's love for them is not everything that it might be. Indeed, precisely the reverse of this is true. A father who spent a great deal of time with his child exclusively for his child's sake would undoubtedly have certain admirable qualities; but most, I think, would find something seriously amiss in his love for the child precisely *because of* this exclusive concern with his child's welfare. Are we then to say that the desire to be with the other which most regard as central to normal love is a desire for the effects which the presence of the other has on *me*: so that we have built an egoistic component into the kind of love which most of us hold up as an ideal? Well, it is true that, in most cases, I enjoy being with the other. That, however, does not show that anything but thoughts about the other draws me to them; and closely connected with that is the fact that we may not be able to characterise the effect which the other has on me independently of a reference to *them*. If, then, we do speak of 'egoism' here what we are speaking of is a long way removed from the model of motivation, familiar in philosophical contexts, which is closely linked with solipsism.

The tangible human being has, then, an importance in our relations with others which will be missed by those who give exclusive emphasis to the first person point of view. I have spoken of the way in which the physical presence of another, the sight of another and physical contact with another matter to us. I want now to turn to another aspect of this: one which will, perhaps, bring more clearly into focus the importance which particular details of the human form have in our relations with each other. I will be concerned now with the role which the other's bodily form may play in our response to their state at a particular time – in our response to their pain, joy or anger. To recognise the richness of this role is to recognise the depth of the difficulty in the idea that we could ascribe these states to beings that had nothing resembling the human form; (and to recognise *that* is to recognise one of the serious distortions introduced by the philosophical mind/body contrast.)

Consider first the fact that my judgements about the states of others are based on my observation of what they say and do, on their facial expression, and so on. Now in some cases I make judgements about myself which are grounded in a roughly analogous way: I come to realise that I am jealous through noticing a pattern in my behaviour which I had previously not seen. Other cases are, however, quite different. My report that I am in pain is not grounded in my observation of my writhings and groans.

Now a recognition of asymmetries of this kind has not discouraged those who insist that my thought about others – for example, my understanding of what it is for another to feel pain – is based on the model provided by my experience of myself: for example of my own pain. For it is insisted that while the human bodily form inevitably plays a role in my coming to *learn* of the states of others it plays no role in my understanding of what it *is* for them to be in that state. For another to be in pain is for them to have something that feels like *this*; and my understanding of that is in no way dependent on my recognition of the forms of behaviour in which pain is characteristically expressed. The asymmetry, then, simply lies in the possibilities of knowledge of the relevant states – not in my understanding of what those states are – and so does not threaten the fundamental, justifying position which is given to the first person point of view.

I will not directly examine the contrast appealed to in my last sentence. Instead, I will suggest in a rather different way that the role which the human form plays in my thought about the other is very much more fundamental than these ways of speaking would suggest. We see this most clearly in the form of my *concern* about the other.

When I am horrified at another's suffering I may have difficulty in looking at them; in particular, I may have difficulty in looking into their face. The sight of intense suffering is difficult to stand. My distress on being directly confronted with the other, or my turning away from the sight of them, are ways in which my horror at their suffering characteristically finds expression. Similarly, the pleasure that we take in another's joy often involves, or is closely connected with, a pleasure that we find in observing the other; and, in particular, in observing their facial expression. The parent delights in the expression on his child's face as she opens her presents. The expression on his child's face, the sound of her laughter, and so on do not simply play the role of *evidence*; the particular way in which he is moved cannot be characterised independently of the pleasure that he takes in her manifestations of joy.

I take it that in one sense these remarks are an uncontroversial characterisation of a familiar and pervasive feature of our normal experience. It might, however, be suggested that the close connection which we find here in practice does not in fact go deep; that my horror at the suffering could in all important respects be the same even though the sight of the suffering person, or vivid visualising of them, is not, in itself, distressing in any way. Indeed, it might be argued that this is the ideal that we should be aiming at in our responses to others: that in so far as we fall short of it what we exhibit is not a pure concern about the other at all, but, in part, something more akin to squeamishness.

The force of the suggestion that what I am speaking of here 'does not go deep' is almost certainly, if unconsciously, in part ethical in character. All I can do (others could do better) is point out that it is not at all clear why we should accept these suggestions. Thus, we can ask: does the charge that what I am speaking of here is 'squeamishness', or 'self-indulgence' of some kind, flow immediately, that is without argument, from the fact that my distress is tied in this direct way to what I see? In so far as it does the question has simply been begged. It is simply being assumed that the behavioural expressions of pain cannot legitimately have for us the kind of significance with which I am concerned.

It might be replied that the assumption is easily defended in the following way: 'The behaviour, facial expression, and so on are not the same thing as the pain. Thus, any distress that I feel over these is to be sharply distinguished from a concern about the pain.' There is, however, an obscurity in this talk of 'concern about the pain'. Rather, if we say that I am concerned about his pain this must not be understood in a way such that it is to be contrasted with my being concerned about *him*. For my response is a response to the *person* on account of the pain that he feels. Now it is very far from obvious that a difficulty in looking at him must be sharply dissociated from any concern that I feel for him in his pain.

This might still be denied. 'For my concern to be focused unambiguously on him' it might be said 'is for me to be concerned about how things are *with* him. That is to say, imaginative identification with his point of view is what is fundamental to pure concern. Now, *his* suffering is quite unconnected with any distress over his behaviour, facial expression and so on. Thus, the purer my concern for him the less I will be touched by these things.' Part of my aim in this section is to re-enforce my earlier worries about the assumption that 'imaginative identification with his point of view is what is fundamental to pure concern'. Thus, I am suggesting that the significance which the other's behaviour can have for us shows that the assumption is, on inspection, rather less plausible than it sounds in the abstract. It is no use, in response, to simply repeat the old claim which is being challenged. What is needed is, rather, a genuine attempt to cast our normal responses here in an unattractive light.

'In so far as it really is the sight of him that fills me with distress my response is a purely aesthetic one. Indeed, it is no different in kind from, for example, my response to an unpleasant smell. With this, my turning away has nothing to do with a concern for him. It is simply an attempt to escape the unpleasant effect which he has on me.' The notion of the 'purely aesthetic' which is appealed to here is unclear; or, if it is clear, the assumption that any direct response to what I see is 'purely aesthetic' is unwarranted. Is the distress that I might feel on seeing a mutilated tree or a disfigured landscape a 'purely aesthetic' response? Well, one thing should be clear. It is not simply the sight of these things that concerns me if that means that I could have the thought: 'What has happened here would not matter provided it was never seen by me, or anyone else; provided, for example, we could keep away from this place or disguise the disfigurement with a bit of plastic and paint.' My distress is a distress over the condition of what I am looking at. Similarly, when I recoil with horror from the sight of the man in terrible pain I do not, or need not, have the thought that things will be all right provided that I can get him out of my sight. It is his condition, not the effect which that has on me, which disturbs me. (Though there are, no doubt, also cases which are correctly described in the latter way.)

If we think, as I believe we are inclined to, that the kind of concern I am speaking of here must somehow be squeezed in between egoism and altruism we are likely to conclude that there is little room for it. Resistance to the idea that the human form could have the kind of importance which I am attributing to it is, in part, a manifestation of the hold which that dichotomy has on our thought. Consider another way in which this resistance may be articulated: 'The response of which you are speaking is one which leads me away from the one in pain; or, at any rate, compromises my ability to help him effectively. From the point of view of the one in pain, help from someone who has, perhaps through long experience, overcome this kind of reaction to the sight of suffering is clearly to be preferred. From that point of view what is most attractive is someone whose "pity" (if that is the right word) can be fully articulated in the thought "This, the pain, is something to be removed." Thus, the kind of horror of which you are speaking cannot be said to manifest a pure concern for the other.' It is not 'for his sake' that I respond with horror to the other's suffering, any more than it is 'for his sake' that I mourn the other's death. So the fact, if it is a fact, that this response is not what *he* would welcome need not lead me to think that there is anything amiss in it. This may be difficult to accept if we do not bear it in mind that the fact that it is not 'for his sake' that I respond in these ways does not show that anything other than thoughts about *him* lie behind the response. If it is felt that the example of mourning does not bring this out, the case in which I am distressed on hearing of a loved one's past suffering may be more helpful. My thought is focused exclusively on the other, my reaction is an expression of concern for the other, but I do not think that my reaction is going to *help* him in any way.

Of course, there are cases in which we will want to say that there is, in one sense or another, something amiss in the response. A mother who is paralysed in the face of her child's suffering will wish that she was not so that she could help him more effectively. Similarly, we want our doctors to have reactions of this kind firmly under control. Quite different from these cases are ones in which we feel that there is room for criticism of the person; think, for example, of someone who wallows in his horror in a way which effectively excludes any serious thought of helping the other. There are, then, cases in which we can criticise the role which the sight of the other plays in my reaction to him. That this reaction can take corrupt forms is, however, hardly a ground for a *general* suspicion of responses to another in which the observable mani- festations of their pain play a crucial role.

I have been considering arguments which purport to show that the role which the other's bodily form may play in our response to his pain is to be viewed with suspicion. I want to return now to the point from which this discussion started. My basic point is that another's pain does not present itself to me as *simply* something to be removed as quickly as possible. It presents itself to me as something in the face of which horror of a quite specific kind is in place. Further, the form of the horror which we generally associate with a clear recognition of another's suffering is one in which the sight of the other, and, in particular, of their facial expression, plays a crucial role. There would be no place for horror of just that form in connection with something that did not have anything resembling the human form, or if the person to whom I am responding was smiling serenely. Now consider someone whose reactions to the sufferings of others totally¹ lacked this dimension. The groans and contorted face are of significance in so far as they are grounds for thinking that the other is in pain; but that is all. There is nothing disturbing *in* them. Thus, once he has recognised that the other is in severe pain the contorted face is neither here nor there. Could the picture of this individual be filled out in such a way that we would be able to see his reactions, not as crucially deficient, but as admirable in a certain way? I am not sure. I have simply wanted to cast doubt on the suggestion that this is *obviously* the ideal to which we should aspire. If anyone does still find this obvious they should consider also the case of our response to another's joy. Consider, for example, a parent who does care about his child in the sense that he is pleased to hear that she is happy, yet who feels no inclination at all to observe or to share in her joy; seeing her laugh or laughing with her are nothing to him. It is with this case in mind that we should ask the question: could our responses to another's joy be what they are in all *important* respects even though the human bodily form, and anything remotely resembling it, was absent? That the other is of a certain bodily form *does* play a significant part in our reactions to their suffering and joy and it is at the very least not obvious that this casts doubt on the purity of the response.

The emphasis in what I have said has been on ways in which my reaction to another's state may be closely bound up with the

manner in which his state is manifested in his behaviour and facial
expression. I must briefly mention a related, but different, way in
which the other's bodily form plays a crucial role in my reactions to
their state. Consider the following striking passage:

> But isn't it absurd to say of a *body* that it has pain? – And why
> does one feel an absurdity in that? In what sense is it true that
> my hand does not feel pain, but I in my hand?
>
> What sort of issue is: is it the *body* that feels pain? – How is it
> to be decided? What makes it plausible to say that it is *not* the
> body? – Well, something like this: if someone has a pain in his
> hand, then the hand does not say so (unless it writes it) and one
> does not comfort the hand, but the sufferer: one looks into his
> face.[8]

The passage raises a number of important issues.[9] What concerns
me at the moment is the way in which Wittgenstein here links the
question of what it is that can be said to feel pain with the question
of what it is that one comforts; and the way in which he links *that*
question with specific bodily features of the other which play a role
in my comforting him. Wittgenstein gives a central place here to
the face. What Wittgenstein is speaking of is, I think, distinct from
the way in which the sight of the other's contorted features fills me
with horror and also from the way in which I might watch the
other's face carefully for signs of an easing of his pain. One *'looks
into* his face' in sympathy. Indeed, we can say more specifically
that one looks into his eyes. Other expressions of sympathy
involve bodily contact; and so, in this society, are generally
restricted to certain relationships or to extreme circumstances. I
hold the other; and that involves putting my arm around, say, their
shoulder, not their knees. I squeeze the other's hand, not their
foot. Of course, bodily contact of *any* kind is better than none at all.
Nevertheless, it does matter to us *what* kind of bodily contact we
make, and so the particular bodily form which the other has is of
importance in our reactions to them.

It is sometimes said that there is a 'conceptual connection' between
pain or joy and the human form. The force of this kind of
suggestion can, however, seem obscure. To insist that the connection is 'conceptual' or 'logical' is, it seems, to insist that it is 'not
simply' of an empirical kind: a connection in the world which could

have been other than it is. Yet is not the alternative to say that the connection is 'simply' of a linguistic kind: a connection in our language which could have been other than it is; and in introducing the notion of the 'conceptual' were we not trying to capture an idea that the connection is one which, in some sense, goes deep? Similarly, Wittgenstein writes 'Only of a living human being and what resembles (behaves like) a living human being *can* one say: it has sensations; it sees; is blind; hears; is deaf; is conscious or unconscious.'[10] Yet in other places he speaks of the 'arbitrariness of grammar' and tells us: 'Do not say "one cannot", but say indeed: "it doesn't exist in this game"'.

The discussion of this section could be taken as an attempt to bring out part of the force of the idea that the connection here 'goes deep'. The other's bodily form plays a central role in our ascriptions of pain and joy to him in the sense that it plays a central role in those responses to the other which are expressive of our recognition of his state. Now perhaps one aspect of this emerged in my discussion of 'arbitrariness' in Chapter 5. The depth of the connection is a depth in human nature: the force of the 'could not' in the claim that 'We could not seriously ascribe pain to a stone' is psychological. ('Just try it and see how you get on.') In this section, however, the emphasis has been different. The difficulty I have tried to point to is a difficulty in seeing what it would *be* to respond to a stone as we might respond to another human being in pain; or to respond to a man apparently at ease and smiling serenely as we might to one who is in agony.

Philosophers, at least of the Western 'analytical' kind, are, for the most part, not very good at producing imaginative depictions of the details of human relationships. I am painfully aware of my own failure to bring any life to my representation of the way in which the human form plays a crucial role in our interactions with each other. Yet the details here are everything. The lack of literary style on the part of philosophers, combined with a certain sense of what is in good philosophical taste, has, I strongly suspect, contributed to serious mistakes in this area. For without a vivid awareness of the details one can too readily think that our relations with each other could have very much the character which they now have even though we lacked anything remotely resembling the human form; and so see no difficulty in the idea that I might think of and treat a brain, or a 'disembodied mind', in all of those ways which are characteristic of the thought that another is in pain.

Since what is required here is not *argument* but reflection on the details of our relationships with each other the best that I have been able to do is to point the reader in the direction of certain features of these relationships, features which I take to be important, and attempt to remove certain obstacles to the idea that these features might be of philosophical significance.

To the extent that I have been successful in this we can conclude that it is not simply, as I argued in Chapter 2, that there is no reason to accept that the extended, tangible human being is not an appropriate object of those responses to others which are central to our thought of them as persons; and so, not simply that there is no reason to accept that it is to something other than the extended, tangible human being that pain and joy are to be ascribed. There is positive reason to reject these suggestions; for such a being is the *only possible* object of the relevant responses in their richest form.

I have been trying to bring out a sense in which, for example, the connection between pain and the human form could be said to go deep. Or perhaps I should say, trying to show what that claim might amount to and to remove certain obstacles to its acceptance. A proper *defence* of the claim would involve a defence of the value of those responses to another in pain which I have stressed:[11] our horror at the sight of his suffering, the way we look into his eyes in sympathy and so on. Thus, if one views all of that as simply froth on the top of what is really serious in our response to another's suffering – this being the attempt to relieve the suffering – matters may look very different: particular details of the human form may not emerge as significant in the sense of which I have spoken. Now I certainly have not shown that that is not the way such responses are to be viewed; I have, at most, simply undermined certain bad reasons for thinking that they *must* be viewed in this way.

I have, in particular, focused on the way in which the 'devaluing' of the extended human form which is a central feature of the philosophical mind/body contrast may flow from the idea that primacy *must* be given to the first person point of view if space is to be left for what is of value in our thought about each other. Such a devaluing of the human form can, however, equally thrive, and does today, in intellectual circles in which the *third* person point of view is given primacy. In the final section of Chapter 7 I will note how the dominant philosophical understanding of that point of view – the understanding which links the third person viewpoint with the scientific – equally deprives the *human being*, that which we encounter in daily life, of its fundamental position in our thought. As with more traditional forms of dualism,[12] those features of our relations with others which are closely bound up with the human bodily form are treated as superficial.

(iv) As I suggested earlier, however, the philosophical mind/body contrast has many sources; and I do not want to suggest that all routes to *something like* this contrast need involve philosophical confusion. Thus, for example, the idea that the first person point of view should be given *the* fundamental position in our thought about each other might be defended by an appeal to considerations of a, broadly speaking, ethical character, rather than simply taken for granted for bad philosophical reasons; and once that is done, the idea that the extended and tangible is to be transcended will, perhaps, be more readily intelligible and more easily defended. In this section, however, I want to look briefly at two considerations of a rather different form which might edge us in a similar direction.

In his discussion, in the *Phaedo*, of the distinction between the soul and the body Plato writes:

> 'Do you think that it is right for a philosopher to concern himself with the nominal pleasures connected with food and drink?'
> 'Certainly not, Socrates,' said Simmias.
> 'What about sexual pleasures?'
> 'No, not at all.'
> 'And what about the other attentions that we pay to our bodies? Do you think that a philosopher attaches any importance to them? I mean things like providing himself with smart clothes and shoes and other bodily ornaments; do you think that he values them or despises them – in so far as there is no real necessity for him to go in for that sort of thing?'
> 'I think the true philosopher despises them,' he said.
> 'Then it is your opinion in general that a man of this kind is not concerned with the body, but keeps his attention directed as much as he can away from it and towards the soul?' 'Yes, it is.'[13]

'The body' is linked here with 'bodily ornaments' and with the pleasures of food, drink and sex. Now it is important to recognise that this notion of 'the body' is not, or not yet, the one that commonly arises within philosophy. We have a familiar contrast between 'bodily', or 'physical', desires and desires of other forms which cuts right across the traditional philosophical mind/body contrast. Thus, the desire for pleasurable sensations or tastes falls unambiguously on the 'bodily' side, and the desire for, for example, philosophical conversation equally clearly on the other side. To link the 'religious' ideal to 'transcend the bodily' with a Cartesian dualism may, then, involve a bad mistake.

When I say that this is a *bad* mistake what I mean is that the differences in the 'mind'/'body' contrasts at work here should not be thought of as a superficial matter of different terminologies. This comes out in, for example, the fact that the object of lust is not the Cartesian lump of matter which happens to be linked with a mind. Thus, to say that he is only interested in a certain woman's *body* is not to deny that it is a crucial feature of his desire that this is a *woman's* body: the body of a *person*. Perhaps he would make do with a lifelike dummy; or, considerably better, an animated one; but it would not be the same. With this, the idea of the bodily as 'base', as it appears in contexts of this kind, must be sharply distinguished from the idea of the body as an object on exactly the same level as other physical things. In explaining the idea of 'baseness' that arises here a reference to the fact that we are speaking of the bodies of *people* is ineliminable. The notion of 'the body' involved here is, then, *derivative from* that of a live human being; not, as we find in the Cartesian picture, the other way round.

I have spoken of a particular notion of 'the bodily' which is linked with a particular range of human interests; and suggested that, on the face of it, this brings us nowhere near what I have called the *philosophical* mind/body contrast. Another dimension of this is seen in the fact that I might, it seems, 'transcend the bodily' in that sense and yet the human form still play a crucial role in my life: at least many of the ways in which the other's form enters into my relations with him may be untouched. Yet there may be difficulties here: difficulties of a kind which could edge us closer to the broad 'philosophical' understanding of what is to be included in the 'bodily'. For the line between those relationships with others which involve an explicitly sexual dimension and relationships of different kinds may be rather less sharp than we sometimes suppose: the different forms of pleasure that we take in, for example, looking at another, or in physical contact with them, merge into each other and can be difficult to categorise. Now a recognition of this might lead someone who had seen the sexual as something to be transcended to view it in a different light. Equally, however, the reverse could happen: most or all normal relationships now being cast in the light previously reserved for the explicitly sexual.[14] In the latter case, the assumption that the sexual is to be transcended will have much wider ramifications: in so far as the other's bodily form plays any important role in my relationship with them that relationship will be viewed with suspicion. Now nothing along these lines will bring us to what we can say just *is* the Cartesian mind/body contrast. It may, however, bring us to a view which has certain affinities with that contrast.

I will say a little now about another path which might lead some in roughly the same direction. This path is tied up with the vulnerability of the human body (and is very closely linked with Martha Nussbaum's marvellous discussion of the *Republic, Phaedo* and *Symposium* in Chapters 5 and 6 of *The Fragility of Goodness*.)

Human beings need sleep and food. The human body is subject to disease and is readily damaged by external forces in many ways. Further, no matter how much care an individual takes, death, and, with that, the disintegration of the body, is, in the end, inevitable. These facts play a crucial role in virtually all of our more important relationships with each other. The same facts do, of course, also play a crucial role in my thought about *myself*. Their role there, however, is, in many ways, importantly different, and the specific point that I will develop does not bear very directly on this. What concerns me, then, is the sense in which any attempt to characterise my understanding of what you are which does not give a central place to the various ways in which you are physically 'vulnerable' will be seriously misleading. To take a very obvious case, think how a parent's relationship to his child would differ if the child was completely invulnerable to physical injury.[15] Now the Cartesian dualist will, no doubt, have things to say about that. What I want to bring out now, however, is the way in which, without denying the centrality of the role which facts like these *do* play in our thought, someone might present as an ideal ways of thinking of each other in which this role is minimised. I will focus on a particular aspect of this: one which is closely related to my discussion in the previous section.

Human beings are vulnerable in the sense that physical damage or disease in another's body can remove the possibility of certain features of those responses to her which were my concern in section (iii). Damage to the face is the most obvious example of what I have in mind: for example, my interactions with another must be significantly affected by the fact that her play of facial expression is totally undermined by paralysis. The loss, deformation or paralysis of other parts of the body could, however, have similar, if less dramatic, implications.

The contrast between a person and her body comes to the fore in our normal thought in contexts of this kind; as it does in those related cases in which we gradually come to realise that within the body, crippled in some way from birth, there is a human being with a rich inner life which is struggling to find expression. Now it might seem that to grant to the human form the kind of importance which I have been discussing is to remove the possibility of making this vitally important contrast. It will be agreed, of course, that in practice this kind of bodily damage is desperately distressing. In that sense the physical *does* play a very important role in our relationships; but does not a consideration of this kind of case make it obvious that we must think of that feature of our thought as something to be transcended? What is of real value in a person is something which cannot be touched by physical damage to the body; and, with that, what is of real value in my relationship to another person is something which cannot be touched by physical damage to her body. What is being disputed is not, then, my empirical claim about the importance of the role which the bodily does play in our personal relationships. Nor is it being suggested that some form of ethically neutral 'metaphysical' investigation will, by revealing what a person is, reveal a confusion in what we attach importance to. What is being disputed is, rather, the *moral* outlook which is involved in the suggestion that the connection between, for example, pain and the human form 'goes deep'. From this point of view that moral outlook hardly appears as one that could be taken seriously.

I have little doubt that considerations of this general form are often an important impetus behind philosophical dualism. On the face of it such considerations can be kept isolated from the philosophical confusions with which they are sometimes linked; and will, when so isolated, still carry us to something quite close to the philosophical mind/body contrast.[16]

We can add: on the face of it the ethical case for movement in this direction is an extremely powerful one. One might say that we appear to have here a serious moral objection to the idea that we can take Wittgenstein's 'Only of a living human being . . . can one say . . .' in the rich way in which he fairly clearly takes it.[17] For to the extent to which one does take this in a rich way one commits oneself to the view that as we move away from the normal human form the possibility of ascribing, for example, pain in the normal sense is compromised.

There may be a number of responses which would, in one way or another, at least blunt the force of the objection. First, one can, perhaps, call a halt to the philosophical use which might be made of such cases by insisting that they are necessarily the exception. (I respond to the smile that I know would be there but for the paralysis.) Again, one might question the sharp contrast drawn between the importance which the healthy human body has for us *in practice* and claims about the importance which it *ought* to have for us: the claim that we ought to 'transcend the bodily' is, we might argue, empty given the degree of involvement which it in fact has in all of our dealings with others. Given our nature – given the forms which our concern for each other inevitably take – there is no more room for the denial that something of fundamental importance is lost with physical damage than there is for the denial that something of fundamental importance, a person, is lost with death. More positively, one might argue that it is not nature that stands in the way of movement in this direction; it is, rather, the value of those forms of concern which we are being encouraged to view as superficial that does so. The suggestion that, for example, the response to another's facial expression (the way I am moved by her smile, say) is not an important feature of my relationship to the other is not, I think, one which we should accept lightly; nor, with that, should we take lightly the suggestion that the *loss* of that possibility through damage to the other's face is not a significant loss.

If some find the implications of my last paragraph hopelessly shocking the outrage may be eased (one should not ask for more) if I stress that to argue in those ways is not to argue that a person becomes of *less* value when they suffer such physical damage. In all of this what is at issue is not the *degree* of value attached to the other but the particular *character* of that value. Thus, for example, there need be no suggestion that my concern for another's physical pain should be *weaker* if the other is, in certain respects, incapable of giving expression to it in normal ways: full room is left for the view that any such weakening of concern is to be severely criticised. The suggestion is, rather, that there are important respects in which the *character* of the concern cannot be the same.[18] More generally, certain forms of physical damage to the other will necessarily involve important modifications in my relationship with her, and so thought about her. The force of the word 'important' here is, in part, that these modifications are not to be thought of as simply 'psychological effects' which the change has on me. The physical damage involves a real loss; but the change in my thought is in no way a matter of valuing her less. (The discussion of this section is linked in obvious ways with questions concerning our thought about animals. In responding to the worries that will arise there I would again stress the central point of the present paragraph. The point should, I think, at least in some ways, be more readily acceptable in that context.)

My purpose in the brief discussion of this section has not been to close any issues. It has been, rather, to give some indication of where I take the real issues to lie: to give some indication of what I take to be the character of certain disputes about the importance of the human form. I suggested earlier that the swift dismissal – or, more common, total ignoring – of the human form which is widespread within philosophical discussions is to be viewed with suspicion. Confusions about the 'grounding' of our thought in the first person point of view, insensitivity to the importance of the detail in our responses to each other, and philosophical muddles about the notions of 'the physical' and 'the body' are often at work here. In other cases, however, the downgrading of the bodily may be strongly linked with religious/ethical ideals which do not involve such confusions. To the extent that that is so the character of disputes concerning the importance of the human form will be very different; and something akin to the philosophical mind/body contrast may emerge as a central feature of a 'metaphysical' outlook which needs to be taken very seriously.

7

Human Beings and Science

(i) A central idea of this book can be formulated in this way: it is a mistake to think that the key to an understanding of what a person is is to be found in the first person point of view. My argument shares that much – an emphasis on the third-person point of view – with the most dominant lines of thought in current philosophy of mind. Beyond that, however, there are quite fundamental differences. First, and most obviously, the focus of my interest is different. I am primarily concerned with the relation between our understanding of people and, broadly speaking, ethical considerations. By contrast the relationship between our normal understanding of people and a scientific understanding is the central concern of contemporary philosophy of mind. Now that difference in interest is, I think, in practice strongly linked with a further difference. The difference is to be seen in remarks such as the following: 'I declare my starting point to be the objective, materialistic, third-person world of the physical sciences'.[1] It is assumed that the third-person world is 'the materialistic world of the physical sciences'. Anyone who combines this assumption with a strong emphasis on the third person point of view is likely to regard questions about the relationship between our normal understanding of people and that offered by the physical sciences as pretty urgent; and may view my preoccupation with ethical considerations as slightly premature.

I want in this chapter to say something about this, the currently dominant, version of the 'mind-body problem'. Since most of what I say will be criticism on a very broad front I should stress that I do not wish to deny that there are real questions to be asked about the relation between our normal understanding of people and the understanding which is presented in various sciences. I *will* deny that we have reason to think that it must be possible to bring our human ontology into relation with the ontology of 'basic' science in any simple way; and I will deny that questions about this relationship have the kind of importance which they are sometimes assumed to have. I will not, however, suggest that we have no grounds for supposing that it must be possible to bring these ontologies into relation with each other in *any* way. For one thing, human beings did, I assume, evolve ultimately from organisms to which characterisations in terms of what I am calling our 'normal human ontology' did not have application: for example, beings to which pains can be ascribed evolved from beings to which they could not. An analogue of this point applies to the development of an individual human being. Now unless one holds that there is simply no such thing as understanding *how* such developments take place one must allow that there is something to be said here about the relation between the two ontologies. Rather differently, while, as I will stress, 'human' and 'physical' character- isations of 'behaviour' are certainly not linked in any simple way they are not, either, totally independent of each other. There are limits on the ways in which this human body might move if it is to be true of me that I act in a certain way. The width of these limits varies with the characterisation of the action; they are pretty wide for 'taking some exercise', but much narrower for 'running a hundred yards'. That there are limits does, however, create a place for genuine questions about the relation between, on the one hand, our normal descriptions and explanations of human be- haviour and, on the other, those descriptions and explanations which are to be found in, more or less, 'physical' sciences.[2] These questions are at least in part philosophical in character but they cannot even be approached without a fairly detailed knowledge of the sciences in question; and it is no part of my purpose to attempt to approach them.

Closely connected with these points is the fact that I will be concerned with arguments of a general kind and will say nothing about more specific questions that might be raised by particular developments within particular sciences. The importance of the kinds of consideration I will raise is, then, dependent on the extent to which people are influenced by a *general* picture of the relation between science and our normal thought. Since I believe almost all of us are influenced by such a picture I am confident that these considerations *are* important. (Proving decisively that the picture is at work in the thought of a particular philosopher would, where it is possible at all, in most cases require more detailed exegesis than I can attempt here. For the picture only occasionally surfaces as an explicitly articulated premiss. The assumption that the picture is at work does, however, explain things that need to be explained; and

I believe that what I say is enough to show that, at the very least, my target is not a completely straw man.)

I said that the relationship between our normal understanding of people and a scientific understanding – the relationship between our human ontology and the ontology of basic science – was the central concern of contemporary philosophy of mind. I then spoke of this as the current version of the 'mind-body problem'. This latter characterisation is, I believe, completely in place. For while it cannot be said that *all* of the traditional philosophical associations of the terms 'mind' and 'body' play a crucial role in contemporary thought about these issues, much that is central to the traditional understanding survives in barely modified forms. On the one hand, we still find the assumption that what is distinctive of our thought about people 'lies behind' what we are confronted with in our daily contact with each other; and this is one of the central assumptions embodied in the philosophical notion of 'the mind'. On the other hand, and closely linked with this, we find the equation of the third-person world – the world of extended and tangible entities – with the world of the physical sciences; and this equation is central to the philosophical notion of 'the body'.

Up to this point, then, we have what I would describe as 'pure Cartesianism'.[3] Divergence only appears with the suggestion that the world as described from the third-person point of view is *the* world. This, combined with the traditional assumptions, yields the view that 'the materialistic world of the physical sciences' is *the* world. There is, then, in the contemporary picture, no other world in which persons might be located; and so a great deal turns on the question of whether there is any room for them in the world of basic science.

We might summarise the impact of the mind/body terminology which I will highlight in this way. Action and expression – and, indeed, the *human being*, where a 'human being' is something that has, for example, a face – are shifted from a central position in the picture. That is to say, those characterisations of what we observe of each other which are linked with the range of interests which we normally have in each other are either overlooked or assumed to be, in some sense, secondary. Now my main point in my next section will be that it is only because matters are viewed in this way that it is taken to be obvious that the relation between 'mental states' and physiological states must have one of certain familiar forms. That is, standard views about how thoughts and sensations are related to a scientific understanding only seem forced upon us because we take for granted a certain view of how *action* and *expression* are related to such an understanding. I will then suggest that behind this outlook lie certain presuppositions concerning our *interest* in what we encounter: presuppositions of a form which we met in Part I. My discussion throughout this chapter will continue to focus fairly exclusively on the third-person point of view since I wish to stress that serious difficulties in standard defences of materialism can be seen clearly from this perspective. As will become clear, those rejections of materialism which insist that it is the first-person point of view which creates *the* difficulty for the views under attack commonly share with materialism the very assumptions which will be the central focus of my criticisms.[4]

(ii) We can begin by sketching in very broad terms some of the commonly perceived options in contemporary discussions of these issues. Perhaps the most alarming suggestion in the field is that science might show that there are simply no such things as minds; or, if this is different, that all talk of 'pains', 'beliefs', 'desires', and so on embodies a pre-scientific myth.[5] Only slightly less disturbing, at least in some eyes, is the suggestion that it could, in one way or another, turn out that when we speak of such states we are speaking of what is, in reality, a complex neurophysiological state of the body. This position can for the moment be taken with the, perhaps slightly different, suggestion that, for example, an individual's thinking is 'realised', 'embodied' or 'instantiated' in, or by, a physiological process. Again, it is sometimes said that the claim that someone is thinking is 'true in virtue of' the fact that a certain physical process is occurring in his brain.[6] Finally, I should mention the suggestion that none of these possibilities is really on the cards since our normal talk of 'pains', 'beliefs', 'desires', 'thoughts', and so on does not commit us to the idea that there really *are* such states. These are simply ways of describing the world which we find useful for certain purposes. Since, then, we never believed that there were such things there is no danger of science showing us that there are not after all, or of its showing us something uncomfortable about the real nature of these states.[7]

The following argument might seem to provide a fairly straightforward route to the conclusion that beliefs, desires, and so on must either be identified with neurophysiological states or else be eliminated from our picture of the world: 'It is now quite clear that all human behaviour is, in principle, explainable in neurophysiological terms and, ultimately, in the physicist's terms. Our knowledge of what science has achieved in other areas, and of the progress which has been made in the explanation of human behaviour, makes it wildly implausible to question this. It is, however, part of our normal picture of people that their behaviour is to be explained in terms of beliefs, desires, sensations, and so on. (It might, indeed, be argued that these states are, in part, *defined* in terms of the role that they play in producing behaviour.) We seem, then, to be faced with a choice. We might argue that the scientist's explanation of a particular piece of behaviour is quite compatible with our normal explanation since the terms which he employs refer to the very same things as are picked out in a different way by the language of 'beliefs', 'desires' and so on; in short, beliefs, desires and sensations are neurophysiological states. Alternatively we might conclude that science is now revealing that our normal explanations are just wrong. There simply are no such things as the beliefs, desires, and so on of which we speak: these concepts form part of a now discredited theory.'[8] (One might, of course, reach a mixed conclusion, believing that some features of our normal thought harmonise with what science is revealing in such a way that they are not discredited by the science while other features have been exposed as simple muddle.)

In response to this argument we can consider, first, what is presented as being the worst possible scenario. Suppose that we were forced by the scientific evidence to grant that all of our normal explanations of human behaviour were completely mistaken – that human behaviour is to be explained in terms of neurophysiology *as opposed to* beliefs, desires, and so on. Would to grant this be to accept that there are no such things as 'minds': that none of our 'mental concepts' in fact have any application in the world? That question cannot be properly answered until we are given some indication of how the terms 'mind' and 'mental' are being used here; for, as I remarked in Chapter 6, it is pretty clear that they are not being used in any normal way. What can be said, however, is that to grant the point about explanation would *not* be to grant that none of those concepts which are distinctive of our thought about human beings have application in the world. For when I describe someone as 'smiling', 'talking about the weather' or 'writing a cheque' I am not, it seems, offering *explanations* of what I observe; I am simply describing it. Yet such characterisations are distinctive of our thought about human beings, both in the sense that they have no application to sticks and stones and in the sense that nothing of this form features in the language of 'basic science'. Since, then, the role of our distinctively human terminology is not purely explanatory, it is in no danger of elimination by scientific advances in the way suggested.[9] (It has to be said straight away that I do not hold out any hope of keeping 'description' and 'explanation' sharply distinguished in the way presupposed in this paragraph. What for one functions as a description of what he is observing, for another plays the role of an explanation: 'Why is he moving his hand in that way?' 'He is waving.' The conclusion *I* draw from this is that the supposition with which the paragraph opened – that all of our normal explanations of human behaviour could be completely mistaken – cannot be seriously entertained. That I draw that conclusion does, however, reflect the particular way in which I view the relationship between the descriptive and the explanatory roles of these terms. Others, as we shall see, view things differently.)

There is a closely connected point which raises a more general worry for approaches of this form. We can ask: is that which we have good grounds for thinking can be explained in neurophysiological terms the same as that which we generally think is explained in terms of beliefs, desires, and so on? Now I take it that if we actually look at what is being achieved by the relevant sciences pretty serious doubts about this begin to arise. As K.V. Wilkes observes:

> For cognitive psychology is seeking to identify and explain the pervasive, fundamental capacities that underlie the purposive behaviour of humans and animals; it asks, for example, how we can store visual or verbal information in short-term or long-term memory; how we perceive; how we set about solving problems of various kinds; and so forth.[10]

By contrast, when, in normal circumstances, we explain his angry words in terms of the fact that he thought the others were making fun of him we do not take ourselves to be saying anything about how human beings are able to perceive. Since, then, what is explained by us, on the one hand, and by the cognitive psychologist, on the other, is different, there is no appearance of competition which needs to be resolved by elimination or identification.

To put the matter as I just have may, however, be slightly misleading. For we must allow that the individual in my example would not have spoken as he did if he had not had the capacity to see. Now this creates the possibility of circumstances – highly abnormal ones – in which the neurophysiology which underlies the capacity *could* be given in answer to the question 'Why was he so angry?' What is explained by the neurophysiology and by his beliefs is, we might then say, the same. It should be clear, however, that the fact that the matter can be put in this way does nothing at all to suggest that it must be possible to bring the two forms of explanation into relation with each other in anything like the ways suggested. There is no more pressure on us to eliminate or identify entities than there is in the case in which I explain why the bumper is dented in terms of the fact that it was kicked and the metallurgist explains 'the same thing' in terms of the atomic structure of chrome.

But do we not have strong grounds, drawn from our experience of what science has achieved in other areas, for believing that it is possible to explain the specific behaviour of a particular individual at a certain time – *as opposed to* the capacities that underlie that behaviour – in physical terms? As the point has been expressed recently: 'our bodily movements, being just so many more physical events, must themselves have entirely physical causes'.[11] Well, we may have grounds of this kind for thinking that our bodily movements are explainable in physical terms. When, however, we ask for and give explanations of human 'behaviour' in terms of beliefs, desires, emotions, sensations, and so on, what we seek to explain is not, generally, why a human body moved in a certain way. We are concerned, rather, with the explanation of a person's actions, words, facial expression, and so on. It is in so far as what I am observing can be characterised as 'writing his son out of his will' or 'smiling maliciously' that I am astonished or puzzled by it and so want it explained. Since it is behaviour in *that* sense which we think is sometimes explained in terms of beliefs, desires and the like, there is, it seems, no competition with the explanations which we have reason to think the neurophysiologist or physicist may come up with.

Some will find that last sentence a little too quick! One response to it would be this: 'Certainly it is under such descriptions that we do, in the normal course of things, ask for and give explanations of human behaviour. That does not, however, alter the fact that *what* we seek to explain is the very same thing as can be explained in physical terms. For what we pick out in these terms is one and the same thing as that which is picked out by a description in terms of movements of matter. In short, actions and so on are bodily movements. Thus the "competition", and so need for resolution, between the two styles of explanation remains.'

Consider an analogy. I point at a man walking down the road and ask 'What is the explanation of that?' The pointing gesture by itself does not show what it is that I want explained. He is walking in a cheerful way down the left hand side of Bridge Street at ten o'clock at night. The explanation of his walking in a cheerful way ('He has just won the pools') may be quite unconnected with the explanation of his walking on the left hand side ('It is safer'); and similarly with the wide range of other descriptions under which this incident might be picked out. Now we do not have to get into any tricky questions about event identity here. Is his walking in that cheerful way one and the same happening as his walking down the left hand side? That I do not have much of a grasp of what might be at issue with that question does not, I think, matter. If it is said that we have here a single thing described in two different ways then we will have to say that whether or not a certain story is an explanation of what happened depends on the terms in which what happened is characterised.

The point is a completely general one. There is one event: the ball rolling down this groove at 10 m.p.h. Yet the explanation of its rolling down *this* groove may be quite unconnected with the explanation of its speed being 10 m.p.h.

To return, then, to actions and bodily movements, I am not completely clear what to make of the suggestion that the descriptions which generally interest us pick out the very same thing as is picked out by descriptions in terms of bodily movements. For our purposes now, however, that does not matter. Even if that is said it will not follow that in explaining, in neurophysiological terms, why a man's body moved in a certain way we explain why he acted as he did. So there will be no pressure here to choose between saying, on the one hand, that our normal explanations refer to the very same things as do the scientist's – and so that beliefs, desires and so on are neurophysiological states – or, on the other, that our normal explanations have simply been shown to be mistaken.

The inclination to think that it must be possible to bring our human ontology into relation with the ontology of basic science by either identification or elimination is powerful and easily kindled. A general awareness of what science has achieved in other areas is thought to be all that is needed to see that movement in this direction is virtually inevitable. I have suggested that this idea reflects the assumption that it is at least clear that what we normally observe of each other is to be spoken of in terms of the categories of (more or less) basic science; for only given that assumption will it seem *obvious* that we are attempting to do with our human ontology the very thing which it is now clear can be done in terms of a 'physical' ontology: namely, 'explain human behaviour'. (Just as, to use a popular analogy, we can now do in terms of modern theories of mental dysfunction what used to be done in terms of the idea of 'demonic possession': namely, explain certain odd patterns of human behaviour.[12]) Now my main point so far has been that our normal characterisations of what we observe of another are characterisations in what I have called 'human' or 'personal' terms. This point, first, I suggested, rules out the claim that all of our uses of such terms involve an attempt to *explain* what we observe and so need to be brought into relation in one of the ways suggested with the explanations offered by science. Further, I argued, when we *do* employ such terms in the explanation of behaviour, since it is behaviour characterised in human terms that we are attempting to explain, our explanations are not, even on the surface, in competition with an explanation in 'physical' terms of the movements of the human body; and so for this reason also there is no need to bring our human ontology into relation with the ontology of basic science by elimination or identification. In short, if we can reject the way of viewing matters which is embodied in the traditional mind/body contrast we will not be confronted with the familiar materialist options.

There is, however, another, more radical, response to my insistence that what we observe, and seek to explain in terms of beliefs, desires, sensations, and so on, is *action* and *expression*, not 'movements of matter': 'What you are calling descriptions of what is observed do, in reality, embody explanatory hypotheses, and so go beyond what is strictly speaking observed. Thus, my description of another as "smiling", "waving" or "talking about the weather" embodies a claim about the cause of what I observe. In this sense, our, so called, "observation language" is theory laden. The language which describes what is strictly speaking observed will be one from which everything which is distinctive of our thought about human beings has been eliminated. Thus, first, all of such language does, after all, have the status of an explanatory hypothesis and so is potentially in competition with the explanations offered by science; and, second, that which the hypothesis is an attempt to explain is behaviour characterised in terms of movements of matter. Thus, we have good reason to think that complete explanations of the same data in scientific terms is possible; and so we are faced directly with the choice between elimination and identification.'[13]

The claim that all characterisations of another in human terms go beyond what we can, strictly speaking, observe of them – that all such characterisations embody an explanatory hypothesis – was discussed in some detail in Part I. The claim may rest, I suggested, on the special position which we are inclined to give to the first-person point of view in the grounding of our thought about each other. The idea that what we can observe of others always leaves room for doubt about their sensations, emotions, desires, beliefs, and so on may play a role. I also suggested that the claim may rest on the idea that nothing in what we observe can show that we are *right* to think of another in human terms; thus, thinking of another as a person involves thinking of him as something that lies behind what I can observe. Closely linked with this is the view that what we observe of another is obviously *not*, in itself, to be treated in the ways which are linked with an understanding of it in human terms. Thus, it might be assumed that what we encounter in the world is, in the absence of reasons for thinking otherwise, to be thought of as something to be used in our attempts to achieve our ends; and so if a person is *not* to be thought of in that way the person must not be what is encountered: our characterisation of another in human terms must embody a theory about the cause of what we observe.

Some of these appeals are not, when explicitly articulated, likely to seem too attractive to the contemporary materialist who gives primacy to the third person point of view. Others, in particular the last, can, in the hands of the materialist, hardly fail to lead to the conclusion that our normal thought about each other is systematically mistaken in a radical way. I will not here add to my earlier criticisms of any of these suggestions. I suspect, however, that something closely related to the last line of thought plays a crucial role in much of the work that is being done in this area. That will be the central theme of my next section.

(iii) I have argued, in effect, that our normal characterisations of
human beings cut across the philosophical mind/body contrast in a
way which creates serious difficulties for certain, currently popular, approaches to the philosophy of mind. Now it will be objected
that this appeal to our normal descriptions of what we observe of
each other simply cannot do the work that I am asking of it. To
think that it can is to be guilty of a form of empiricism – of
conceptual conservativism – which has been exposed as quite
untenable. For nothing in what we observe can, it will be argued,
show in what terminology it is to be characterised: the language in
which we normally speak of each other's behaviour is, as all
language is, subject to revision in the light of empirical discoveries.
Thus, the fact that our normal descriptions of human beings are
not couched in the language of the physical scientist does nothing
to show that the third-person world is not the materialistic world of
the physical sciences.[14]

This protest normally emerges as a response to the claim that the
materialist view of persons could not possibly be correct, or is
unintelligible. For example, it is argued by critics of materialism
that to speak of an emotion as a neurophysiological state makes no
sense since it makes no sense to speak of the spatial location of an
emotion; and it is replied that the fact that our current ways of
speaking leave no room for this is, at the very least, not decisive.
Now I must stress that my appeal to our normal human characterisations is *not* part of an attack on the conclusion of the materialist
argument. I agree that there can be reasons for thinking that our
language should be revised in certain ways; and so the fact that a
particular materialist view involves a commitment to such revisions is not, in itself, grounds for rejecting the view. My point
was a point about the *argument* for the materialist view; or, perhaps
better, a point about the general picture which inclines many to
feel that, given our knowledge of what the physical sciences have
achieved in other areas, a materialist view of persons *must* be
correct. A standard line of thought, I suggested, involves the
assumption that a pure characterisation of what we observe of
another will be couched in the terms of the physical scientist rather
than in those of our normal human ontology; it is only in the light
of that assumption that it will seem clear that what we do not
observe – namely, the sensations, emotions, thoughts, and so on
which explain the behaviour – must, if they are to be anything, be
physical states.

My appeal to our normal characterisations of human behaviour is not, then, a reflection of the empiricist idea that the language in which we speak is somehow vindicated by our experience of human behaviour: that the appropriateness of such characterisations can be 'drawn from' what we observe. It is, rather, a reminder that some work needs to be done before we can take even the first step in the simple materialist argument outlined in section (ii). Indeed, it is tempting to reverse the charge of empiricism: to suggest that the failure to see the need for this work is a reflection of the assumption that physical movements are 'the given': the assumption that the appropriateness of characterisations in terms of movements of matter can be 'drawn from' what we observe. However, while I suspect that something like this is one of the forces that is sometimes at work here, this can hardly be the end of the matter. For we will still need an explanation of how it could have been thought that such characterisations can be 'drawn from' what we observe in a sense in which characterisations in human terms cannot. Now it is, I believe, with this explanation that we reach the most fundamental assumptions of contemporary materialism in its various forms.

We can best approach this point through a consideration of a straightforward sense in which characterisations of each other in human terms can be said to be 'basic'. Our normal characterisations of human behaviour – characterisations in terms of action and expression – are basic in our thought in the sense that it is these characterisations which reflect and serve the kinds of interest that we generally have in each other. That 'He smiled' when he saw her in that dress tells me what I want to know; as a description in geometric terms of the movement of his facial flesh does not. That 'He cut his daughter out of his will' tells his daughter what she wants to know; as a physical description of the movements of his body through space does not. My suggestion that what we observe of each other is to be characterised in human terms[15] is not, then, an expression of the idea that the appropriateness of such characterisations can be drawn from what we observe. My point is rather that we find significance *in* what we observe. I speak of you as a person who 'smiles', 'looks at me', 'cries out in pain' and 'treats me badly'; and, with that, your smile warms me, I hide from your look, I respond with sympathy to your pain, and am hurt by your hostility.

While this point will not, perhaps, be disputed, its significance certainly will be. One response will insist that no observations concerning what *interests* us can show us anything about the character of what we are confronted with when we are confronted with another human being: it can show us nothing about the form which a 'basic' or 'pure' characterisation of what we are confronted with would take. Our speaking in the ways that we normally do, it will be argued, is purely a matter of convenience: descriptions of what we observe in terms of action and expression collect together the basic data of our experience – that is to say, movements of matter – in the ways that bring out what is of interest to us.

In response to this objection I should stress that my point is not that the character of our normal interest in each other reveals something about the character of what we are confronted with when we are confronted with another human being. I speak of our normal interest in order to bring out the sense in which certain forms of description can be said to be basic for us. My point is that in so far as *this* sense is rejected as irrelevant to the discussion we stand in urgent need of an explanation of the supposed sense in which *movements of matter* can be said to be 'the basic data of our experience'. Is it being assumed that there is a sense of the term 'basic data of our experience' which is quite distinct from the notion of what is basic in our thought: that, perhaps, characterisations in terms of movements of matter can be said to be a 'pure reflection' of what is there in the world, in the sense that this form of language is in no way a reflection of a certain kind of interest that human beings have in what surrounds them? Or is the assumption, rather, that a particular form of interest, the form linked with such characterisations, is, in some sense, 'basic' to our thought about the world; so that our normal forms of interest in other people can be said to be 'secondary', and the descriptions that go with them merely 'a matter of convenience'?

Suppose that it was assumed that, in some sense, our primary, or basic, interest in other human beings lies in the fact that they make a difference to what happens in the non-human world. Suppose that it was assumed that the, in some sense, basic reason why they feature in my thought at all – feature in my thought, that is, *as* human beings: beings that smile and act, that have beliefs, desires, emotions, and so on – lies in the fact that thinking in those terms enables me more readily to predict and control what happens in the world. Suppose, that is, it was assumed that our 'primary' interest in other human beings was, as I expressed it in

Chapter 2, a 'functional' interest. In what light would such an assumption present our characterisations of human behaviour in terms of smiles, greetings and dancings of the Highland fling? Well, if what you are interested in is, for example, whether this ceiling is going to collapse it is quite irrelevant whether the person in the room above is doing a Highland fling or is stamping with rage provided that the impacts on the floor are of the same force. So far as this particular interest goes that distinction has no role to play. With that, the fact that what is taking place upstairs is 'the same as' what took place upstairs yesterday, namely, a dancing of the Highland fling, is, from this point of view, of no significance in itself: if it is prediction and manipulation you are interested in to say that 'the same' thing is taking place will be seriously misleading if yesterday it was a five-stone child and today a fifteen-stone man doing the dance. This similarity will not, then, be marked in an ultimately acceptable ontology. Relevant similarities, as with relevant distinctions, will be captured in descriptions in terms of movements of matter.

Now it is true that the similarities and distinctions rejected as irrelevant in the above example *can*, in other cases, play a role in prediction and manipulation. If we want to know what mood the 'dancer's' girlfriend will be in in ten minutes time it may be relevant to know whether he is dancing or stamping with rage. Similarly, if I want to upset Sally, or to make her leave, the *distinction* between a visual and a verbal insult may be irrelevant; as will be the *similarity* between my utterance of the words 'You have a fat face' and my utterance of the words 'Life is a rat race'. In these cases the distinctions and similarities marked in our normal descriptions of behaviour appear to play a crucial role in prediction and manipulation. It will be clear, however, that this role is, in one way or another, ultimately eliminable. For all examples with this feature are ones in which someone's behaviour has effects on another person (or, perhaps, animal). Now on the assumption which I am considering our 'primary' interest in those effects lies in *their* significance for prediction and manipulation. The assumption is that human beings only feature, or, perhaps, only *legitimately* feature, in our thought – only feature *as* human beings – in so far as thinking in terms of them enables us more readily to predict and control what happens in the world. The term 'the world' here can, then, only mean 'the world as described in non-human categories'. My rude gesture, as opposed to the movement of my finger described in geometrical terms, has a basic place in our thought only if reference to it plays an ineliminable role in predicting and controlling the way in which matter moves. It is a very short step from here to the conclusion that my rude gesture does *not* have a basic place in our thought. For, if it is not a conceptual truth that nothing but a knowledge of movements of matter can be required for the prediction of movements of matter (for the prediction of what happens characterised in these terms), it is at least a thoroughly well embedded assumption of contemporary thought.[16]

The assumption that an interest in prediction and control is, in some sense, what is basic to our thought about each other would, then, fill what seems to be a gaping hole in popular defences of materialism. For in the light of this assumption it will, as I have argued, seem obvious that a 'basic' characterisation of human behaviour will be in geometric terms; and so seem obvious that our normal explanations of human 'behaviour' in terms of beliefs, desires, sensations, and so on are potentially in competition with explanations in physiological terms.

The assumption is explicitly articulated by Paul Churchland in the following passage:

> Beliefs, desires, and the rest of the folk psychological ontology are all in the same position (as the ontology of witches, demonic possession and so on.) Their integrity, to the extent that they have any, derives from the explanatory, predictive, and manipulative prowess they display.[17]

The claim is that beliefs, desires, and so on are only truly ascribed to human beings in so far as making such ascriptions facilitates our attempts to explain, predict and manipulate what happens: where 'what happens' is characterised in non-human terms. Churchland does not deny that talk of 'beliefs', 'desires', and so on may play other roles in our lives. He does, however, insist that this role is basic; such ways of speaking are to be assessed in terms of their success in that role: in terms of the success with which they serve this particular human interest.

While this assumption is rarely articulated as explicitly as it is by Churchland, various commonly discussed views can, I believe, be usefully presented in terms of it. The 'eliminative materialist' holds that our normal human ontology displays a predictive and manipulative prowess which is very meagre indeed by comparison with that possessed by the ontology of the scientist, and so should be eliminated in the latter's favour. Other forms of materialism hold that the explanatory, predictive and manipulative powers of at least much of our normal thought are pretty satisfactory. In learning that Jones believes it is raining we do learn something important about how to predict and control his behaviour; but, further, the scientist who knows that Jones is in a particular neurophysiological state has knowledge which, so far as the prediction and control of behaviour goes, puts him in exactly the same position as we are in with our knowledge of Jones' belief. To express the same point in another way: the neurophysiological condition plays the same 'causal role' as does the belief. We should conclude, it is suggested, that the belief and the neurophysiological state are one and the same thing identified in different ways. Finally, the 'instrumentalist' suggests that the question of *what* we are referring to when we speak of 'beliefs', 'desires', and so on does not arise: '*What it is* to be a true believer is to be an *intentional system*, a system whose behaviour is reliably and voluminously predictable via the intentional strategy.'[18] Beliefs and desires are to be ascribed to a creature on the basis of the fact that making such ascriptions serves this human interest: our interest in being able to make predictions.

The fact that a significant range of materialist views can be formulated in terms of the assumption that an interest in prediction and control is, in some sense, what is basic in our relations with each other does not prove that that assumption lies behind these views. Still, the suggestion that this assumption is at work at some level would, as I have argued, explain things. Further, since this assumption, or something very like it, is central to the consequentialism which dominates contemporary philosophical thinking about morality, it would hardly be surprising if it was at work here. I believe that Occam's Razor is, at least often, roughly the same assumption in a different guise.

One writer in which this last connection becomes explicit is Richard Rorty. Rorty defends a form of 'eliminative' ('disappearance') materialism which holds that the relation between physical events in the brain and mental events 'is not strict identity, but rather the sort of relation which obtains between, to put it crudely, existent entities and non-existent entities when reference to the latter once served (some of) the purposes presently served by reference to the former'.[19] It is suggested that, for example, talk about 'sensations' serves the same purposes, plays the same role in our lives, as does (or might) talk about brain events. What Rorty takes that role to be emerges most clearly in his discussion of the, supposedly analogous, elimination of demons from our ontology: 'Demon-discourse is one way of describing and predicting phenomena, but there are better ways' (ibid, p. 36). Now it is clear that it is 'predicting', as opposed to 'describing', that is doing all the work here; for it is only in terms of relative predictive power that it is clear what 'better' means. The way in which we speak of 'sensations' is, then, to be assessed in terms of its predictive powers; it is in terms of its usefulness in that role that our sensation discourse is to be judged. If we balk at this use of Occam's Razor we are referred to 'the practical advantages gained by the use of the Razor in the past' (ibid., p 30).

Dennett, defending as he does a position often thought of as a long way removed from 'eliminative materialism', provides another instructive example. His 'instrumentalism', summarised in a passage already quoted, faces the objection that intelligent Martians might be able to predict the movements of our bodies without ascribing beliefs and desires to us. Dennett replies that these Martians would be missing real patterns that there are in human behaviour: the patterns which are captured in our descriptions in terms of beliefs, desires and actions; but, and this is my point, he locates the significance of *that* in the fact that such patterns provide us with shortcuts in the making of predictions – the prediction, for example, that 'a large metallic vehicle with rubber tyres will come to a stop in the drive within one hour' – which would not be available to the Martians (Dennett, 1987, pp. 25–7). He takes this difference in the way the Martians and we are able to satisfy *that* interest to be *the* significant difference between our understanding of each other and the Martian's understanding of us.

I suggested in Chapter 2 that what I called the 'functional' paradigm of rationality in action may be an important motivating force behind traditional mind-body dualism. It is assumed that only if the person lies outside the world of extended and tangible beings will there be room for the idea that another person is not to be thought of simply in terms of his usefulness in bringing about certain states of affairs. Thus, what lies *in* the world of extended, tangible beings entirely lacks those features which are distinctive of persons: what lies in that world is a mere 'body'. I have suggested in this section that the same paradigm of rationality in action may lie behind contemporary materialist views of the person; and have linked that suggestion with the role still played by the traditional understanding of the human 'body': by the idea that 'the objective, third-person world' is 'the materialistic world of the physical sciences'. From this perspective we might, then, describe the movement that has taken place in these terms: the contemporary materialist acquiesces in the paradigm of rationality in action which the traditional dualist attempts to escape. My suggestion has been that we can bypass this choice by rejecting that paradigm.[20]

(iv) I have suggested that the idea that an interest in prediction and control is what is basic in our relations with each other may play a fundamental role in contemporary materialism. I would, however, not suggest with any confidence that it plays *the* fundamental role, and want now to consider briefly another consideration which may dovetail neatly with this one.

I have stressed that my appeal to our normal ways of speaking of each other is not a reflection of the empiricist idea that the language in which we speak is somehow vindicated by our experience of human behaviour. What we observe cannot be said to show our language to be 'correct'; and so materialist views cannot be ruled out simply on the grounds that they are in some kind of tension with our normal ways of speaking. I share *that* much with most of those who are sympathetic to some form of materialism. Beyond this shared rejection of empiricism, however, there are major differences. At its most simple the difference comes to this. While philosophers such as Rorty, Feyerabend and Churchland suggest that our normal forms of description reflect certain general beliefs or 'theories' about human beings, my point throughout this book has been that these forms of description reflect certain kinds of *interest* that we have in human beings. Now a worry that some will feel about my emphasis is this: assuming that there is, in the end, no such thing as assessing our *interests* as correct or incorrect there will, on the view I have defended, be no such thing as assessing the language which is linked with those interests as 'correct' or 'incorrect'; and, with that, no such thing as assessing one form of description as more, or less, 'adequate to the world' than another. I suggested that dualism may be, in part, an attempt to overcome this worry by providing a touchstone by reference to which our forms of concern about each other *can* be assessed. Materialism might be seen as, in part, an attempt to overcome the worry by a different route: by presenting a certain form of concern (or group of such forms) as a background in terms of which *all* forms of language are to be assessed.

Consider the suggestion that the terms in which we describe each other are 'theory laden'. The importance of this suggestion from the materialist's point of view lies, in large measure, in the fact that it provides him with a way of undercutting objections which appeal to our normal ways of speaking and acting. Central to the suggestion is, I take it, the idea that the adequacy of our language is to be assessed by empirical investigation, and that the language can be shown to be 'correct' or 'incorrect' by such investigation.[21] That is a claim which, on a broad reading of 'empirical investigation', it shares with traditional empiricism. If, however, one rejects the traditional empiricist picture of the direct vindication of our language in sense experience an account of what the criteria of assessment are is required. Some picture of how the results of an empirical investigation are to be brought to bear on the forms of our language must, explicitly or implicitly, be at work here. Now my point here is that in so far as a certain form of concern, a certain form of interest in a phenomenon, is taken as given, a choice between alternative forms of description of that phenomenon will, in the way required, present itself as a matter to be resolved by empirical investigation.

I have already quoted, and commented on, remarks by Rorty concerning 'better ways of describing and predicting phenomena'. Feyerabend writes in a similar vein:

> in order to defeat the materialist it must also be shown that a language structured in this way will describe the world more correctly, and more efficiently than any language the materialist could develop.[22]

Perhaps the term 'more efficiently' provides a strong clue to what the words 'more correctly' mean here; but my central point is that these words *do* stand in need of explanation; and that the assumption that all forms of language are to be judged in terms of the way in which they serve a single human interest, or range of human interests, would provide that explanation.

Consider again the most popular analogy of the eliminative materialist. To hold, as perhaps most contemporary philosophers would, that talk about 'witches' is theory laden is to hold a particular view about the role which talk of 'witches' played in the lives of those who engaged in it. Thus, someone who takes it to be obvious that contemporary science has overturned all talk about witches or demonic possession is someone who takes it to be obvious that those who have spoken in these terms have been engaged in an enterprise which is, at some fundamental level, of the same form as that of the contemporary scientist who explains the failure of the crops in terms of the quality of the soil or a particular individual's strange behaviour in terms of hysteria. It is only if those who have spoken of 'witches' and 'demonic possession' were trying to do what the contemporary scientist is trying to do that there is room for the claim that the contemporary scientist does 'it' better. Furthermore, nothing is achieved by the suggestion that clearly both *are* trying to do the same thing: namely, 'describe what is going on'. For, apart from anything else, that answer, by itself, tells us nothing about how the merits of the two forms of description are to be compared.

Now it may seem obvious that the 'fundamental' role of talk of witches and demonic possession, wherever such talk has flourished, has, as Churchland assumes, lain in the way in which thinking in those terms has facilitated attempts to predict and manipulate the environment (or has been thought to do so.) My aim here is not to dispute that. (Though, as will be clear, I would be very suspicious of any claim that this is obvious which was not backed up with detailed information about the lives of those who have spoken in these ways.) I introduce the example simply in order to illustrate the following point: empirical investigation, on its own, will be able to adjudicate between different forms of description only if those forms of description are to be judged in terms of how well they serve a single human interest (or range of such interests.) One who holds that there must be such a thing as assessing all language as 'correct' or 'incorrect' may thus be under considerable pressure to give such a place to a single form of human interest.

My suggestion, then, is this. The idea that a 'functional' interest in phenomena is 'fundamental' – an idea which I have suggested may lie behind materialist views of persons – may not flow solely from any intrinsic attractions of a consequentialist ethic. The idea that it must be possible to adjudicate between different forms of description of a phenomenon by appeal to empirical evidence has a power of its own. This idea can only be satisfied if some form of interest is taken as 'fundamental' in the sense that it is in terms of that interest that assessment is to be made. Now it is true that the possibility of such assessment does not depend on one particular form of interest being taken as fundamental. Considerations of other kinds may, however, make the move towards giving priority to the 'functional' virtually irresistible. The test for ontology which will then emerge is one in which the 'real' is strongly linked with the 'causally efficacious'. Provided that I can count on someone being concerned about future experiences[23] I will be able to say that anything which might be causally significant to that ought to feature in his picture of the world; we will, that is, be able in principle to settle all disputes about the reality of particular kinds of thing.

It may be worthwhile to sketch, against the background of this point, various connections of ideas which would deserve further exploration. I suggested in Chapter 6 that it is often thought that unless pains have location in the same sense as bullets and bones do then a pain is not a 'real thing' in the rich sense in which bullets and bones are. This point can be linked with Dennett's suggestion that almost everyone now accepts the 'double standard' introduced by Quine in *Word and Object*:

> If we are limning the true and ultimate structure of reality, the canonical scheme for us is the austere scheme that knows no quotation but direct quotation and no propositional attitudes but only the physical constituents and behaviour of organisms.[24]

This thought may be reflected in such questions as 'What, if anything, is the property of believing that p to be identified with?' and 'What' in the case of silent thought 'does constitute the thinking?'[25] Such questions cannot go on for ever. ('What is the property of being round to be identified with?', 'What, in the case of a ball rolling down a hill, does constitute the rolling?') Those who insist that there clearly *is* room for such questions in the case of thinking or anger must, then, be working with some picture of the kind of answer to them which would put an end to further questions of the same form. The picture is, I suspect, often Quine's. That picture, it should be noted, may be shared by philosophers who insist that it is a mistake to expect answers to these questions. The picture is still at work in so far as it is thought that the reason these questions do not arise is that nothing in our normal practice commits us to the idea that there really *are* such things as pains, thoughts, beliefs or anger.[26]

There is room for many fine shades of position here: the shade turning, in part, on the precise force which one gives to phrases such as 'the true and ultimate structure of reality'. (See, for example, the shifting focus in Dennett's treatment of the terms 'real' and 'true'; pages 72–3 of *The Intentional Stance* contain an interesting instance of this. See also Wilkes' telling use of the phrase 'truth by correspondence': *Inquiry*, 1984, p. 357). In so far, however, as one thinks that a phrase such as 'the true and ultimate structure of reality' usefully marks some contrast between, on the one hand, 'physical' states and processes and, on the other, states and processes of other kinds one is giving a special position to some particular 'criterion of the real'. A full explanation of this criterion would require a full exploration of the force of the word 'physical' as it appears here. I take it to be clear, however, that the idea of what is 'causally efficacious' is central to this idea of the 'physical'; and, with that, central to the contrast between the senses in which the bone and the pain are located in the foot.

These remarks do no more than suggest possible connections between ideas in this area. I have, in particular, wanted to suggest that there may be links between the idea that the 'causally efficacious' is *the* test for 'the real', a consequentialist picture of human concern, and the search for a form of 'metaphysical grounding' for our thought about each other. I suggested in Part I that the search for 'metaphysical grounding' is, within traditional empiricism, characteristically sought within the first person point of view. I am now, in effect, suggesting that the idea that 'immediate experience' can provide the required grounding has been replaced, for some, by the idea that science can. Now, as with the appeal to 'immediate experience', the idea that science can provide grounding of *that* form can, of course, only flourish so long as it is not acknowledged that science itself is the expression of a particular human interest or range of such interests. I will close this section with some further remarks on this point as it may be here that many will feel that my discussion is most seriously misleading.

It might, first, be argued against my presentation of materialist thought in section (iii) that whether or not a certain procedure is an effective means of manipulation and prediction is a completely objective fact which is in no way dependent on human interests. This response, however, misses the point. For it is equally true that whether or not there is anger to be seen in his features is a completely objective fact which is in no way dependent on human interests; at least, reason has yet to be given for doubting this. It is the *acknowledgement* that there is anger to be seen there that is dependent on the particular kind of 'interest' that we have in what confronts us. Now the acknowledgement that something is an effective means of manipulation and prediction is, equally, dependent on the fact that we have some interest in both the future and the past. In the life of a being whose horizon of concern did not extend beyond its current sensations there would be no place for that acknowledgement. ('But if someone failed to make the acknowledgement, insisted that a particular procedure was not an effective means of manipulation and prediction, would he not just be *wrong*?' If he shares enough with us to *deny* what we say he is certainly wrong.)

Another consideration that may be relevant here is this. An interest in prediction and manipulation *is* basic in the sense that the possibility of living any kind of life is dependent on having some kind of predictive and manipulative hold on the world. Further, one aspect of this is that the possibility of having any kind of relationship with another person is dependent on being able to predict and influence their behaviour to some extent. Now, it might be argued on these grounds that my use of the term 'interest' here is badly misleading, suggesting as it does that we are speaking of something which is an idiosyncracy of people, or even of a particular group of people. (With that it will be argued that it is far from clear that we can understand the suggestion that there could be a being whose horizon of concern does not extend 'beyond the present'.)

All of that seems to me correct and important. None of it, however, can do the work required unless it is argued that prediction and manipulation are the only things basic to human life in this sense. It seems, to say the least, highly likely that a defence of that claim will run into difficulties. We need not, however, pursue that since even if that *was* argued we would still be faced with the question: how does it follow from this that predictive and manipulative prowess are the ultimate test of ontology? The grounds for saying that we should reduce our ontology to that required for a 'minimal' life seem to be no better than those for saying that we should strive to reduce our life to this form.

Further fuel for the picture articulated by Churchland and implicitly endorsed by many others comes from a rather different understanding of the idea that one must reduce one's ontology to a minimum. It might be thought that if it is possible to explain how things of a certain kind (phlogiston, witches, beliefs) come to feature in our thought about the world without committing oneself to the existence of things of that kind then the entities in question have no legitimate place in our thought. It is, that is, demanded that we view our own thought about the world as a feature of that world about which we must ask: what needs to be postulated in order to predict and manipulate *this*.[27] In the suggestion that this is the decisive question the scientific paradigm is combined with a philosophical demand for 'grounding' in a way which is extraordinarily hard to resist. I do not for a second suppose that my limited and separate attacks on each of these ideas will appear very persuasive to many of those who find this suggestion transparently correct. I have, however, done as much as I can now see how to.

(v) I want, finally, to highlight an aspect of all of this which has important links with a recurring theme in this book. We can ask: how does the notion of a person, of a human being, fare in the light of Churchland's test for an acceptable ontology? Is the predictive and manipulative prowess of this notion sufficient to make the role which it plays in our thought a significant one? Well, at the moment the answer to that question might seem to be 'Yes'. As things are now, one who is concerned to predict and manipulate the course of events would be well advised to treat the *human being* as a significant unit. Thus, if I want to predict where this car will be in an hour's time it would, as Dennett often reminds us, generally be a serious mistake to conduct my thinking exclusively in terms of the smaller units which feature in the phsysicist's or neurophysiologist's ontology. I will, rather, listen to what people say, observe their facial expression, observe what they are doing, and so on. A statement of the grounds for my prediction will speak, not of the movements of neurons, or even hands, but of the behaviour of *human beings*. Similarly with manipulation. It may be true that if I want his lower leg to jerk in a funny way I should focus my attention on a point just below his knee; but in most cases, judging purely in terms of effectiveness of control, I will do best to treat the human being as the significant unit.

As things are now one who adopts the normal approach will

generally beat the physicist or neurophysiologist hands down. In so far as our interest is exclusively in prediction and manipulation, however, the significance which the human being has for us may appear to be simply a function of our ignorance. At any rate we will have to agree that we have no reason whatsoever for thinking that the human being will ultimately emerge as a unit of ontological significance. The most effective means of prediction and manipulation may dispense entirely with that notion. The fact that the brain, or central nervous system, rather than the human being is regarded as *the* significant unit in much recent philosophy of mind is, I take it, one indication of the power of this line of thought. Though there is, I suppose, no reason to think that this process of decomposition will stop there; no reason to think that in the end even this shadow of our idea of the individual person will appear in a purified ontology.

In Chapter 6 I followed Wittgenstein in suggesting that our ascriptions of beliefs, desires, emotions, sensations, and so on are very closely tied up with the fact that the beings to whom we ascribe these states have something resembling the human form. To the extent that that is so the disappearance of the human being from our ontology would take with it beliefs, desires, emotions, sensations, and so on. In so far as my argument in Chapter 6 had any force, however, its force was dependent on the particular ways in which ascriptions of belief, desire, emotion, and so on are linked with certain responses to the other: the responses only being possible in relation to a being having something resembling the human form. To the extent, then, that one does not regard such responses as being of deep significance in our relations with each other one will not think of the 'conceptual connections' stressed by Wittgenstein as running very deep. Thus, if what was of most significance about beliefs, emotions, sensations, and so on was the role they may play in enabling us to predict and manipulate the course of events – and, with that, the role they may play in 'causal' explanation – the suggested difficulty in ascribing such states to beings (such as human brains) which totally lack the human form would not be a significant one. The approach which looks to basic science for an understanding in this area converges dramatically at this point with that which looks to the first-person point of view.

While I assume that this convergence is noteworthy I am not completely certain what we should make of it. A consideration which should, perhaps, prevent us from making too much of it too quickly is this. As I suggested, to the extent that one's interest in others is exclusively an interest in prediction and control there is no reason to suppose that *any* notion corresponding to that of the individual person will be left in a finally purified ontology. By contrast an emphasis on the first-person point of view might seem to leave us with a clear notion of 'the self' whose states and activities these are. It might, however, be that this apparent contrast between the approaches will tend to disappear if matters are pressed further. I will, in Chapter 12, consider one way in which this might happen: one way in which an emphasis on the first-person point of view can lead to the disappearance of the individual from the picture.

In the introduction to this chapter I noted that the approach I have followed shares with currently popular ways of thinking in the philosophy of mind an emphasis on the third-person point of view. With this, there is a common emphasis on the spatial and tangible. In the one case, however, that takes the form of an emphasis on physiology while in the other on the human being. While that difference is in part simply a reflection of a difference in interest it is, I have suggested, not only that. For it is a reflection also of different models of what is central in relationships between human beings. Thus, viewed in the light of the approach followed by Churchland, Dennett and others, what is to me most striking in our relationships with other people is the *limits* that we acknowledge in our treatment of them. To recognise this as a person is to acknowledge that this is *not* just something to be used in our attempts to predict and control what happens in the world. This was my central point in Chapter 1. Another person is not simply something to be used to attain my ends: her pain, for example, makes a demand on me which is quite independent of what my ends happen to be. In my next chapter I will discuss limits of a different kind on how another is to be treated: limits which are not subservient to *anyone's* ends. There are, in addition to this, fundamental aspects of our thought about each other which may not be helpfully spoken of in terms of the idea of a 'limit' but which are, equally, not subservient to an interest in prediction and manipulation. The daughter who learns that her father has cut her out of his will because he violently disapproves of her life style is, no doubt, on the basis of that, able to make certain predictions about her future and to see how she might improve it. Unless, however, her relationship with her father had already totally broken down the significance of what she has learned will not be fully captured in any such terms as these. My primary aim in this chapter has been to suggest that facts of this kind, given the weight that they ought to be given, reveal a crucial confusion which lies near the centre of much recent philosophy of mind. (Is that a philosophical 'ought' or is it a moral one? To what extent are the differences between philosophers here differences in understanding of what actually goes on and to what extent differences in 'ethical' outlook? I don't know; but I suspect that it would not be easy to make any very sharp distinctions here.)

8

Human Beings and Homo Sapiens

(i) I opened this book with the question: what is it to recognise the reality of another human being – to recognise them *as* a human being? In having this question at its centre my approach contrasts sharply, in at least two ways, with philosophical discussions which take as their fundamental question 'What is a person?' First, my choice of the term 'human being' is, of course, closely tied up with the central importance which my discussion gives to the human bodily form. While that point will play an important part in this chapter I want, for the moment, to highlight the other obvious contrast: that between the *form* of the two questions. (It will make my discussion of *this* point easier if, for the moment, I use the terms 'person' and 'human being' fairly interchangeably: that is to say, roughly as we normally use them.)

Many, I think, would regard with suspicion the suggestion that we should formulate our central question here in the terms that I have. Thus, it might be felt – as it has been felt about Wittgenstein's discussion of such issues – that in focusing attention on my responses to the other, rather than directly on the character of the other, this approach betrays a leaning towards idealism. In particular, it might be thought that this approach reflects the idea that what features something (say, a person) has is not independent of how we think of it.

The worry about 'idealism' is one which I touched on in Chapter 5 and to which I will return in the postscript. Here I will simply note a contrast between the path which I am following and one which has had some prominence in recent discussions of the notion of a person. Daniel Dennett and Kathleen Wilkes, among others, have, as I have, given a central place in their account of our thought about each other to the fact that we characteristically have a certain attitude towards others.[1] They have, however, done so without abandoning the basic framework provided by the question 'What is a person?' Thus, that others have a certain attitude towards this individual is represented as a condition of his *being* a person. Now I

107

would not suggest that this is as absurd as would be an analogous remark about, say, trees: there may well be truth of some kind in it. Nevertheless, a consideration of this position should encourage those who see a latent idealism in Wittgenstein's approach to think again. For there is, as I have stressed, nothing in that approach which implies that whether or not this is a person is in any way dependent on my attitude towards him. It is giving the central place to the question 'What is a person?', not to the question 'What is it to think of another as a person?', which leads to that conclusion. (Ironically, Dennett's search for 'conditions of personhood', for necessary and sufficient conditions of being a person, appears to flow from a worry about a form of idealism: a worry that it might turn out that 'the concept of a person is only a free-floating honorific that we are all happy to apply to ourselves, and to others as the spirit moves us, guided by our emotions, aesthetic sensibilities, considerations of policy, and the like' (Dennett, 1978, p. 268). In fact, this conclusion would no more follow from the fact that there is no such thing as a set of necessary and sufficient conditions for being a person than does the analogous conclusion follow from the fact that we cannot state necessary and sufficient conditions for being red.)

My choice of question does not, then, rest on the assumption that whether or not something is a person is dependent in some way on how we think of it. My reason for placing at the centre the question I have is that I do not believe that there is much of philosophical interest to be said in answer to the question 'What is a person?' – in so far, that is, as this question is to be contrasted with the question 'What attitude towards persons is appropriate?' Indeed, the view that there *is* often rests, I suspect, on philosophical confusion and issues in moral confusion. The philosophical confusion lies in what I have argued is a misguided picture of the 'grounding' of our thought; the moral confusion in attempts to say *what* it is about human beings which gives them the kind of importance which we ascribe to them. I want now to develop these points, focusing on what I take to be a serious gap in the main discussion of Part I.

There is, I suppose, no single form of interest which counts as a philosophical' interest in the question 'What is a person?' One central form of philosophical interest, however, involves an exploration of those features of human beings which play a crucial role in the distinctive kind of relations which we have with each other: which mark our relations with another human being off from, for example, our relations with a stone. Now those features of human beings which were central to the discussion of Part I – the fact that they think, act, see, get depressed and angry, feel pain, and so on – are features of that kind and so can form part of an answer to the question 'What is a person?' If we wish to say what marks our thought about other human beings off from our thought about the higher animals we will clearly have to add to this list: noting, perhaps, that human beings are characteristically rational beings, are capable of verbal communication or have a certain form of self-consciousness, to mention three of Dennett's conditions. To suppose, however, that even with these additions any answer of this form can take us very far is to suppose that my thought about another can be said to be the product of my acknowledgement that he has each of these features. Now I suspect that it would be closer to the truth to say that my recognition of the other as a person is a *condition* of my seeing him as a being that acts, sees, and so on.[2] My main point, which can stand independently of that suggestion, is, however, this. There is no reason to suppose that any answer along these lines – any answer in terms of conditions which are necessary for being a person – could be complete. To suppose that it could be is to suppose that the term 'person' or 'human being' can, without loss, be eliminated from our language in favour of a terminology which does not presuppose those categories; and there is no reason to accept that that is possible. In so far as such elimination is the aim of 'conceptual analysis' the idea that the main task of philosophy is conceptual analysis is seriously confused. For there is no reason to suppose that I can say why this, with which I am confronted, is to be treated in certain ways without employing the notion of a 'person' or a 'human being'. (The idea that the notion of a 'person' or 'human being' can be 'analysed' in terms of the notions of 'mind' and 'body' – the idea that *the* morally significant feature of human beings is the fact that they 'have minds' – is a particularly pernicious version of this confusion. I will come to that in the final section of this chapter.)

I have already touched on certain features of our thought about each other which could be used as illustrations of this point. In Chapter 1 I quoted Simone Weil's observation that 'A person who crosses our path does not turn aside our steps in the same manner as a street sign.' In Chapter 6 I spoke of the kind of importance which the presence of another, and contact with another, can have for us. In this chapter, however, I will place at the centre of the discussion two other pretty fundamental features of our thought about others: another person is not to be killed, nor eaten once dead. What I believe all of these examples share is the way in which an aspect of our thought about others need not be linked with a particular feature shared by all, or most, human beings – apart from the fact that they *are* 'human beings'. Simone Weil expresses what is, perhaps, in part the same point in this way: 'There is something sacred in every man, but it is not his person. Nor yet is it the human personality. It is this man; no more and no less.'[3] 'It is a human being' may be the most direct statement possible of my reasons for treating this, with which I am confronted, in certain ways.

I focus on the examples of killing and eating primarily because there is a considerable literature on these topics in which that claim is vigorously resisted. It is argued that if our attitudes in this area are not hopelessly misplaced it *must* be possible to say what it is about human beings that makes it inappropriate that they be killed or eaten. This is to insist that the question 'What is a person?' must have an answer of the kind I am rejecting: one which brings out all that is significant in our thought about people yet makes no reference to the attitudes we take to be in place towards them.

(ii) I said that another person is not to be killed, nor eaten once dead. My point was in part that these features of our thought about others are of such central importance that we might say that thinking of another in this way is part of what it is to recognise them as a person. Such a suggestion does, however, need to be treated with care. Thus, most, or at least many, will suggest that there are extreme circumstances in which another can be killed or eaten. Some hold that there are circumstances in which another *must* be killed; and not simply in the sense that the reasons that there are for killing him clearly outweigh the fact that this is a human being and human beings are not to be killed. Rather, this human being, on account of what he has done or because he is one of the enemy, *is* to be killed. Similarly, some cultures have had a place for the thought that certain human beings *are* to be eaten. Such differences between individuals or cultures are pretty radical. Suppose, however, that we try to imagine an individual or a culture for which the killing or eating of another human being is, in itself, always a matter of complete indifference. Imagine, for example, an individual who spoke of his dead 'loved ones' in this way: 'There is very good reason why we should ... eat such of them as we like to eat: we are the better for it, and they are never the worse.'[4] There is a *radical* contrast between this case and that of, for example, a group whose insistence that outsiders *are* to be eaten rests on their acceptance that to act in this way is to violate a norm in our relations with others. Similarly, someone who thought the killing of another would be fully justified if we could truly say of them 'We should be the worse for their living, and they are never the worse for being dead' – someone who thought that with these words the moral issues were exhausted – would be a *long* way from those defenders of capital punishment who hold that certain people are to be killed on account of the enormity of what they have done. Such a defence of capital punishment, in sharp contrast with any purely utilitarian approach, rests on an acceptance that to kill another is a terrible thing.

The thought that another person is not to be killed, nor eaten once dead, is, I take it, reflected in some, however restricted, way in the lives of virtually all of us. I am not, however, insisting that there *could not* be a recognisably human culture in which it was, in certain ways, not like that. Perhaps we can imagine a society in which the eating of the dead is an expression of one's respect for them. Such a society would still be recognisably human: what they shared with us would be *much* more important than what they shared with a group of people who simply found human flesh rather tasty. Still, we are not such a society, and it is the prevalent attitudes in our society which will be my primary concern in this discussion.

It will, perhaps, be readily agreed that an individual for whom the killing or eating of human beings was never a matter of significance would be, perhaps, as alien as one who was invariably completely untouched by the pains of others. Even if this is agreed, however, it will be said that such 'attitudes' towards others are quite distinct from our understanding of what it is we are confronted with; and so that it is quite misleading to say, as I did, that thinking of another in this way is part of what it is to recognise them as a person. 'To deny this,' it will be argued, 'is to allow ethics to infiltrate the philosophy of mind in a way which is bound to cause trouble. The philosophical question "What is a person?" is certainly connected with the question "How is it appropriate to treat people?'' There must, however, be room for *some* distinction here. That a person is, for example, a being of a kind that feels pain is a point about what a person *is* in a sense in which the fact that a person is not to be eaten is not. How exactly the line between these two different kinds of claim about people is to be drawn may be unclear. However, that there is *some* kind of line to be drawn here is undeniable. It is also important in that to deny this is to leave no place for the question "What is it about people that makes it appropriate that they be treated in these ways?" '

The point is worth developing a bit further. In practice, when I recognise that it is a human being that is being spoken of I do not ask why he is not to be killed or eaten; and if I did not realise that it was human flesh on the table I would accept the information that that is what it was as giving a reason for the horror that others displayed. It is insisted, however, that we must raise the question: *which* of the features which human beings, or at least most of them, possess are we taking to be morally significant? 'For', it will be argued, 'if these ways of thinking about others are not simply misplaced – or, more positively, if we are to regard them as *in place* – there must be something about people, a feature which they possess, in virtue of which this is so. Just as it is in virtue of the fact that people feel pain that we are not to strike them and that they are sometimes to be pitied, in virtue of the fact that they act that responses of resentment and gratitude towards them are sometimes appropriate, and so on. Thus, rather than being a direct expression of our recognition of another's reality these ways of thinking must be *grounded in* our recognition of some feature of the other; and so we are faced with the question: *what* is it about people that grounds these ways of thinking?'

When we try to answer this question, when we try to say what it is about human beings that makes them beings of a kind which are not to be killed or eaten, the answers that we come up with seem to many to be quite unsatisfactory. When a particular feature, such as our rationality, is picked out as being the thing that is really doing the justifying work here we feel, not simply that this does not take us behind the 'more superficial' articulations of reasons with which we normally operate, but, worse, that it is a step in quite the wrong direction. The most obvious expression of this is the fact that any such suggestion will imply that the morally significant boundaries between beings lie at rather different points from those which we normally accept: for example, not all human beings will emerge as beings who are not to be killed or eaten. No less important, how-ever, is our sense of the ludicrousness of the proposed justifica-tion.

The situation is a familiar one within philosophy. While in one sense it is recognised that chains of reasons must come to an end somewhere it is felt that the point at which we allow them to come to an end in daily life cannot really be a satisfactory stopping place.[5] The moral defective who insists that we must be able to give him some *reason* for thinking that it is really not on to eat, say, the victims of road accidents is transformed into a philosophical hero. Now this move may, in some cases, be motivated by a sense that there is something *morally* unacceptable in our normal patterns of justification. In other cases, however, a central role is played by a philosophical picture which dictates that, quite independently of any moral considerations, the process of giving reasons *could* not stop at the points at which it might appear to in practice. (I take it that in many, perhaps most, cases the 'moral' and the 'philo-sophical' are tightly intertwined here. Further, while at the begin-ning it will be useful to try to prise them apart I suspect that after a certain point it will prove impossible to draw any useful distinction between these.)

In practice, the words 'It is a human being', or 'It is a person' – or, perhaps more naturally, 'It is a woman', 'It is a man' – put an end to 'Why?' questions of a certain form. As I said, however, certain philosophers see a danger here. Thus, Tooley suggests that it is a 'philosophically dangerous' feature of our normal use of the term 'human being' that little room is left for questions that must be asked.[6] We might express the point by saying that the term has two faces. On the one hand, it is correctly used of, and only of, all members of the biological species homo sapiens; on the other, it carries the implication that a being so identified is to be treated in certain ways. Thus, the term stands in the way of our asking why all members of that biological species are to be treated in these ways. Tooley argues that we can leave a place for this question if we treat 'person' as a 'purely moral' concept and replace the term 'human being' by 'some expression that is more naturally inter-preted as referring to a certain type of biological organism charac-terized in physiological terms, such as "member of the species *Homo sapiens*".' Thus, in describing a being as a 'person' I am claiming that it ought to be treated in a certain way and am saying nothing about what 'properties of a purely descriptive sort' it has.

That then leaves a clear space for the question: what 'purely descriptive' properties ground that moral claim?

The danger Tooley sees here is not of a purely abstract kind: it is closely bound up, he suggests, with serious moral confusion. The confusion is seen in, for example, the way in which Judith Jarvis Thomson appeals in her discussion of abortion to the fact that by the tenth week the foetus has a face, arms and legs, fingers and toes. Tooley insists that we need to ask: 'But what do such physiological characteristics have to do with the question of whether the organism is a person?' He adds 'Thomson, partly, I think, because of the unfortunate use of terminology, does not even raise this question. As a result she virtually takes it for granted that there are some cases in which abortion is "positively indecent"' (Singer, 1986, pp. 61–2). Now I am not sure that I would even try to discuss abortion with somebody who did not take *that* for granted. So I find nothing unfortunate in a terminology which leaves little room for that question. Tooley's moral outlook is obviously very different. What concerns me, however, is what he has in mind when he speaks of Thomson's terminology as *'philosophically* dangerous'.

Consider a case which might appear to provide an analogy. The term 'susceptible to pain', we might say, has two faces. On the one hand it is used to ascribe a property of a purely descriptive sort, namely 'susceptibility to pain'. On the other hand, it carries the implication that a being that has that property is to be treated in certain ways: once I recognise that this is a being of that sort I accept, without further 'Why?' questions, that there is reason not to do certain things to it. (At any rate, some use the term in this way, and that is all I need for my point.) Would Tooley insist that we must ask the question: what does the fact that a being is susceptible to pain have to do with the question of whether it is all right to cut it open without anaesthetic? Would he insist that a terminology which stands in the way of our asking this question is 'philosophically dangerous'?

Well, I suppose he might. If he does, however, he will, I take it, be asking this question confident that it can be answered; but what answer could be given? It might be thought that, while there is nothing which we can *say* in answer to this question, there is an answer which I can, in some sense, give to myself: I *recognise* why the fact that a being is susceptible to pain can be a reason for giving him an anaesthetic in my experience of my own pain. We might, perhaps, articulate this idea in this way: 'What it is about pain that makes it something to be thought of in this way is what it feels like.' I argued, in Chapter 4, however, that all of this is simply an illusion. There is no such thing as seeing *why* another's pain constitutes a reason for feeling and doing certain things; and with that the idea that it is something 'about' pain, namely, 'what it feels like', which makes it such a reason must be rejected.

Some feel that there *must* be room for the question 'What does the fact that a creature (say the foetus of ten weeks) has a face, arms, legs, fingers and toes have to do with the question of how we should treat it?': that if we cannot answer that question the significance we attach to facts of this kind is misplaced. I am suggesting that this idea may be dependent on the way in which we are inclined to set up a certain kind of case – in particular, the case in which I am concerned about another's physical pain – as a paradigm of grounded concern for another. For it is these cases which provide us with our model of what would constitute an answer to that question. I have argued, however, that the model is a philosophical illusion. Our acceptance that another's pain is a reason for feeling and acting in certain ways is not grounded in a way which is different in *kind* from that in which our response to the physical form of the foetus at a certain stage of development is grounded.

I suggested in section (i) of this chapter that there is little of philosophical interest to be said in answer to the question 'What is a person?' in so far as that question is contrasted with the question 'What attitude towards persons is appropriate?' My point there could be expressed in this way: any answer to the question 'What is a person?' will, in so far as it is potentially of significance in our relations with others, already reflect a particular attitude towards others. There is, for example, no such thing as first acknowledging that a particular class of creatures feel pain and then, on the basis of that, coming to accept that certain forms of treatment of them are appropriate.[7] Now we are inclined to resist this. Thus, we have a picture of a 'recognition of others as people' which *does not reflect but does call for* a certain attitude on the part of the observer. The philosophical question 'What is a person?', as it is commonly asked, is a request for an articulation of the content of this recognition; as is the question 'What is it about human beings that grounds the special ways in which we think they should be treated?' We derive the picture which is at work here from a consideration of certain states in which a form of the grounding we require seems to be provided within the first person point of view. This, however, is an illusion: in all cases, a recognition that a particular attitude is called for is dependent on existing shared reactions at some level. When we appreciate this we should be free to accept at face value justifications which come to a halt with the words 'It is a human being'; dependent though these are on reactions for which we have no justification. To accept *that* is to accept that there need be no philosophically significant answer to the question 'What is a person?' or 'What is a human being?'

(iii) But this may not get us to the bottom of the matter. For it might be argued that it is quite clear that the insistence that there *must* be room for Tooley's question does not spring from this philosophical confusion. What makes that clear is this. It is not simply that we do not know how to show that membership of a particular biological species, or having certain physiological characteristics, is morally significant; as we do not know how to show that pain is of moral significance. Rather, as soon as the thought is explicitly articulated – as soon as Tooley raises the question 'What do physiological characteristics, or being a member of a particular biological species, have to do with the question of whether the organism is a person?' – we find that we are *not* ready to endorse the suggestion that these features are morally significant. By contrast we have no hesitation in endorsing the suggestion that pain is of moral significance.

This argument appeals to a contrast between 'being a member of a particular biological species', or 'having certain physiological characteristics', on the one hand and 'being susceptible to pain' on the other. To describe our normal thought in terms of that contrast is, however, to seriously *mis*describe it; or, at any rate, to present it in a seriously misleading light. The light in question is, I think, that of the philosophical mind/body contrast. We are being asked to view our thought about each other in terms of a division of a form which drains the observable and tangible of all moral significance. In opposition to this I will argue, first, that there is no reason to suppose that the characterisations 'member of this biological species', or 'having these physiological characteristics', are the ones which are operative in our thought; to insist that it must be these characterisations which are at work is to refuse to acknowledge the irreducible place occupied in our thought here by the notion of a 'human being'. The other side of this is that the contrast fails to highlight the role played by 'the physical' in *both* cases: the significance we attach to the fact that another is in pain is grounded in a response to the 'physical' at least as directly as is the significance we attach to the fact that another is a human being. I want now to develop these points, beginning with some brief remarks about the second.

The human form is clearly of great significance in our relations with others in a wide variety of ways. We ascribe sensations, thoughts, emotions, intellectual abilities, and so on to others on the basis of their behaviour and expression. What they *say* also, of course, plays a crucial role here; but our confidence that we understand the other's words is closely tied up with the connections that we see between their words and their behaviour. Now some hold that none of this suggests that there is any difficulty in the idea that a being with nothing resembling the human form should undergo these states or have these abilities. In Chapter 6 I linked that suggestion with the suggestion that there is no difficulty in the idea that we could have with beings whose form in no way resembled the human form relations which, *in all important respects,* exactly resemble those which we can have with other human beings; and I tried to bring out some difficulties with that suggestion.

If the general direction of those remarks is accepted then it cannot be right to suggest that the human bodily form could not possibly be of any moral significance (if we are going to use the word 'moral' here). Still, it might be argued that considerations of that kind do not touch directly on the issue with which we are concerned. The point there was that certain forms of concern for another are dependent on the other possessing a particular bodily form: nothing could be just *that* form of concern in the absence of an object with a bodily form of this general kind. 'What we are now concerned with', it might be said, 'is, however, quite different. For, first, there is no difficulty in the idea that I should view the killing or eating of something, say a cabbage, whose form in no way resembles the human with just the horror that I view the killing or eating of a human being. And, second, even if there were that would not touch the question: *why* should moral significance be attached to something purely physical, such as the possession of a certain bodily form or membership of a certain species?'

The first of these suggestions is highly dubious. Does the difficulty that most would find in eating another human being have nothing to do with thoughts about which part of the person this, and this, is? Suppose that particular parts, the eyes for example, were clearly recognisable. Think also of the kind of difficulty which, for most of us, would be involved in, say, stabbing or strangling another: I mean, those dimensions of the difficulty which are tied up with the 'purely physical' character of the act. Now is it *obvious* that this kind of thing should be spoken of as 'just squeamishness and so not of moral significance'? I suspect, though perhaps not with adequate grounds, that only those guilty of the kind of philosophical confusion with which I am concerned in this section will be inclined to find that obvious. I will not, however, pursue that since it is the second point – the suggestion that nothing 'purely physical' could possibly be accepted as being of moral significance – which really concerns me now.

When terms such as 'member of the species homo sapiens' and 'physiological characteristics' are used the idea that the 'purely physical' could not possibly have the kind of moral significance we are concerned with here sounds very plausible; but have we been given good reason to think that these *are* the characterisations which are relevant here? Can we not insist that this terminology simply distorts our normal practice? Can we not argue that the characterisations which are of significance to us are ones in terms of the notions of 'human being', 'person', 'man', 'woman', and so on; and that this terminology cannot be eliminated without leaving out the very thing which is significant to us?

Well, if the 'cash value', the 'descriptive content', of the term 'human being' is not 'member of the species homo sapiens' what *is* it?

Those born of human parents have a recognisable human form and generally live a recognisable human life. What I mean by this last phrase covers an enormous range of features. A recognisably human life is a life in which there are recognisable sensations, emotions and interests, in which there are manifestations of intelligence of the distinctively human forms, a life in community of various forms with other human beings, a life which goes through recognisable stages of physical development, which is physically vulnerable and which ends in death, and so on. There are tight connections between all the features in this list, and between these features and others, such as the use of language, which I have not explicitly mentioned. There are, further, tight connections between all of these features of a human life and the possession of a human bodily form; and also between many of them and being born of human parents. What primarily concerns me here, however, is that even where it does make some sense to isolate one feature from others there are no grounds for thinking that one, or even a limited group, of these features is what is *really* doing the moral work. There is, for example, no reason to think that our horror at the thought of eating another human being is to be fully understood independently of a reference to this complete background.

Having said that it must also be said that the human form has a powerful impact on almost all of us even in cases in which most of the rest of this background is clearly absent. We might try to articulate this point by saying that the live human form, in itself, has an impact on us.[8] Now care is needed here. For the fact that the human form *generally* has the connections I have spoken of is not irrelevant to the character of its impact in particular cases. Further, later developments in particular cases could have a decisive effect on that impact. Most strikingly perhaps, if the facial features contort into utterly unexpected forms the character of the impact may be transformed. Still, there is point in saying that the live human form, in itself, has an impact on us. What this way of speaking brings out is, for example, the way in which few are completely unmoved by pictures of a foetus with face, arms and legs, fingers and toes. While, as I have stressed, it is not incidental to this that foetuses generally develop into adult human beings, the impact remains even when, in a particular case, we know that that will not happen. Further, and perhaps even more important, speaking in this way serves to highlight the extent to which our recognising 'psychological' features in another – say intelligence or a sense of humour – is *dependent upon* the bodily form that he has; as opposed to the significance of the human form being, as is often suggested, entirely dependent on the connection which it standardly has with 'psychological' features.

But now, in acknowledging that the live human form, in itself, has an impact on us are we not acknowledging that the other's 'physiological characteristics' have an impact on us; and so are not Tooley's suspicions concerning what is at work here confirmed?

What is true is this. On the basis of watching an individual for a moment I will be prepared to say, without hesitation, 'That's a human being', 'That's a person' or whatever ('It's a woman', 'It's a boy'.) In a few cases – perhaps with the foetus at a certain stage of development – there may be some hesitation even after I have observed the individual closely for several minutes. These cases are, however, the exception. Suppose now it is asked: in virtue of what features do you identify this as a human being? I can answer that question in the sense that I can say that it is on the basis of what it looks like and how it behaves that I judge it to be a human being; just as I can say that it is on the basis of what it looks like that I say that the car is green. If, however, the question is a request for a statement, in some quite distinct terminology, of necessary and sufficient conditions for something to count as a human being there is no reason to suppose that that can be given. For one thing, as I have already noted, there may *be* no sufficient conditions in that however careful my observation of the other there would always be room for a further development which would throw me into chaos. More important, however, is the fact that there may be no other 'more basic' terminology on which I can fall back. Thus, if in a particular case – say that of a foetus at a certain stage of development – I and another differ over whether we are yet dealing with a 'human being' ('person') there may be no other level of description to which we can move in the hope of resolving our difference. Of course, I can point to 'the face', 'the hands', and so on; we might speak of this as 'another level of description' and I might be able to move him in this way; but I might not: where I see 'eyes' he sees only 'things that will develop into eyes'. If there is a form of description in whose terms we can reach agreement (geometrical descriptions of arrangements of flesh perhaps) I might be quite incapable of relating a description in those terms to my original characterisation of this as a 'face', or the whole as a 'human being'.

   While I am not entirely clear what the force of the term 'purely descriptive' is supposed to be in these contexts I take it that none of what I have said so far casts any doubt on the claim that the term 'human being' is a 'purely descriptive' one. The claim that it is not certainly does not follow from the fact that there could be disagreements about its application in particular cases which cannot be resolved by appeal to some 'more basic' level. At least it had better not. For *that* much is true of *any* term.[9] So on the basis of what has been said so far there is no reason to say that we ought to be able to spell out the 'cash value', the 'descriptive content', of the term 'human being' in some other terminology; and so no reason to say that we had better replace the term 'human being' by 'member of the species homo sapiens' if we want to avoid philosophical and moral trouble.

With my unhesitating insistence that this is a human being goes the fact that I would not, except perhaps in the most extreme circumstances, dream of killing or eating this being. Further, the words 'It is a human being' do, on the lips of many, function as a pointing to a serious moral obstacle to such actions. We might, then, say that we learn what a human being is, in part, through coming to accept such obstacles to our actions.[10] Now it is at this point that the objection will arise. 'For to say this', it will be said, 'is to acknowledge that the term "human being" is not morally neutral. That is why it is so important for philosophical and moral clarity to distil off a "purely descriptive" component, as, for example, Tooley does.'

It is, however, very difficult now to see what the objection can possibly amount to. The difficulty emerges in the fact that it seems that we can meet it by a simple shuffle in our terminology. We can say that the term 'human being' is 'morally neutral': in describing an individual as a 'human being' or 'person' we are not, as such, making any judgement about how that individual is to be treated. These are 'purely factual' judgements. They do, however, function for most of us as a *basis* for certain moral judgements; that it is a 'human being' is a reason for not killing or eating him. If it is asked just what the 'purely factual' content of the judgement that another is a human being *is* we will, as before, have to reply that there is no reason to suppose that that can be given in any other terminology.

I am not suggesting that this is the way the matter ought to be put; for I do not find the terms 'purely descriptive', 'morally neutral' and so on, as they commonly arise in discussions of these issues, at all perspicuous. My point was simply that if we *are* going to speak in these terms there is nothing in our normal use of the words 'human being' or 'person' which forces us to choose between saying that they are 'purely descriptive' or 'morally loaded'; and so, even within the terms set by philosophers such as Tooley, there is nothing here which forces us to search for some 'purely descriptive' terminology which plays a more fundamental role in picking out the group of beings with which we are concerned. Thus, the fact that we are inclined to agree that, for example, membership of a particular biological species, or possession of a particular physiological structure, could not, in itself, possibly be of moral significance is quite irrelevant to our normal practice. For it is not in so far as an individual can be characterised in *these* terms that we judge that he is to be treated in certain ways.

These remarks will certainly be regarded with suspicion by

philosophers of a certain kind. For they, of course, are well aware that we do not, in practice, express our reasons in biological or physiological terms: they are well aware that we might, for example, express our horror at one group's treatment of another in the words 'These are human beings!' What concerns philosophers such as Tooley and Singer is the fact that the term 'human being', as it is used here, is itself the expression of a certain attitude which most of us have towards members of a particular group. The whole point of their procedure, as they see it, is to take us behind this attitude and to make room for the question 'What is there in what we see which justifies the attitude?'

A central theme of Part I of this book, a theme which has re-emerged in this section, is that the idea that we must, for philosophical reasons, attempt to 'go behind the attitude' is a confusion. I have found the example of our response to another's pain particularly helpful here. I will close this section with one more attempt to bring out its bearing on the issues central to this chapter.

'My attitude towards him is an attitude towards a soul.' The sight of a human foetus at a certain stage of development has an impact on us: we could not for the life of us think of it as just a fleshy growth inside the woman's body. Compare this now with the way in which the sight of another human being obviously in acute pain has an impact on us. We might say that it is on account of what he is feeling, not on account of how he is behaving, that he is to be pitied. For all that, if someone, confronted with such behaviour, seriously, and in the absence of any special background, asks 'What bearing does this have on what I should do and how I should feel?' there is nothing further to be said. There is no such thing as 'Giving him reasons for thinking that one who behaves like this is in pain and so to be helped and pitied.' I presented a certain way of thinking within the philosophy of mind – that which sees a place for the argument from analogy and which leaves room for philosophical scepticism – as a futile attempt to resist this conclusion.[11]

If we say that the term 'human being' is 'morally loaded', and so has two faces, then we must say the same of the term 'pain'. For the use of both terms is, in our society, closely tied up with certain ways of thinking and acting which, most of the time, go completely unquestioned. Further, our finding it transparently clear that one who is in pain is to be helped and pitied is as much a reflection of the way in which we respond spontaneously, without reason, to what we observe in another as is our finding it transparently clear that a human being is not to be killed or eaten.

As I said, however, I do not find the 'purely descriptive'/'morally loaded' terminology helpful here and I suspect that the position is better expressed in terms that cut across this distinction. Thus, while it is true that in describing an individual as a 'human being' I am committing myself to certain claims about how he is to be treated, the kind of commitments with which we are concerned – the kind of presuppositions which the use of the term has – are too basic to be spoken off as 'moral': the difference between most of us and someone who spoke of the eating of people as Bentham speaks of the eating of animals, arguing that 'we are the better for it, and they are never the worse', is below the level at which we can speak of 'moral disagreement'. The same point fairly clearly applies to the term 'pain'. If, then, there is an oddity in the suggestion that our use of the term 'human being' or 'pain' expresses a particular moral outlook – as there undoubtedly is – this is a reflection of the extent to which these ways of responding to others are a feature of the lives of any with whom moral dialogue could even begin.

(iv) I opened this chapter with the observation that there are two ways in which my discussion is marked off from many contemporary treatments of issues in this area. The first lay in the way in which my central question gives a primacy to our 'attitude' towards each other; the second, in the position that I give to the notion of a 'human being'. I must now say a little more about this latter point as many will feel that the most serious difficulties that arise here have, by no means, been adequately dealt with. In particular, it will be pointed out that the term 'human being', as used by most of us, is *coextensive* with the term 'live member of the species homo sapiens'. (Though a slight qualification may arise in connection with the very earliest stages of the development of the individual.) So even if it is said that the latter characterisation is not the one which is, for us, morally significant, our moral discriminations do in fact coincide with the border between our own species and others. This, it will be felt, is highly suspicious.

Dennett opens his paper 'Conditions of Personhood' with one formulation of this worry:

> I am a person, and so you are. That much is beyond doubt. I am a human being, and *probably* you are too. If you take offense at

the 'probably' you stand accused of a sort of racism, for what is important about us is not that we are of the same biological species, but that we are both persons, and I have not cast doubt on that. One's dignity does not depend on one's parentage even to the extent of having been born of woman or born at all. We normally ignore this and treat humanity as the deciding mark of personhood, no doubt because the terms are locally coextensive or almost coextensive. At this time and place, human beings are the only persons we recognize, and we recognize almost all human beings as persons, but on the one hand we can easily contemplate the existence of biologically very different persons – inhabiting other planets, perhaps – and on the other we recognize conditions that exempt human beings from personhood, or at least some very important elements of personhood. For instance, infant human beings, mentally defective human beings, and human beings declared insane by licensed psychiatrists are denied personhood, or at any rate crucial elements of personhood.[12]

To give the position that I have to the notion of a 'human being' is, then, to be guilty of a sort of racism. In making this charge Dennett is clearly working with a picture of 'what is important about us' which is significantly different from that which I have taken for granted. For to the extent that the argument of Chapter 6 was correct there is much of importance in our relations with other human beings which is such that it cannot be said to be merely incidental that they *are* human beings. Now nothing that I have said rules out the possibility of a different conception of what is important in our relations with each other; and, with that, nothing in what I have said rules out the possibility that there could be beings not of our species who are to be treated in all 'important' respects just as we think other members of the species homo sapiens are to be treated. My point is just that considerable care is needed here. As they stand, Dennett's remarks about the relation between the notions of 'person' and 'human being' ('locally coextensive', 'easily contemplate') appear hopelessly exposed.

The conception of 'what is important about us' with which Dennett is working is, in fact, fairly clear from the first two sentences of the passage I have quoted. In the emphasis which he gives to 'the intellect' Dennett's approach reflects one important strand of Cartesianism. I want, however, to focus on contemporary ways of thinking which pick up another central strand of Cartesian thought: the position that is given to the first-person point of view. The clearest expression of this is to be found in certain attempts to articulate what is to be objected to in our current treatment of animals.

I suggested in section (iii) that we are inclined to set up a particular kind of case – that in which I am concerned about another's physical sensations – as a paradigm of *grounded* concern for another. We are, with that, inclined to set this case up as a paradigm of *concern* for another; and so to think in terms of a *single* morally significant divide in nature. Much of the philosophical discussion of our treatment of animals is conducted in these terms. Now the point I will stress is that to think in these terms is to have a seriously impoverished view of what could be of moral importance in our relations with others. This brings me back to the idea that it is helpful to articulate what marks people, and perhaps animals, off from, for example, sticks and stones in terms of the fact that a person 'has a mind'.

The philosophical notion of 'the mind' is, in part, an expression of the idea that there is something that can be spoken of as *the fundamentally* significant feature of persons: the fact that they are 'conscious', 'have experiences', 'have a point of view' or that there is 'something that it is like' to be one. Consider in this connection Descartes' observation that 'it is more probable that worms and flies and caterpillars move mechanically than that they all have immortal souls'.[13] Whether Descartes actually maintained, as has sometimes been thought, that animals are automata – that they have no thoughts, feelings or sensations – there appear to be strong pressures within his philosophy, pressures which are clearly reflected in the above remark, to move in this direction. From the fact that a creature has the capacity for thought or feeling of any kind it does, for Descartes, follow immediately that it has an immaterial mind or soul; and from this, in turn, it follows immediately that it possesses what is for Descartes the most fundamental kind of value: immortality. Finding the conclusion that there is *no* fundamental contrast to be drawn between human beings and animals intolerable Descartes was left with no option but to place them on the other side of the great divide.

Now the idea that there is something that can be spoken of as *the* fundamentally significant feature of persons, and that this lies in the fact that they 'have experiences', 'have a point of view', and so on, is clearly reflected in many modern philosophical discussions

of our relations with animals. Thus, many quote with approval
Bentham's observation that: 'The question is not, Can they *reason*?
nor, Can they *talk*? but, Can they *suffer*?'[14] That animals are, like
us, capable of suffering is taken to be *the* fundamental truth about
them which is relevant to our treatment of them. A closely related
idea is sometimes expressed in terms of the fact that animals do,
like us, have interests. Thus, Peter Singer writes: 'Taken in itself,
say the animal liberationists, membership of the human species is
not morally relevant. Other creatures on our planet also have
interests.'[15] What concerns me here is the implication that the only
morally significant fact about a creature with which we are confronted is the fact that it 'has interests'. In a similar way Wilkes
attempts to account for the special obligations which we have
towards a human foetus or infant in terms of the fact that it will
develop into a being with the full range of normal, adult human
interests.[16] Again, Tom Regan writes: 'We are each of us the
experiencing subject of a life, a conscious creature having an
individual welfare that has importance to us whatever our usefulness to others.' Regan adds '*All* who have inherent value have it
equally, whether they be human animals or not'; and 'Inherent
value, then, belongs equally to those who are the experiencing
subjects of a life.' Finally here, I should mention the idea that it is
helpful to discuss our moral relations with other beings exclusively
in terms of their '*right*' to be treated in certain ways – an idea which
we find in, for example, Tooley's discussion of abortion and
infanticide.[17] The effect of this terminology is, again, to represent
the point of view of the other as occupying *the* fundamental place
in all of our moral relations with others.

There are important differences between these writers. Bentham,
for example, is a (consistent) utilitarian in a way in which none of
the others is. (His strongly utilitarian remarks concerning the
eating and killing of animals, which I made use of earlier in this
chapter, are, for fairly obvious reasons, quoted rather less often by
defenders of 'animal liberation' than is the remark which I quoted
in my last paragraph – even though they occur in the very same
paragraph of Bentham's work.) What they share (at any rate in
some of their remarks) is the suggestion that there is a *single*
morally significant division between beings in the world; and
perhaps more fundamentally, a certain picture of the *kind* of
division that is. Now that idea is a fundamental strand of the
Cartesian notion of 'the mind'.

In this sense Cartesianism still has a strong hold on much moral thinking. There are, however, also important contrasts with Descartes' outlook. Since few today will find it easy to deny that animals – at any rate, the higher animals – are capable of physical suffering the other side of Descartes' coin is likely to seem more attractive. In so far as we are thinking in terms of a great divide in nature we will be more inclined to place animals on the same side of that divide as ourselves. The way for this conclusion is perhaps eased by the fact that the stakes are in one sense not quite as high for most of us as they were for Descartes. As our picture of the kind of value possessed by a human being has grown thinner so it has become easier to grant value of that kind to, at any rate, the higher animals. While for Descartes the matter of an immortal soul hung on the question of physical pains and pleasures it often seems that for us little is at issue but the sensations themselves.

I should stress here that when I speak in this way I do not mean to suggest that the issue of physical pleasures and pains is a trivial one. I have no doubt, for example, that Peter Singer is correct when he suggests that there is a great deal in our current attitude towards and treatment of animals which can be condemned solely in terms of the fact that we are responsible for much suffering – both physical and mental – on their part. Indeed, while I do not accept it I do not find obviously absurd the suggestion that this fact is the overwhelmingly most significant feature of our current relations with animals. What I *do* find obviously absurd is the suggestion that everything which is important in our thought about and relations with other human beings can ultimately be understood in anything remotely resembling these terms. (The suggestion of a contrast in these two sentences may well reflect the fact that I give much less thought than I should to our relations with non-human species. Perhaps I should find the suggestion about animals obviously absurd; as I take it Cora Diamond does: see her discussion in 'Eating Meat and Eating People'. I should, however, stress that what is at issue here is *not* speciesism as Singer understands this: that is to say 'a prejudice or attitude of bias toward the interests of members of one's own species and against those of members of other species' (Peter Singer, *Animal Liberation*, p. 7.) For the distinctions I am speaking of have nothing to do with the relative importance to be attached to the 'interests' of human beings and animals.)

I have given examples of what I have in mind here at various points in this book; and will give further examples in Part III. The examples, such as that concerning the killing and eating of human beings, would, I suspect, be quite uncontroversial were it not for our tendency to seek a form of metaphysical grounding for our thought about each other in terms of an appeal to the first-person point of view; and the closely related tendency to view our relations with each other exclusively in terms of the egoism/ altruism contrast. In any case, once it is granted that we cannot understand everything which is of moral significance in our relations with others in terms of the model provided by our obligation to relieve their physical pains, there appears to be no reason to suppose that everything which is of moral importance in our relations with another is *grounded in* a single feature that they possess. That is to say, if our obligations towards another do not lie solely in ensuring that things are all right from his point of view there is no reason to suppose that all of our obligations towards another are grounded in the fact that he *has* a 'point of view'. Thus, when we abandon the unified picture of our moral relations with other human beings we can also abandon the idea that there is something that can be spoken of as *the* fundamentally significant feature of persons. We can, that is, abandon the philosophical notion of 'the mind'. To abandon that is to remove what should be acknowledged, by all but the purest of utilitarians, to be a serious obstacle to clear moral thinking. For only then is a place left for distinctions in our moral thought which few will abandon lightly. To insist that the suffering of animals is to be taken much more seriously than most of us take it – indeed, to insist that it is to be taken just as seriously as the suffering of human beings – is not to be committed to the claim that the distinction which is marked in our language by the terms 'human being' on the one hand and 'animal' on the other is not a deep one. It is not, for example, to be committed to the claim that, other things being equal, infanticide or euthanasia are to be viewed in the same light as most now view the act of 'putting an animal out of its misery'. A failure to leave a space for an acknowledgement of this seems bound to, and I believe clearly does, cause trouble.

I have, in Part II, discussed three general ways in which the notion of a human being may, in philosophical discussions, become displaced from its fundamental position in our thought. In Chapter 6 I considered the way in which the philosophical mind/body contrast involves a focusing of attention away from the importance which the extended and tangible human form has in our relations with each other. In Chapter 7 I discussed the tendency to assume that characterisations of persons in terms of the categories of 'basic science' are, in a crucial sense, more fundamental than characterisations in human terms. Finally, in Chapter 8, I have looked at the common insistence that the notion of a human being could not legitimately have a fundamental position in our ethical thought. It will not be doubted that there are strong links between the topics I have discussed in these chapters but I will close this Part of the book with a reminder that one of my central points is that these links are not of the form that one might suppose; and, indeed, not of the form that might be suggested by the order of my presentation. Thus, to express the matter very schematically, it is not that we can *first* settle the question of whether people are basically just 'physical objects' and *then*, on the basis of our conclusions there, resolve the question of whether it is all right to eat the dead. Rather, it is the fact that it is *not* all right to eat the dead – along with other facts of the same form – which reveals the confusion in philosophical talk of people as basically just physical objects. Another way to express this point is to say that the discussion of Chapter 8 has been a *direct* contribution to 'the philosophy of mind': a direct contribution to an answer to the question 'What is a person?' The idea that we can, and must, answer that question *before* moving on to the ethical issues is a serious philosophical confusion; (but see section (i) of the Postscript). Further, it is, I think, a philosophical confusion which is closely linked in one way or another with serious moral confusion. For the idea that we can get our metaphysics straight before moving on to the moral issues can only survive so long as a certain ethical outlook is so deeply engrained in our thinking about these issues as to go unnoticed. That ethical outlook is, in contemporary discussions, utilitarianism. While I have not directly argued that utilitarianism is a moral confusion I hope that I have said enough to show why I believe that it involves a dramatically restricted understanding of what matters to human beings. It is the idea that we must squeeze all value into this mould that leads to moral confusion.

Part III
Identity and Particularity

9

The Identity of Human Beings

(i) The thought that a person with whom we are confronted is a particular individual, an individual with a particular history, can be important to us in a number of different ways. I may be relieved when I recognise the man coming down the road as John, who I know has trained as a mechanic, because I badly need some help with my car. I may feel respect or contempt for another on the basis of my understanding that he is the one who did certain things in the past. I may, in the same way, think him deserving of reward or punishment, or of my gratitude. I may feel particular obligations towards someone on account of certain facts about our mutual history: he saved my life once. I may feel particular emotions in the light of my recognition of this as someone with whom I have a certain relationship: I am comforted by the presence, in the alien environment in which I find myself, of Jim, a long-standing friend; I am horrified at the suffering of Jane, my child, in a way quite different from that in which I am horrified at the suffering of others.

We might summarise this general point by saying that, in our relations with others, we do not begin from scratch on each occasion that we meet them. Our thought about and treatment of another, and our understanding of how it is appropriate for us to think of and treat another, is, at least in many cases, crucially dependent on facts about their past. Our understanding of *who* this is, in this sense, is important to us.

There are, however, distinctions to be drawn here. First, the first of the cases I mentioned is importantly different from the others. In this kind of case we might say that this fact about his past, this fact about who he is, is of no importance *in itself*; its importance lies only in what it is evidence for. That he has trained as a mechanic is important to me only because it is grounds for thinking that he *will* be able to do something. If it ceases to be grounds for thinking this, say because I realise that he is hopelessly drunk, the fact that he

133

has trained as a mechanic ceases to be of any significance for me. Similarly, my recognition of this as Jones, the man I was rude to last week, may be important to me simply in so far as it is a guide to expectations that I can reasonably have for the future: his behaviour towards me is likely to be hostile. On the other hand, that it is him may, in this case, have an importance for me which has nothing to do with expectations for the future: I feel shame in his presence and an obligation to apologise to him. That he is the one matters in itself. Of course, many cases will be mixed and it will often be difficult to know just how a case is to be described. No doubt, most apologies are both forward and backward looking. Punishment is another obvious case in which the fact that this is the one who did it can be thought to have importance both in itself – 'He deserves to be punished' – and in so far as it is a guide to the future – 'He is likely to act in that way in the future if we do not teach him a lesson.'

Another distinction within the cases I mentioned is this. In some our concern that this is, as I put it, a 'particular individual' is a concern that this is the individual who did or underwent a particular thing in the past: for example, he saved my life. In others there is no *particular* fact about the past which plays this role; this is Jim, a long-standing friend, or Jane, my child. Thus, in most cases it would be wrong, I think, to suggest that there is a particular fact about the past – the fact that he fathered this girl – which the father has in mind when he is moved by his recognition that this is Jane, his child. No doubt there are cases which are like that. A man is confronted with a twelve-year-old daughter whom he never knew existed; if it turned out that he did not father her after all he would lose all interest in her. Such a case would, however, be the exception. A father who has for twelve years taken a particular girl, Jane, to be his daughter and then discovers that he did not, in fact, father her will, presumably, be badly shaken. That supposed fact was an important component of his picture of her. He will not, however, immediately feel that his conception of who this girl is, in the sense that concerns me, has been completely undermined. He will, for example, still be horrified at her suffering in a way different from that in which he is horrified at the suffering of others.

The father is concerned in a quite special way about the well-being of his daughter; that it is her, this particular individual, who is suffering enters in a crucial way into the character of his distress about the suffering. He cares that it is *this* individual. Which individual? The most direct answer may be simply 'Jane'. Any other answer, such as 'my daughter' may be misleading in so far as it suggests that there is one particular feature of this individual's past which plays the decisive role in his conception of this girl; but there is no such feature. We cannot, then, explain what he means when he says 'It is Jane' in terms of any such single feature. To do that we will have to speak of an enormous range of features of this individual's history, some of which will be more important than others. The discovery that this individual's history lacks one of these features – she was fathered by someone else – will not by itself undermine his thought that 'It is Jane'. If, however, we imagine a case in which I come to suspect that I was misled about a great deal of what I took to be this individual's history the case may be different. Think, for example, of a pair of twins playing a cruel joke on a man who, not realising that there are two of them, takes himself to be falling in love with 'Mary'. When he discovers the deception he may no longer be able to think of either of them 'This is Mary'; neither of them has a history with enough of the features which played a role in his conception of 'Mary'. (The thought 'This one is called "Mary"' is, of course, quite a different matter.)

The way in which I have been speaking of our understanding of this as being a particular individual needs, I think, to be distinguished from something else. It might be said that most people have 'a conception of who they are', 'a conception of themselves' or 'a sense of their own identity'. What people have in mind when using phrases such as these is, I think, often distinct from, though related to, the kind of thing I have been speaking of. They might, for example, be thinking, at least in part, of the conception that an individual has of the *kind* of person that he is. He thinks of himself as kind but firm, intelligent though not always terribly practical, and so on. Also relevant to what we could speak of as the individual's 'self-image', however, are considerations of a slightly different kind. Each of us has some conception of our place in things. This is, in part, simply a matter of knowing certain things about myself; of knowing, for example, where I come from, what kind of work I do, that I am married and have a certain number of children, and so on. It is, however, also a matter of my attaching a special importance to some of these facts: to the fact that I am Scottish, to the fact that I once swam the Channel, to my relationship with this individual, and so on. Clearly individuals weigh things very differently here. For one person the fact that she is, say, a doctor may be of central importance in her thought about herself; for another, that he is a doctor may have only a marginal place in his conception of himself.

I mention this notion of 'self-image' or 'self-identity' simply in order to distinguish what I am centrally concerned with from it. When I speak of the idea that this is a particular individual I am concerned with the idea that this is an individual with a particular history; for example, this is the one who swam the Channel last July. This kind of thing is a crucial part of an individual's 'conception of himself' in the sense of which I spoke in the previous paragraph; but it is not the whole of it. Now there is, no doubt, room for dispute about the precise character of the relationship between these two notions. My aim, here, however, has simply been to draw attention to this distinction since a failure to keep it in mind does, I think, sometimes cause trouble.

(ii) Besides the idea of this as being a particular person we can place the thought that something with which we are confronted is a particular tree, a particular car, a particular stone, and so on. Many are inclined to say that there are crucial differences between the first of these ideas and the others; and differences of one kind are, perhaps, fairly obvious. The kind of importance which we attach to the identity of a person, to the question of who this is, is, in many cases, quite different from that which we attach to the identity of, say, a tree, a car or a stone. For example, the question of which stone this is rarely matters to us in anything like the way in which the question of *who* this is can matter to us in a personal relationship.

This kind of difference is, however, felt by many to be connected with another. It is suggested that if we want to do justice to the kind of *importance* which our recognition of this as a particular individual does, or should, have for us we must acknowledge that the *content* of our judgements of identity is of a certain particular form. Thus, in his discussion of personal identity John Locke draws a distinction between 'same man' and 'same person' which implicitly or explicitly plays a crucial role in the thought of many on this topic.[1] He suggests that it is one thing to judge this to be the same man, or, as I will express it, the same human being, as was encountered earlier and quite another to judge it to be the same person. We are confronted with the same human being if we are confronted with the same solid, extended, living organism. Now, we do, of course, in practice take the fact that we are or are not confronted with the same human being as a pretty reliable guide to whether we are confronted with the same person: if the human being before me now was in London when the bank was robbed in New York this could not be the person responsible for the robbery. It is suggested, however, that the fact that this is the same human being as the one who committed a crime is only *evidence* that it is the same person. That is to say, its being the same human being is of no importance *in itself*. The significant connection between an individual now and one encountered earlier, the connection which we have in mind when we speak of this as being the same person as the earlier one and treat them accordingly, is of quite a different kind. It is the kind of importance which we attach to the idea of this being the particular individual that he is which shows that this is so. The point could be put in this way: the importance which we attach to the idea of this as being the same person as the earlier one only makes sense if we agree that it is sameness of mind, not sameness of body, which is crucial to its being the same person.

Quinton presents us with one clear version of this idea:

'For why, after all, do we bother to identify people so carefully? What is unique about individual people that is important enough for us to call them by individual proper names? In our general relations with other human beings their bodies are for the most part intrinsically unimportant. We use them as convenient recognition devices enabling us to locate without difficulty the persisting character and memory complexes in which we are interested, which we love or like.'[2]

Quinton goes on to suggest that our concern and affection for another is tied to the character and memory complex of that person and that in so far as we have an idea of another as a *person*, as opposed, for example, to an idea of them as a purely sexual object, 'it will be as a unique cluster of character traits and recollections'. It is, then, continuity of character and memory which is crucial to the idea of this as being the same persisting individual over time. A consideration of the way in which we care about another in a personal relationship – of the way in which the question of who this is matters to us in a personal relationship – shows that the notion of 'who this is' must be carefully distinguished from that of 'which human being this is'. It is 'psychological continuity', not 'bodily continuity', which is crucial to personal identity.

Quinton imagines that someone might object that he has a sentimental view of the nature of personal relations. This seems to me to be an extraordinary worry. His view of personal relations strikes me as being profoundly cynical. I suppose that he is comparing his view with one which holds that we identify others primarily in terms of their bodily characteristics and that we are inclined to lose interest in another in so far as their bodily characteristics change in ways which we don't find attractive. His view is, perhaps, marginally less cynical than that; but only marginally. To the extent that my commitment to another is dependent exclusively on their retaining a set of psychological characteristics which I find attractive I can, surely, hardly be said to have a commitment to, or relationship with, the *person* at all. I *like* his cheerful manner and the stories he tells; just as I might like a particular set of bodily characteristics. There is, however, hardly room here for talk of affection or friendship; and if we speak of loving a 'persisting character and memory complex' that is surely a very different thing from loving a person.

I can find no better way of characterising the defect in Quinton's account of personal relationships than by saying that it leaves out the very thing which he is trying to understand: that is to say, our concern about the *identity* of the other. Quinton's friends are completely substitutable. Anybody with the same personality and apparent memories would do just as well. Now it may be true, as Quinton suggests, that the complexity of personality and apparent memories involved here is such that, the world being as it is, we can be quite certain, in every case, that no relevantly similar set of psychological characteristics will be found. I will return to that response in the next chapter but for the moment we can see that this does not help matters by approaching the issue from a slightly different direction. Quinton's relationships are all completely conditional. If just that sparkling sense of humour which played an essential role in first attracting me to someone disappears, then the very basis of the relationship disappears with it. A commitment to another can only survive such a change in so far as the lost characteristic is replaced by some other suitably attractive psychological feature. To put the objection to this in a fairly weak form: surely a central feature of, at any rate, certain forms of love is their resilience in the face of change of this kind.[3]

It is true that in many cases what first attracts us to someone, what leads us to enter into any kind of relationship with them, is, to some extent at least, what might be described as their psychological characteristics. It does not follow that once the relationship is established what binds us to them is solely the persistence of that particular set of psychological characteristics. What binds us to them is, at least in part, *who they are* – where this cannot be understood in terms of the persistence of such a set of characteristics. To bring out the force of the words 'who they are' here one would have to speak of the way in which the history of the relationship enters into my feelings towards the person now. My feelings towards them now are not, as Quinton appears to suppose, grounded solely in the psychological characteristics which they now possess.

It is, perhaps, worth stressing in this context that some of our most important relationships with others are not ones which we chose to enter into as a result of being attracted by the other's psychological characteristics. We do not enter into a relationship with our parents or with our children because we like their personality. Quinton asks: 'What is unique about individual people that is important enough for us to call them by individual proper names?' (Quinton, 1962, p. 402). It is slightly ironic that in the one context in which we are generally in a position to actually *give* somebody a name Quinton's answer to this question is manifestly outrageous. I do not give my child a name because he has a set of psychological characteristics which I wish to keep tabs on. The character of my love for my child has, at this stage, nothing whatever to do with a set of psychological characteristics which mark him off from any other infant twenty minutes old.

Of course, as a unique personality develops the character of my feelings towards my child will, as in any other relationship, change. One certainly cannot separate the character of the relationship which it is possible to have with another from the psychological make-up of that person. I cannot, for example, feel towards an individual who, in an important sense, has no life of his own just that kind of love, I cannot have with such an individual just that kind of friendship, which is possible in the context of a relationship between two normal adult human beings. To say this is, however, very different from saying that the *persistence* of a relationship with another is dependent on the persistence of a particular set of psychological characteristics. The mother's love for, and commitment to, her developing child is fairly obviously not tied in this way to the thought of this individual as a persisting embodiment of a particular 'character and memory complex'.

Perhaps the point is clearer in the case of a continued commitment to the brain damaged or senile. We do, of course, say in such cases 'He is not the man he once was.' Such remarks need, however, to be treated with care. If we ask who is being spoken of the answer is, for example, 'John' or 'My father'. We only understand the remark, we only know who the word 'He' refers to, if there is no doubt in our minds that the individual before us now *is*, for example, 'The one I used to play darts with.' Now this is not 'simply a point about the grammar of the remark'; it is a reflection of crucial features of our reactions to such cases. That I am in no doubt about *who* this is shows itself in my feelings about them; in, for example, the special responsibilities which I feel towards them and the anguish with which I am filled by my recognition of their condition.

I have been considering a suggestion which could be formulated in this way: 'If we look at the way in which people do care about the identity of another, at the way in which the question of *who* this is matters to people, we will see that what we are thinking when we think of this as being the same person as the one encountered previously is closely bound up with the idea that they possess the same "character and memory complex". Locke was right to suggest that there is a crucial distinction between the idea of this as being the same man and the idea of it as being the same person. For if we are to do justice to the kind of importance which we attach to the identity of others we must acknowledge that it is continuity of psychological characteristics, not the physical continuity of the human being, which is crucial to the idea of the identity of a person over time.' I have suggested that this argument rests on a dramatic misrepresentation of the character of our relations with others. Now it might be objected that the plausibility of my remarks here crucially depends on my choice of examples. Thus, beside the cases in which commitment to another survives radical change in their characteristics we must place the many cases in which an individual who undergoes such changes is rejected by his or her loved ones. Think, for example, of children disowned by their parents or of ageing parents virtually abandoned by their offspring in geriatric wards. In such cases is there not a very real sense in which, as a result of the dramatic changes in the other's psychology, we no longer think of this as being the child or parent we once knew? If, then, we are concerned with the way in which the idea of this as a particular individual does in practice feature in our thought must we not agree with Quinton that the idea of a 'persisting character and memory complex' should be at the centre of the picture?

In response, I should say first that I am pretty confident that the ways in which I spoke in the last paragraph do, at the very least, leave out a crucial dimension of most cases of this kind. It is precisely because there is no doubt in my mind about who the person in the hospital is that the thought of visits is such a nightmare. Similarly, the disowned son is not a stranger; his parents, after all, refuse to speak to him, as they do not refuse to speak with strangers. There is, however, a further point, of a different kind, which needs to be made about such examples. Thus, while it may be true that in some of my relations with others the other is for me essentially a particular 'character and memory complex' might I not regard this as a *failing* in my thought about them? I might, at any rate, be horrified at the prospect of a world in which all relationships between people approximate to this form. Now how am I to articulate the worry that I have about such ways of regarding others? The overwhelmingly natural articulation would, I think, be of the form: 'He treats his own daughter as a stranger.' That is to say, an articulation of the worry requires a language in which it can be acknowledged that this is unambiguously the same individual – his daughter – despite radical changes in her psychological characteristics.

Someone who has a different conception of the ideal in our relationships with others, who thinks, perhaps, that continued commitment through radical change involves 'sentimentality' on our part, will not require such a language. Thus, those who suggest that continuity of psychological characteristics should be at the centre of our picture of sameness of persons may be appealing not so much to how we *do* think of others in personal relationships as to how, in their view, we *ought* to. We are being offered an ideal of personal relationships; and, to match that ideal, a, possibly reformed, understanding of what is required for this to be the same individual over time. Whether or not Locke's distinction between 'same human being' and 'same person' is reflected in the way most now think, it will, on this suggestion, be reflected in the thought of those whose relationships come closer to the ideal. Now it will be clear, I suspect, that I have little sympathy with this ideal. My aim, however, has not been so much to defend my way of looking at this as to show that there is at least room for a view of a different kind: room for a view which insists that to give continuity of psychological characteristics *this* kind of significance is not to care about the other as an individual at all.

I suspect that this possibility is obscured, in part, by the terminology which is often employed in the discussion of these issues; we ask ourselves whether it is 'having the same mind' or 'having the same body' which is crucial to being the same person. The suggestion that 'the body' should have that kind of importance somehow sounds grotesquely wrong, and so we are left with the idea that it is 'the mind' which plays this role. Connected with this terminology is a picture of the options which are open to us in our relations with others. I must be interested either in the other's body or in their mind; that is to say, the other is for me a purely sexual object or an interesting personality. Thus, if we do not want to suggest that lust is the norm, or the ideal, in our relations with others we must think of personal relationships in the way that Quinton does.

Consider in this light a suggestion which Bernard Williams makes in one of his powerful attacks on the kind of approach followed by Quinton:

> While in the present situation of things to love a person is not exactly the same as to love a body, perhaps to say that they are basically the same is more grotesquely misleading than it is a deep metaphysical error.[4]

To suggest that loving a person is basically the same as 'loving a body' is certainly grotesquely misleading. Indeed, while this odd phrase is dramatically ambiguous, the suggestion is surely, on any non-technical reading, grotesquely false. For example, Quinton and Parfit are clearly right to insist that it simply will not do to suggest that love is 'basically the same as' sexual lust. Again, loving a person is *utterly* different from 'loving a corpse' (whatever that might be). Now it might be replied that this kind of appeal to normal usage pushes the point in the wrong direction. Williams, it might be said, uses the word 'body' here to remind us that the kind of affection we may feel for another human being may, in certain respects, be more closely linked to what we may feel for a house or a tree than we sometimes suppose. Yet, if this is Williams' purpose it needs to be pointed out that there is something very odd in the way in which he expresses himself. For houses and trees neither are, nor have, 'bodies'.[5] Now it might be replied that this protest still reflects a slavish adherence to normal linguistic conventions and so fails to touch the spirit of Williams' thought. Should we not take the word 'body' here to mean simply 'extended and tangible being'? One difficulty with this suggestion is that the word 'body' does *not* mean that. Another is that such a reading confronts us with the question: why does Williams think that loving this person is 'not exactly the same as' loving this extended and tangible human being?

The idea that these questions need to be pressed does not rest on the view that normal linguistic usage is sacrosanct. It rests, in part, on the view that when thinking philosophically about these issues we are inclined to use the terms 'mind' and 'body' in a technical way without making it clear to ourselves, or to anyone else, how we are using them. Further, this technical use – reflected in Williams' suggestion that loving a person is 'not exactly', but 'basically', the same as loving a body – may well reflect 'a deep metaphysical error': namely, that cluster of ideas which represents all interest in, all concern about, extended and tangible entities as being of fundamentally the same form.

Be that as it may, once we free ourselves from blinkers which are, perhaps, partially induced by the terminology, it becomes clear that there is a wider range of options in our relations with others than is sometimes acknowledged. For example, relations with others which are resilient in the face of changes in his or her psychological characteristics need not be purely lustful. Again, my continuing commitment to this individual is conditional neither on his retaining this particular psychological make-up nor on his retaining these particular bodily features; and in so far as I suspect that my commitment is conditional on either of these I might regard this as a failing on my part. With this we can say that my conception of *who* this is, my acknowledgement of this man as, for example, my son whom I have not seen for ten years, is dependent neither on the thought that this individual has the 'same mind' nor on the thought that he has the 'same body' as the child I remember.[6] My recognition that he and that child are one and the same person is, we can say, my recognition that they are one and the same *human being* – the same solid, extended, living organism.

(iii) There are, I think, some who would have complete sympathy with most of what I have said about personal relationships and yet who would totally reject the suggestion in my last sentence. They would insist that it is precisely because of these points about personal relationships that we must take Locke's distinction between 'same human being' and 'same person' seriously. The kind of commitment to another of which I have been speaking only makes sense in so far as we think of the real person as being something quite distinct both from the human being that we see and from the psychological characteristics manifested by the human being. For there is nothing in what we actually observe when we look at another which could justify that kind of commitment. Unless the connection which links the different stages of a human life together was of a deeper kind than anything which can be found in the publicly observable empirical world the kind of significance which we attach to the idea of this being a particular individual would make no sense.[7]

This idea of 'depth' is one which we have met before (see Chapter 2). The issues which it raises here are, in part, of much the same kind. We must ask why we should accept that the kind of commitment to others of which I have been speaking is dependent on the idea of a 'deeper' level in the sense suggested. Is the point one about human psychology: human beings simply would not care in the way that they do about *who* this is if they did not believe that behind the observable links between the stages of a person's life were links of another kind? Why should we accept that? Compare the way in which I care about who this is with the way in which I might care about which ring this is – namely, my wedding ring. Consider again the way in which it mattered to believers whether the Turin Shroud really was the shroud that covered Christ; or the way in which I might be moved by the fact that *this* is the house in which my grandmother grew up. If we look at these cases in a certain light the significance which we see in such facts can seem utterly mysterious. 'Its being the shroud that covered Christ', it might be said, 'consists in no more than its being spatio-temporally continuous with the shroud that covered Christ'; and why should we see any significance in that fact? Well, we do. The ways in which we care about *who* this is are of course very different from the kinds of concern which arise in these three examples. Nevertheless, reflection on such examples may help to remind us of the variety of ways in which the identity of solid, extended things in the empirical world can have significance for us. It then becomes unclear why we should accept that we would not care about *who* this is in the ways in which we do unless we believed that behind the fact that it is this particular human being there lay another fact of a quite different kind. Why should the fact that this is the human being who saved my child from drowning not *in itself* have significance for me?

Perhaps, however, the point was a different one. It was not a point about what people *do* attach importance to but, rather, a point about what they *ought* to attach importance to. The relationship of 'being the same human being as' is not one to which it is appropriate to give a significance of these kinds. But now how is this suggestion to be defended? Is it being assumed that the significance of the fact that it is *this* one can in the case of solid, extended things only lie in the way in which that can serve as a guide to its likely future behaviour; as the significance of the fact that this is the car I drove last week might be dependent on what I learn from that about the condition of its gear box? Why should we accept *that*? There are, of course, people who are inclined to view the ways of caring about the identity of rings or houses which I mentioned as inevitably involving 'sentimentality'. There may be nothing we can say to show that there is some confusion in the thought of such people. Equally, however, there appears to be nothing they can say to show that there is some confusion in the thought of the rest of us. In the same way, it needs to be shown why the kinds of significance which we attach to the fact that this is a particular individual would not be appropriate if his being that particular individual consisted in no more than his being that particular human being. In the absence of further argument here one can only suppose that it is being assumed that a 'functional' attitude towards that with which we are confronted is the norm: that the '*basic*' kind of significance which things have lies in their usefulness in promoting our ends. I suggested, in particular in Chapters 2 and 7, that this assumption may be at work in many discussions of closely related issues. I argued too, in Chapter 2, that if one assumes in this way that the world of extended and tangible beings is a world to be *used* by us it is far from clear why the same should not be said of a world which supposedly lies behind this one. Thus, suppose that we agreed that there was some other kind of connection which 'lies behind' this observable continuity of the human being. We would still need to ask: why is it *more* appropriate to care in the special ways that we do about connections of *that* kind?

It might be replied, however, that there is real reason to deny that the *human being* could be the bearer of the kind of significance which is in question. 'For', it might be argued, 'there must be something in common in the individual which confronts me at successive instants to underpin the common concern which I have for her at successive instants. My love is for the individual that confronts me now and so must be in virtue of features she now possesses. Thus, an unchanging commitment requires an unchanging object: if this is, in the important sense, the same individual it must be in virtue of something unchanging in her. The human being, however, is in a constant process of change: the atoms which compose the human being are completely replaced every seven years. So there is no important sense in which this *is* the same human being as the one I met seven years ago, or, indeed, three weeks ago. Now since the kinds of commitment of which you have spoken are only intelligible in so far as there is something unchanging in the person, and since there is nothing unchanging in the human being, such commitments are only intelligible if there is a persisting, unchanging core which lies behind the being we encounter in the empirical world.'

I have imagined these words in the mouth of someone who deplores the picture of personal relationships which I discussed in section (ii). The notion of an unchanging core behind the changing surface is introduced in order to combat the idea that our commitment to others must be conditional on a reasonable constancy in their psychological characteristics. Yet one who argues in this way shares a crucial assumption with those who defend that picture of personal relationships: the assumption expressed in the words 'an unchanging commitment requires an unchanging object'. The only point at dispute between the views is an empirical one: *is* there such an unchanging core?

I suggested that the earlier picture of personal relationships leaves out something which is crucial to such relationships: namely, our concern about the *identity* of the other, about *who* this is. Another way to express this would be to say that it leaves out the way in which the *past* can matter to us. The same comment is in place here. The suggestion that, for example, love is dependent on the idea of an unchanging object is simply another manifestation of the failure to acknowledge the irreducible significance that the past can have for us. My commitment to another now need not be dependent, in the way suggested, on any feature that she *now* possesses. Indeed, in so far as my commitment is dependent on the idea of an unchanging core it is unclear in what sense I can be said to have a commitment to the *person* at all. To the extent that it matters to me *which* individual this is my commitment to her is grounded in the past and so its persistence does not need the support of a persisting unchanging object.

It is suggested that the special kinds of significance which we attach to the question of who this is only make sense if we acknowledge that what we are concerned about when we are concerned about the identity of a person is something quite distinct from the identity of the publicly observable human being. Thus, it is held that to put the persisting, though changing, human being at the centre of the picture is to leave no room for things that are of fundamental value in human life. The defences of this suggestion which I have looked at in this and the previous sections rest on a, more or less, dramatic failure to recognise just what *is* special in our thought about who a particular person is. The philosophical notion of 'the mind', as it appears in this context, is, we might say, an attempt to plug the gap left by a failure to appreciate the significance which the *past* can have for us.

10

The Irreplaceability of Persons

(i) In Chapter 9 I suggested that there was a fundamental and crucially important distinction between 'loving' a particular set of psychological characteristics and loving a person. The emphasis of my discussion there was on the fact that to the extent that I am committed to an *individual* my commitment will survive changes in his characteristics. The other side of this, on which I touched briefly, is the fact that in so far as I am committed to an *individual* I do not think of him or her as a *type*; what is crucial to my thought about the other is not, or not simply, the fact that he or she satisfies a certain description which another person could, in principle, satisfy. There is an idea of irreplaceability which is central to the love of a particular individual.

It is on these grounds that Gregory Vlastos criticises the view of love which he finds in Plato's *Symposium*:

> We are to love the person so far, and only insofar, as they are good and beautiful. Now since all too few human beings are masterworks of excellence, and not even the best of those we have the chance to love are wholly free of streaks of the ugly, the mean, the commonplace, the ridiculous, if our love for them is to be only for their virtue and beauty, the individual, in the uniqueness and integrity of his or her individuality, will never be the object of our love. This seems to me the cardinal flaw in Plato's theory. It does not provide for love of whole persons, but only for love of that abstract version of persons which consists of the complex of their best qualities. [1]

Commenting on this passage Martha Nussbaum asks 'what this uniqueness and individuality come to'. [2] She goes on to suggest that Plato himself was well aware of the importance which 'uniqueness and individuality' have in relationships between people as is shown by the following passage from the *Symposium*:

One could find many other wonderful things about Socrates to praise. But these same virtues one might attribute to someone else as well. The really wonderful thing about him is that he is not similar to any human being, past or present . . . . This man is so strange – he himself and his speeches too – that you could look and look and find nobody even near him.[3]

The idea of 'uniqueness' which we find here is then linked by Nussbaum with the speech of Aristophanes. Each of us once formed one half of a sphere. Separated from our other half we are, as individuals, incomplete beings who strive to become whole by uniting ourselves again with our other half. The cut, Nussbaum stresses, was a jagged one. There is, thus, no reason to think that there is more than one individual who, having a jagged edge which perfectly matches mine, will fit together with me to form a whole (Nussbaum, 1986, p. 173).

The imagery here is very rich. One dimension of it is, surely, the insistence that the other is not for me simply an object of contemplation. I have a relationship with the other – am in interaction with the other. Thus, it is of crucial importance that the other's character (and life) should 'fit' with mine. I might find a particular individual both admirable and attractive and yet recognise that, in view of my own particular characteristics, it is unthinkable that we should have a satisfactory relationship. The other, then, is not for me simply a set of 'good and beautiful' characteristics, and so readily replaceable by someone else who comes up to the same mark. He is an individual in the sense that he has a quite particular set of characteristics which relate in the appropriate way with my own characteristics. The myth, as Nussbaum takes it, asks us to think of the details of these characteristics as all important.

This stress on the notion of a relationship, with the concomitant stress on the complex and particular details of the other which play a crucial part in my thought about her, is clearly a very important advance on the picture of love which Vlastos finds in the *Symposium*.[4] Nevertheless, there are, perhaps, doubts of various kinds which one might have about it. The one which concerns me is the question of whether it does, as Nussbaum suggests, capture the idea of 'uniqueness and individuality' which plays a crucial role within personal relationships. Consider the following passage from Nussbaum's discussion:

Nor are love objects interchangeable for these people, as seats of abstract goodness or beauty might be. The individual is loved not only as a whole, but also as a unique and irreplaceable whole. For each there is, apparently, exactly one 'other half' (192B6, 191A6). Although upon the death of the half each will begin a search for a replacement, there is no evidence that this search will bring success. There is nothing like a general description of a suitable or 'fitting' lover, satisfiable by a number of candidates, that could serve as a sufficient criterion of suitability.[5]

'. . . there is no evidence that this search will bring success.' On this view, however, I could say what 'success' would *be*. Even if I cannot give a 'general description of a suitable or "fitting lover"' (and it is not quite clear to me how that follows from this account) I can at least say that my 'problem' would be solved if I could find another whose 'jagged edges' were the exact complement of mine. Now many will feel that to the extent to which my situation can be represented in this way my concern for the other cannot be characterised as, in the fullest sense, a love for the individual. There is a sense of 'individuality' which has been completely lost as soon as there is room for talk of the chances of finding a substitute; and the remoteness of the chances does nothing to change that.

Can any sense be made of such a notion of 'individuality'? It has been argued – by Josiah Royce and, more recently, by Stephen Clark – that, while this notion is very important to our thought, sense can only be made of it on the assumption that the other, in some sense, lies behind the surface that we encounter. 'Individuality', writes Royce, 'is something that we demand of our world, but that, in this present realm of experience, we never find.'[6] Thus, 'Love and loyalty never directly find their unique objects, but remain faithful to them although unseen.' Clark argues in a similar vein that unless my wife is a being who is distinct from her properties and so is unknown by me, 'then in loving "her" I only love her characteristics, and should be satisfied by them wherever they may be'.[7] It is not quite clear to me how Clark makes the step to his striking conclusion that 'If there is no eternal life, then the demands of personal love are utterly mistaken.' What primarily concerns me, however, is the negative stage of the argument. This might, I think, be summarised in this way: 'When I try to describe the individual that I love I only manage to produce a description that another could, in principle, satisfy. That is to say, all of the observable characteristics of the individual I love are repeatable in principle. Thus, to think of the other as unrepeatable, as irreplace-able in the sense with which we are concerned, I must think that the essential person somehow lies behind those characteristics.'

What is right in this is the insistence – in opposition to what we find in Quinton and, in a more sophisticated form, in Nussbaum – that no amount of fineness of detail in the observed characteristics of the other can take us a single step closer to the idea of irreplace-ability which is relevant here. Consider again Alcibiades' speech. It is noteworthy that the fact that Socrates is utterly different from anyone else is itself represented as one of the striking things, indeed as the most striking thing, about him. The rest of us, even such exceptional men as Pericles and Achilles, are not so *very* different from others who have lived (*Symposium* 221 C–D). In so far, then, as we find an idea of individuality in the speech it is an idea which, at least in the view of the speaker, has much clearer application to Socrates than to most others. If I speak of the rather unremarkable boy next door as an irreplaceable individual the force which my words can legitimately have – can have if they are not to be an expression of woolly wishful thinking – is quite different from that which they have when used of Socrates. Rough approximations are available. If it is objected that this remark shares with Alcibiades' speech a gross insensitivity to the fineness of detail which we find in personalities I would reply, first, that I do not believe it[8] and, second, that it is, in any case, irrelevant. For the fundamental point here is this. If we understand the notion of irreplaceability in this way my thought of my son as an irreplace-able individual is a hostage to fortune.

The idea of 'irreplaceability' which is appealed to here should not be seen as one which, being tied to a quite particular concep-tion of love, most of us would not seriously miss. The idea cannot, I think, be separated from a form of concern about, say, the suffering of another which is quite fundamental to anything which most of us would recognise as love or friendship. I am horrified in a quite particular way at the suffering of John, my child. The thought that it is *that* individual is central to my horror. Now suppose that the force of the words '*that* individual' could be brought out in terms of a detailed description of his personality.[9] This will open up the possibility that there is another child, whom I have never met, whose suffering is something for me to be dis-tressed about in exactly the same way as is the suffering of my own child. Now I do not want to suggest that that idea, as it stands, need be absurd. (I will return to claims of this form in Chapter 13). What I think *would* be absurd is the suggestion that my thought about my child is of a form such that empirical discoveries could bear on it in the way suggested. For example, if I do not know my child well it is possible that another should fit any description that I can give of the object of my concern *better* than does my child. Perhaps, then, my distress over the suffering of the boy who lives in the same house as me is invariably misplaced! Now the point here has much more general application, and so is not vulnerable to the objection that parents obviously generally know their children well enough to exclude this possibility. I am distressed in a quite particular way about the suffering of the man from whom I have bought a paper every day for twenty years; yet the character sketch which I can give of him might be extraordinarily thin. It might be quite clear that there are many others who would fit it as well as, and perhaps better than, he. If, then, we understand the notion of 'individuality' in the terms suggested by Quinton and Nussbaum we will have to agree that the appropriateness of the quite particular distress that I feel on learning of his painful illness depends on whether or not this is so. It is this conclusion which I take to be clearly absurd.

(ii) Royce and Clark are, then, right to insist that there is a notion of individuality, or irreplaceability , which is crucial to our normal thought and which is lost as soon as we think that the irreplaceability of an individual is to be captured in a description that another could, in principle, satisfy. The sense of 'irreplaceability' which is involved here is *utterly* different from that involved in the business-man's thought that his secretary is, in virtue of her qualities, 'irreplaceable'. This leaves open the question of what sense, if any, can be made of this notion of 'irreplaceability'. Since all of my wife's characteristics are, apparently, repeatable in principle in what sense can it be denied that my wife is repeatable in principle? Now the vague gestures which Royce and Clark make towards a realm behind the surface of observed characteristics are, I think, no more than gestures.[10] Clark, for example, tells us nothing of how the 'unknowable quiddity' of which he speaks would satisfy the requirement of individuality any better than do the familiar beings in this world. More serious, however, is the fact that these gestures, in so far as we understand them, are, I believe, gestures in quite the wrong direction.

Consider the distinction, stressed by Clark, between my wife and her characteristics. We can, when speaking of objects in space and time, draw a distinction between the thing and its properties which does not involve any idea of the thing itself being unknowable. There are, of course, a number of familiar philosophical problems in this area but I hope that what I need here is reasonably uncontroversial. We can distinguish between, say, a chair and its properties in the sense that we can speak of two distinct chairs having the same properties. We can do this because chairs can be individuated in spatio-temporal terms. With this goes the fact that by building into my characterisation of the chair an account of its spatial relations to other things at a particular time I can produce a description which *could not* be satisfied by more than one chair.

This does not, by itself, ensure that we will understand someone who insists that a particular chair is 'irreplaceable' in the sense that we are concerned with. For it does not follow from the fact that we understand her when she says that that, over there, is a different chair from this one which has the same properties, that we understand her when she insists that it *matters* that it is a different chair – that it would *not* do just as well as this one. How, we might ask, can the fact that the chair is over there, as opposed to here, possibly have any bearing on one's thought about the chair itself? We might continue: 'Mere difference in spatial location is simply not the right kind of thing to influence one's feelings about the *chair*. After all, each chair could just as easily have been in the position that the other one now occupies. This brings out that any difference in attitude towards them, any insistence that the other will not do just as well as this one, must, to be intelligible, be based on some difference in the "intrinsic features" of the two chairs. Thus, the familiar ways in which objects with identical properties can be individuated are quite irrelevant to any sense that can be given to talk of an individual as "irreplaceable". We are pushed back to the conclusion of Royce and Clark that such talk only makes sense in so far as we can hold that behind the surface properties of a person there are "intrinsic features", unknown by us, which are, in some sense, necessarily unique to this individual.'

This argument moves very rapidly from a plausible claim about one example involving chairs to a general thesis about what could possibly be of significance to us in our thought about any individual.[11] The move is obviously far *too* rapid. We understand someone who insists that it matters to him that Van Gogh sat in this chair – that that fact makes a difference to his thought about the chair. Yet, it might be said, what marks off this chair from the one over there which is exactly like it is 'merely that it once stood in a certain spatial relation to Van Gogh'.

Now consider a suggestion which was central to Chapter 9: the suggestion that an individual's history may play a crucial part in my thought about them now. Does this suggestion help in the attempt find sense in talk of a particular individual as irreplaceable? That depends on how we understand the notion of an individual's history. Taken in one way it makes *sense* to suppose that another should have a history which is identical with that of my wife: both fell off a horse on their tenth birthday, loved music from an early age, and so on. Here we have a list of characteristics which are repeatable in principle. However, by building into the history references to her spatial relations to other things at particular times we can produce a description which necessarily individuates: picks out a single individual. For example, the precise time and grid reference of our birth individuates each of us.

Now I am not, of course, suggesting that *that* individuating fact is what is crucial to my conception of my wife, or anybody else. Apart from anything else there is, as I stressed before, no reason, in most cases, to suppose that my conception of another is tied in this way to a *single* feature of their history. I take it, also, that in most cases characterisations of the other's history which involve indexicals in a fairly explicit way[12] are of central importance in our conception of the other: she is 'the one I first saw standing in that odd posture by the stream', 'the one I built this house with', 'the one who looked at me in that amused way when I said that', and so on. The philosophical terminology and the list of definite descriptions no doubt sounds quite odd in this context; and in a way it certainly *is* odd. Nevertheless, it does pick out crucial features of our normal thought. What, in practice, corresponds to these definite descriptions is a series of memories of her in particular situations which I observed and of things we have done together. Now my point is that such memories are likely to be central to my conception of someone who matters to me and that no more than one individual *could* satisfy the descriptions encapsulated in these memories.[13] The series of memories necessarily individuates. (It is, of course, possible, that *no one* satisfies the whole series of descriptions; my point is that not more than one could.)

Here, then, we have a notion of irreplaceability which satisfies the requirement of which I have insisted: the requirement that this notion should be such as to leave no *sense* to the idea that a substitute for this individual is possible. On this understanding of the notion of irreplaceability nothing could count as a solution to my problem when my wife dies; nothing could count as a suffering to be horrified at in *just* the way that the suffering of John, my child, is to be horrified at; and so on. There is no room for sense in these suggestions since the characterisation of the individual which is central to my understanding of who this is involves uniquely individuating references to history. We can say that what individuates this person – that in virtue of which he is irreplaceable – is something that 'lies behind the observable surface'; but what lies behind the surface is the individual's history – not an impenetrable realm beyond the normal world of experience. [14]

(iii) I have placed at the centre of the picture a notion of *who* this is which is to be understood in terms of this being an individual with a particular history; and have argued that any attempt to understand our concern about the identity of the other exclusively in terms of a concern about a particular set of characteristics which they possess is bound to be desperately misleading. The reference to the past is, I suggested, ineliminable. It will be replied that a consideration of the character of grief on the death of a loved one reveals that this is quite wrong. For what is it that is unbearable about the death of a loved one? How are we to characterise the horror that I feel on hearing of such a death? Is it not clear that what is unbearable is the realisation that I will never see her again? I think back on her mannerisms, the particular character of her responses in certain circumstances – the particular way in which she would use that phrase, smile on those occasions – and so on. It is the thought that, for example, I will never see that smile again which is unbearable. What I want, and realise that I will never have again, is moments just like that. This, surely, if not the whole of grief, is undeniably at its very centre. If this is correct, however, it seems that I have just done what I insisted in my discussion of Nussbaum could not be done. I have said what would constitute a 'solution' to my troubles when a loved one dies: namely, more moments just like those ones. With that the idea of irreplaceability, and so of individuality, can no longer be understood in the terms which I have favoured. The history of the person who has died,

that which I have suggested is fundamental to the idea of irreplaceability, only enters in in this way: it is a reminder of the kind of
moment which will almost certainly be wholly absent in the future.
Other smiles may come close but none of them will have just those
nuances and so could move me in just that way. The particularity
of the other can thus be understood in terms of the particular set of
characteristics which she instantiates; and her irreplaceability in
terms of the fact that it is, in practice, utterly inconceivable that any
other individual should possess all of these characteristics which
were important to me in her.

It is, I think, fairly clear that nothing like this can be the whole
story. Think, for example, of grief on the death of one whom I
never expected to see again in any case; or of the contrast, of which
I have spoken before, between our response to death and our
response to the other's loss, through brain damage or senility, of
most of the characteristics which were central to our picture of
them. It is clear that these responses cannot be understood
exclusively in the terms outlined in the previous paragraph.
Nevertheless, there must be *something* in the ways in which I spoke
there. It can hardly be denied that the fact that I am never going to
see her again and, more specifically, that I am never, for example,
going to see her smile in just that way again, are central to grief on
the death of a loved one. This suggestion, properly understood, is
not, however, in competition with the view that the past – the
thought of the one who has died as an individual with a particular
history – is central to grief. For the sense in which my thought is
focused on the future itself involves an ineliminable reference to
the past.

Consider, for example, my thought that I will never see that
smile again. What do I mean when I speak of 'that smile'? It is
clear, I take it, that what is being spoken of here is a *response* to
something. That is: its being *that* smile is not independent of what
it is a response to. What I think of when I think back is her smile on
catching my eye, or the smile in response to a humorous absurdity
of the particular kind which struck her. It would hardly be '*that*
smile' if 'it' was a response to the sight of another's suffering.[15] At
any rate, the sight of that facial configuration in *those* circumstances, so far from being a joy to me, would be positively night-
marish. When, then, my distress focuses on the thought that I will
never see that smile again what is at issue is not simply, as I put it,
a particular 'facial configuration'; there is a reference to context

which is crucial. Now there *may* be cases in which we can capture the force of the words 'that smile' without spelling out a context in a way which involves a reference to the *past*. There are, however, clearly cases in which this *cannot* be done. For example, I spoke of her smile on catching my eye. It would not be *that* smile, in the sense that concerns us here, if she had been a total stranger. What to the camera might be indistinguishable responses would for me be responses having an utterly different significance. When I reflect, on her death, that I will never see 'that smile' again it is a smile on the lips of *that* individual, with whom I share a history, that I am thinking of.

What is fairly obviously true of this case is, I suspect, true in more subtle ways with smiles of other kinds. Her smiling response to an absurdity is only fully understood as the response that it is in the light of connections between this situation and others she and I have experienced. That is to say, an amused response could be, for me, *that* response only if it was her, the one with that past, who was responding.

Consider another dimension of my grief. I look back on conversations that we had and reflect with despair on the fact that there will be no more conversations like that. One might again think that since it is 'conversations like that' which are at issue I must at least have an understanding of what it would be to have the relevant kind of conversation with another. This suggestion would, however, be misconceived in much the same way as the parallel suggestion with smiles. There *may* be certain kinds of conversation that we had of which something like this can *almost* be said. I enjoy talking about films and anyone whose knowledge, tastes, and so on dovetail in the right way with my own would fill this aspect of the gap which has been created in my life reasonably well. Even here we will, I think, often be a long way from really understanding what a replacement would be: for it is almost inconceivable that our shared history should not enter in an important way into my understanding of the conversations that we had. In any case, if there is room for doubt here there is none in the case of talk of other important kinds where the reference to the past is explicit. Most obviously, of course, many people find great pleasure, or comfort, in talking about their shared past. It is clear that the pleasure, or comfort, which each finds in such talk is dependent on the idea that the other is the one with whom one went through that experience.[16] Equally important, however, is the fact that we talk about people or places that we have encountered together – whether it be five minutes ago, last week, or twenty years ago. Our talk is in the present tense but it is crucial to its character that we both *know*, that is, have had contact with, the person or place about which we are talking. Here again, then, the significance which the conversation has for me is crucially dependent on my understanding of *who* it is I am talking with. While we might say that it is the other's words that matter to me this is not to say that 'the same words' on other lips would serve just as well.

I have been concerned with the question of whether grief on the death of a loved one can be said to be entirely forward-looking in this sense: we can say what would constitute a 'solution' to my troubles.[17] This question arose through the bearing which it has on the idea of the other as an irreplaceable individual. Now I have not suggested that all aspects of my response on the death of a loved one will inevitably involve a reference to the past of the form I have been discussing. Perhaps I am going to sorely miss the delicate consistency of my wife's omelettes. I could say what would be a replacement for *that* loss. I will not discuss the question of how we should think of this kind of thing as being related to grief; nor that of whether the triviality of my example is significant. What concerns me here is simply that there is much which is central to grief that is *not* like that. While my thought may be focused on the desolate future the character of the desolation can only be captured by saying that it is a future without *her*. The smiles, the mannerisms, the conversation are in that sense secondary. While they may be at the centre of my picture the fundamental notion is that of the particular individual whose smiles, mannerisms and conversation they are. My point here might, then, be put in terms of the following reversal of views such as Quinton's and Parfit's: it is not that my concern about 'who this is' is dependent on the significance which this set of psychological characteristics has for me. Rather, the significance which the characteristics have for me is dependent on who this is; and the force of the words 'who this is' can only be brought out in terms of the idea that this is an individual – a human being – with a particular history.[18]

11

Personal Identity and the First Person

(i) In my treatment of identity and individuality I have so far focused exclusively on the third-person point of view. I have been speaking of the ways in which the idea of this as being a particular individual enters into our thought about another and have said nothing about the role which my conception of *myself* as a particular individual with a particular history plays in my thought. Now while this is clearly a major gap in my discussion it will be felt by many to be more than that. For it will be said that the first person point of view is fundamental; that if we want to get clear about our thought of *another* as being a particular individual we must begin with the individual's thought about himself as being a particular individual.[1]

One aspect of this line of thought would be this. A person, it might be said, is in some sense in a privileged position when it comes to the question of who he himself is; and, further, this fact creates serious difficulties for any suggestion that there is a close connection between the idea of 'sameness of person' and that of 'sameness of human being'. 'For', it might be argued, 'my judgement that I am DC is not based on observation of my bodily features. It must, therefore, be based on my knowledge of my mental features – either on my knowledge of my psychological characteristics or on my direct acquaintance with something more fundamental than this: the mind that has them. We can conclude that it is "sameness of mind", in one of these senses, as opposed to "sameness of living human being" which is crucial to this being the particular individual that it is.'

There *is* a sense in which I am in a privileged position when it comes to the question of who I am. I can, as no one else can, characteristically say who I am without taking note of any of my personal characteristics. When I wake in the morning I can tell you who I am – that I am DC, who grew up in Edinburgh, now works in Lampeter and so on – without, for example, glancing in the mirror 'to see who this is'. However, the argument outlined in my previous paragraph reflects a failure to appreciate just how radical the difference between the first and third person case is. It assumes that since my claim that I am DC is not based on my observation of bodily features it must be based on my recognition of *other* features which I possess. The way I expressed the point, however, was that I can say who I am without taking note of *any* of my personal characteristics. Certainly I would be in a bad way if I could not say who I was without taking note of my physical features. Would I be in much, or any, better shape if I could not say who I was without taking note of my mental features?

I have noted a sense in which I am in a privileged position when it comes to the question of who I am. One might be tempted to connect this notion of being in a privileged position with another: supposing that the individual cannot be mistaken about who he himself is. Now this idea – the idea that the individual inevitably has an overriding authority to say who he himself is – is clearly in tension with any suggestion that 'being the same person' is closely tied up with 'being the same human being'. For the question of whether this is the *human being* who did certain things in the past is one which others may sometimes be in a better position to answer than the individual himself. Thus, we will, it seems, be forced to conclude that in taking myself to be an individual with a particular history I am making a judgement about a 'private' entity to which I have 'immediate and infallible access'; and so that it is the identity of this entity, not that of the publicly observable human being, which is crucial to the identity of the person.

One comment on this tenuous line of thought will suffice. It does not follow from the fact that I do not characteristically need *grounds* for my claims about who I am that I cannot be mistaken in such claims. I do not base my claim that I am the one who, say, broke the vase on evidence which indicates which human being broke the vase. It does not follow that I am not *committing* myself to the claim that this human being broke the vase; and, on the face of it, I clearly am committing myself to such a claim. If someone presents me with what appears to be clear evidence that this human being, the human being that I am, could not possibly have broken the vase since he was somewhere else at the time I will take this evidence to be in direct conflict with my claim that I broke the vase. Whether and how I resolve the conflict will depend on the circumstances. The crucial point, however, is this. While it is certainly an important truth that people are generally correct in their memory judgements about their own past we do, in special cases, readily allow that an individual can be mistaken in such a judgement. Indeed, even if we cannot convince him that he is not the one who made that clever remark in the discussion last year that need not make us hesitant in our judgement that it was, in fact, someone else.

A rejection of the kind of claim made in my previous paragraph is central to Geoffrey Madell's argument against the 'bodily criterion of personal identity'. Madell quotes with approval the following remark by Shoemaker: 'Where the present-tense version of a judgement is immune to error through misidentification relative to the first-person pronouns contained in it, this immunity is *preserved* in memory'.[2] It is, however, far from clear that this claim can be read in a way such that it is both true and in tension with the kind of position which I have given to the identity of the human being. One possible reading would be this: 'If I could not have been mistaken at the time in thinking that it was me who was making that remark my present memory impression that it was me who made it cannot be mistaken.' As I have already noted, however, this suggestion is, on the face of it, simply untrue. Its falsity arises from the fact that our memory impressions are not always conditioned solely by our experience of the incident at the time: wishful thinking, what others tell us and so on can, and commonly do, introduce distortion into the memory impression. Now Shoemaker might reply that his claim is restricted to cases in which no distortion has been introduced: 'My memory report could of couse be mistaken, for one can misremember such incidents, but it could not be the case that I have a full and accurate memory of the past incident but am mistaken in thinking that the person I remember shouting was myself' (Shoemaker, 1984, p. 20). To create any difficulty for the 'bodily criterion' this claim needs to be more than the trivial truth that we will not call it a 'full and accurate memory' if it turns out that I am mistaken in my impression that it was I who shouted. Yet if it is not this trivial truth it is, as before, not clear that it is a truth at all. Could my memory not be 'full and accurate' in the sense that I can give a word-perfect report of what was shouted and yet, perhaps as a result of wishful thinking, remember it as having been me who shouted when it was in fact someone else? It might be said that there is some other sense of the phrase 'full and accurate memory' – perhaps a sense which involves the idea of 'reliving the incident from the inside' – which is such that this possibility is excluded. Again, however, what is needed is a defence of this claim which does not reduce it to the trivial truth which will not do the work required. For example, we might refuse to call it 'reliving the incident from the inside' if it was, in fact, someone else who spoke the words; or we might refuse to say that the incident was 'preserved in memory' if wishful thinking played some role. This will leave us with something which is close to the form of Shoemaker's claim but which will not do the work which Madell asks of it since it will not give to the individual's own view of his past the particular kind of privileged position which Madell supposes it to have: it will not render his memory impression immune from revision in the light of the discovery that this, the human being that he is, is not the one who did the deed.

I am not suggesting that the only truth to be found here is the trivial one that we would not say that he 'remembers performing the action' if it turned out that he was not the one who performed the action in question. Shoemaker argues with great plausibility that there could not be a world in which most 'memory impressions' do not correspond to things previously experienced by the one who 'remembers'; or, perhaps, that in such a world our knowledge of the past would be very limited indeed. Thus, it is not simply an empirical discovery on my part that most of my memory impressions are of incidents which I myself witnessed. We might, then, say that the first-person point of view – my impression that I am the one who shouted – does have a privileged status. It is a necessary truth of some kind that such impressions are generally veridical: the link between 'being the person who did it' and 'being the one who has a memory impression of having done it' is not a merely contingent one. This, however, does nothing to suggest that the link between 'being the same person' (for example 'being the person who did it') and 'being the same human being' is a merely contingent one. On the contrary, it is central to Shoemaker's argument – appealing as it does to the idea that it is important that we should have some conception of the spatial location of the remembered incident – that this is not so. (See section III of Shoemaker's paper.)

If Shoemaker is right, as I take it he is, there is a link of fundamental importance between 'continuity of the human being' and 'continuity of memory impressions'. This will, then, mark a crucial difference between the identity of people over time and the identity of other things. With this, it ensures that once we enter the realm of science fiction, imagining that the world was different in certain very general respects, cracks will appear in our thought about people which will have no direct analogue in our thought about trees or cars. (Not because cracks cannot be made to appear there too; but because a different kind of strain will be required to produce them.) Connected with this is the possibility that we can envisage circumstances, perhaps of the kind associated with, for example, Ian Stevenson's work on reincarnation, in which the richness of 'accurate memory impressions' would lead us to identify an individual before us now with an earlier individual with whom he could not conceivably be physically continuous. To grant that, is, I take it, to grant that personal identity cannot be 'analysed' in terms of physical (spatio-temporal) continuity; but then, there is, I take it, no reason to suppose that an 'analysis', in that sense, should be possible. (It is perhaps worth adding that I take *that* point to apply equally to the identity of trees, cars or anything else.)

We can argue that my memories of what I have done occupy a position which is, in a certain sense, privileged yet still allow that the judgement that another makes about who this is *can* be better informed than that of the individual himself. All of us, I believe, readily acknowledge this latter point in practice. Some, however, are inclined to resist it when thinking more abstractly about the issue. This resistance may spring in part from an idea that it is an individual's *right* to say who he himself is. To allow that others could be in a better position than the individual to say who he himself is is, it might be felt, *morally* objectionable: it involves us in imposing on the individual something, a conception of who he is, which, if nothing else is, should be left exclusively in his hands.

We must distinguish what is at issue here from questions concerning what I called the individual's 'self-image' or 'sense of his own identity' (cf. Chapter 9 section (i)). It might, for example, be insisted that the individual has not only a right but a duty to decide for himself which are the *important* features of his life. If the fact that he is a doctor, or that he once wrote a successful novel, does not have a central place in his conception of himself who are we to argue that it should? Well, however one feels about that suggestion the issue it raises needs to be carefully distinguished from another. It is one thing to suggest that it is 'up to him to decide' what importance to attach to the fact that he once wrote a successful novel. It is quite another to suggest that he has the last word on the question of whether he *did* once write a successful novel – that it is the individual's right to say who he himself is in *that* sense.

If, on reflection, someone continues to press the latter suggestion we might reply: as soon as one enters into a personal relationship with another, and we are all born into some relationships of this kind, one gives up this supposed exclusive right. The person in the geriatric ward may have no idea who he (or anyone else) is. Should that make me more hesitant in my thought that this is my father; and more hesitant in the reactions to him which go with that thought? Again, suppose that he is making what everyone else takes to be completely wild claims about who he is. There *might* be something morally objectionable in my not 'playing along with him'; though, depending on the precise circumstances, many may feel that a proper *respect for him* places severe limits on what is acceptable in this direction. Would it, though, reflect a failing in me if my thought of this as my father was in no way shaken by his claims? Well, there may be room for different answers to this question. It does, however, need to be *argued* that it is obviously morally objectionable to allow that others may be in a better position than the individual to say who he himself is.

(ii) Let us turn now to the way in which the thought of another as a particular individual *matters* to us. In this connection, the idea that the first-person point of view must play the fundamental role in any treatment of these issues comes to this: the way in which another's thought of this as Jane, that particular individual, matters to the other runs through his conception of how it matters to Jane herself. An individual's thought about *herself* is the model on which the thought of others about her is based insofar as they are thinking of her, and caring for her, as a person.

What are we to make of this? Consider the following remark of Wittgenstein's: ' "When I say 'I am in pain', I do not point to a person who is in pain, since in a certain sense I have no idea who is." '[3] Rather than focus on this directly I want to bring out the truth in a closely related claim: when I am in pain there is a certain sense in which I do not *care* who is in pain. Now we have to be careful here for there is of course a clear sense in which I do care who is in pain when it is I that am in pain. This sense in which I care may find expression in, for example, my wishing that it was someone else who was suffering. The insistence that there is a sense in which I do not care who is in pain when I am in pain is quite compatible with the acknowledgement that most of us are strongly self-centred. In *that* sense I may care a great deal who is in pain. The sense in which I do not care is this. When I am in pain it does not matter to me that it is David Cockburn, the person who grew up in Edinburgh, now teaches philosophy in Lampeter, and so on, that is in pain. Thus, if I get into a state in which I begin to think that I may be in a muddle about who I am – perhaps I am not DC after all – that will be no consolation at all in the face of the pain that I am now feeling. Again, consider my selfish wish that it was someone else who was suffering this pain. The basic articulation of this wish is *not* 'I wish that DC was not in pain'. That a person with this particular history is in pain is quite irrelevant to my concern. Now, we can contrast this with a case in which someone I care about, say my child, is suffering. Here the thought that it is *John* is crucial to the form that my concern takes. When I see a child in the distance fall and hurt himself I have the thought 'He is in pain'; but there is a further question, the question 'Who is that child in pain?', that will be important to me if I suspect that it may be my child; as the question 'Who is this man who is in pain?' is *not* important to me when it is I who am in pain.[4]

With this in mind we can return to the idea that an individual's concern about *himself* must be taken as the model on which the concern of others is based. When my child is in pain she does not care that it is Jane who is in pain; the thought of herself as *that* individual, the individual with that history, does not enter into her concern in any way. If, then, the form of my concern about her is to be modelled on the form taken by her concern about herself something which is central to the concern which most feel for those close to them will drop out. I am not saying that our concern would be *weaker* than it now is (partly because I am too unclear what 'basing my concern about her on the model of her concern about herself' would come to); but something will be missing. While some may hold that what drops out – the thought of this as that particular individual – ought to drop out, not everyone will agree. The suggestion that the ideal form of concern about others must be modelled on the individual's concern about himself is not one which we *have* to accept; and in so far as one holds that the idea of this as being the particular individual that he is, the idea of the identity of the individual, is of central importance it is not a suggestion that one *will* accept.

When I am in pain there is a certain sense in which I do not care who is in pain. We might express this by saying that my thought about myself is, in this respect, essentially impersonal: the idea of particularity, of the *particular* person, which characterises our thought about certain other people does not here characteristically play a role in our thought about ourselves. The point is a more general one. Compare my concern about the fact that my child is *going* to suffer severe pain tomorrow with my concern about the fact that I am. Of course, there is, in the latter case, one sense in which I care who is going to suffer. I care that it is going to be *me*; that is, we might say, I care that the individual who is going to suffer is the very same person as this one, the one that I am. As before, however, *which* individual that is is quite irrelevant to my concern. Now it is clearly quite different when it is my child who is going to suffer. Indeed, we could say that the situation is reversed here. That it is 'John' who is going to suffer is of crucial importance to me; and that it is 'This one' (pointing to a person) is, in itself, of no importance to me. (Imagine that I discover that this one is not, as I took him to be, John.)

Consider now a case from further afield: my concern about how I act. For various reasons this case is potentially more complex than that involving physical pain. Consider, for example, a situation in which I feel terrible about the way in which I have treated someone. One form that my feelings could take might be expressed in this way: 'This life (that is, mine) has been tarnished with this terrible action.' Here it seems that there is a sense in which thoughts about the identity of this individual who has done this terrible thing are playing an important role. My feelings crucially involve thoughts about *who* I am: for example, 'The Emperor's son' or 'The man who did that fine action, and that one and that.' There is, presumably, a variety of kinds of case we can imagine here at least some of which, most will want to say, involve moral self-indulgence. However that may be, it is clear that my feelings need not take any such form as this. My horror that 'I did that' may be totally impersonal in the sense that no thoughts about *who* I am need be a part of it. Compare this with my horror that this man, who is my son John, has acted terribly. The thought that it is *John* who acted terribly is fundamental to the character of my horror.

Finally here, consider our 'horror at death'. I place these words in quotes in order to stress that there is an important ambiguity here. On the one hand there is the terror that I may feel in the face of my own death, and, on the other, the desolation that I may feel on the death of a loved one. Now this ambiguity is important in that the relation between these forms of 'horror' is a good bit more distant than might be supposed. One might, for example, imagine that they are connected in this way: 'Death is a terrible thing. It is because of this that both my own death is something to be feared and the death of loved ones something to be very upset about.' Well, no doubt a lot of people will find things to complain about in *that*. The asymmetry which I want to stress, and which is obscured in this formulation, is, however, this. My fear at my own death characteristically has nothing to do with a horror that this in-dividual, DC, will no longer exist. That the life which is nearing its end is *this* life – the life with these particular features – is characteristically quite irrelevant to the form of my fear. In this sense, as with fear of pain, I do not care *who* it is that is dying. By contrast, a conception of *who* this is is central to my concern about the death of a loved one. That it is John who is dying or has died, that particular individual, the individual with that particular history, is what is unbearable.

The way of speaking which I have just criticised does not give a primacy to the first person point of view. It at any rate leaves open the possibility that the 'terribleness of death' can be recognised in an equally fundamental way from either the first or third person perspective. Thomas Nagel seems to present us with what is, perhaps, a more tempting view in the second sentence of the following quotation:

> Your relation to your own death is unique, and here if anywhere the subjective standpoint holds a dominant position. By the same token, the internal standpoint will be vicariously dominant in your attitude towards the deaths of those to whom you are so close that you see the world through their eyes.[5]

Well, there is *something* in this. If I care for another I will feel for him in the terror that he feels in the face of death. That terror may be important in my thought about his death both before and after he has died.[6] Assuming that I do not think he *has* an 'internal standpoint' after he has died that is all the identifying with his standpoint that I will be able to do. Now, if this was the whole of, or even the most important part of, the story concerning my thought about the death of a loved one the ambiguity in the phrase 'horror at death' would be less significant than I suggested; the form of the two kinds of horror which I distinguished would be very closely related. It is, however, fairly clearly *not* like that. When I vicariously adopt the 'internal standpoint' of my dying child, wife or mother I find a glaring gap in the concern that is felt. What is for me an overwhelmingly significant fact – the fact that it is *Jane* who is dying – is barely registered in the internal standpoint. We are not, then, going to get clear about the way in which the idea of who this is enters into our thought about death by giving *the* primary place to the first-person point of view.

The suggestion which I have been moving towards in this section might be expressed in this way. The notion of a person has its fundamental place within the context of a personal relationship. It is in our thought about those who are close to us that the idea of someone as a particular individual is seen most clearly at work. By contrast the first-person point of view is, in a sense, essentially impersonal. That I am this particular individual does not characteristically matter to me in that way. Thus, if we take the first-person point of view as the model on which all our thought about people is to be based the idea of the particular individual will lose the crucial hold which it now has on our thinking about certain individuals. In my next chapter I will say something about views of this kind: views, that is, within which the idea of the particular individual has no significant place. In Chapter 13 I will return to the personal: suggesting how ways of thinking which have their central home within the context of a personal relationship might be linked with a 'metaphysical' picture of what a person is.

12

Self and No-self

The mental and the material are really here,
But here there is no human being to be found.
For it is void and merely fashioned like a doll,
Just suffering piled up like grass and sticks.[1]

Buddha has spoken thus: 'O Brethren, actions do exist, and also
their consequences, but the person that acts does not. There is
no one to cast away this set of elements and no one to assume a
new set of them. There exists no Individual, it is only a conventional name, given to a set of elements.

But setting aside some metaphysicians of this kind, I may
venture to affirm of the rest of mankind, that they are nothing
but a bundle or collection of perceptions, which succeed each
other with an inconceivable rapidity, and are in a perpetual flux
and movement. ... They are the successive perceptions only,
that constitute the mind.[2]

These remarks might initially strike one as hopelessly obscure.
How, one might ask, can there be an action without there being
someone who performs it? Similarly, the suggestion that the
person just *is* the 'successive perceptions' – the denial that the
person is something that *has* the perceptions and so is quite distinct
from them – is not easy to grasp. The image of a pain which is not
had by anything, is one which, I think, baffles most of us even if we
are not sure how to say just what is wrong with it.

One way in which one might try to bring out the difficulty here
would be by way of the fact that there is no way to identify which
pain we are speaking of without making a reference to which
individual is in pain. Closely related to this is the connection
between, on the one hand, beliefs about the existence of pains and,
on the other, responses of pity. If there is a pain there is a place for
pity; and so for the question 'Who, or what, is to be pitied?' Thus,
when, in a defence of a Buddhist ethical outlook, Steven Collins
writes 'But I do want to see suffering-experience, and *not* persons,

as basic to moral theory and practice'[3] we should, from one point of view, be struck by the absurdity of his suggestion. It is as if, confronted with a man with a severe pain in his leg, Collins would say: 'It is not the man I am worried about; it is what he has in his leg that concerns me.' This, surely, is not simply morally outrageous. Indeed, it is not that at all. We simply do not understand it. For what would it be to be concerned about a pain except by way of being concerned about the person (or animal) who is in pain?

Philosophers, such as Hume, who conduct their thinking about 'the self' exclusively in first-person terms are not likely to be impressed by these points. When it is my own pain I am thinking of can I not identify the pain for myself directly: without, that is, an intermediary identification of a person? With this, when it is my own pain that I am concerned about it is far less clear in what sense a concern about the pain necessarily involves a concern about the *person* in pain. The tendencies to turn away from the sight of the suffering person, to comfort the person, to look into the person's face, and so on are central to my response to another's pain but seem to have only weak, if any, analogues in my response to my own pain. A philosopher who insists that my thought and concern about myself is the model on which all genuine thought and concern about persons is to be built may, then, hold that these difficulties that I have touched on are merely superficial. Though he will, of course, owe us an account of just how my concern about another's pain is to be modelled on the form characteristic of my concern about my own.

I will not add to my earlier remarks, in Chapters 4 and 6, which bear on these points. For I wish to explore a rather different way in which we may be able to make sense of the denial of the reality of 'the self' or 'the individual'. We can approach this by noting that the way in which I spoke of 'which individual is in pain' contains a significant ambiguity. Thus, to the question 'Who is in pain?' different kinds of answer can be given. On the one hand there are answers of the form 'That man' or 'The woman next door'. On the other hand, there are answers which make an implicit or explicit reference to the individual's past: for example 'The man who used to work here' or 'John'. Now the reference to history here may be simply a matter of convenience. The nurse would have said 'The man in the bed at the end is in severe pain', only he has disappeared so she is forced to say instead 'The man who had the fit last week'. She picks out the individual in this way simply because in these particular circumstances, this is the most effective way of leading the doctor to the relevant patient. In other cases, however, the reference to history functions in a totally different way. The contrast comes out clearly if we think of a case in which the doctor knows who is in pain in the sense I have just been speaking of but has not yet realised that the man in pain is the man he used to work with, or John, his son. Now the reference to history here is not simply the most convenient way of locating the individual in question. For he had already done that. The vital new thing which he has now learned is who this, already located, individual is. To insist that 'There exists no Individual, it is only a conventional name given to a set of elements' may be, in part, to insist that the significance which we attach to the question of *who* this is rests on a misunderstanding. ('At the beginning of their conversation the king politely asks the monk his name, and receives the following reply: 'Sir, I am known as "Nagasena"; my fellows in the religious life address me as "Nagasena". Although my parents gave (me) the name "Nagasena" ... it is just an appellation, a form of speech, a description, a conventional usage. "Nagasena" is only a name, for no person is found here.'[4]

How might this claim be defended? One possible defence would run through a criticism of the way in which we generally think of people as beings who persist through time. For the idea that a proper name is something more than a convenient, conventional device for identifying which individual one is speaking of is directly tied up with that way of thinking: if there is no significant sense, no 'deep' sense, in which it can be said that an individual at one time is the *same* individual as one at another time then the reference to history, to who this is, embodied in a proper name is not something of significance.

I want to focus on this more general claim – the claim that there is no significant sense in which people can be said to persist through time – for a moment. The claim would be that, for example, there is no significant sense in which it can be said that this person in front of us now is the one who broke a vase last week. To insist that there is no 'significant' or 'deep' sense in which this can be said is not to deny that there is *any* sense in which it can be said. When we say '*He* is the one who broke the vase' there is some relevant connection between this man before us and the man who broke the vase; when I say it was him and not her who did it I am latching onto some relevant distinction between the two; but the connection between this man and the man who broke the vase does not have the kind of importance which we generally ascribe to it. Indeed, in itself it is of no importance at all. The only importance which such identity claims can ever have lies in the way in which they may serve as a guide to the future. One example of this concerns the group of reactions connected with the notion of desert. To insist that there is no 'deep' sense in which it can ever be said that this individual is the one who did a certain thing is, in part, to insist that remorse, blame, resentment, gratitude, punishment, and so on are never in place except in so far as they are attempts to modify the individual's future behaviour. That it was him that did it is not in itself a fact of any significance.[5]

Another way in which the claim that there is no deep sense in which we are beings who persist through time would find expression in our thought is this. I do, in practice, have a quite special form of concern about what I think of as 'my' future well-being. For example, I fear the pain that 'I' will feel and fear 'my' death as I do not fear anyone else's. Now the suggestion is that the connection between me now and the individual who will suffer pain tomorrow is not of a kind which justifies this special form of concern. There is *some* connection between me now and the individual who will be in pain tomorrow, and so the claim that it will be me who is in pain is not *completely* empty. Further, I might legitimately attach a *certain* kind of significance to this connection. For example, knowing that it will be 'me' who is in the dentist's chair I have some indication of how to go about reducing the pain that will be felt; indeed, I know that the pain that would otherwise have been felt can be eliminated altogether if I ensure that this body is given an anaesthetic. Further, what I think of as 'my' well-being might legitimately be of special interest to me in the sense that I am generally particularly well placed to have some control over it. This, however, is the only kind of special interest which could be appropriate. That it will be 'me' who suffers should not, as I put it, *in itself* have any significance for me. I may be upset that there will be suffering. The character of my distress should, however, in no way be affected by my recognition that it will be 'me' who is in pain. For that fact, the fact that it will be 'me', is not a deep fact.

How is it to be decided whether the kind of connections which hold between an individual at one time and 'the same individual' at another time are 'deep' ones in the relevant sense? Many of the more familiar arguments to show that they are not are the other side of considerations which arose in Chapter 9. The most common, perhaps, is that which appeals to the fact that there is nothing unchanging in us. Collins writes: 'For Buddhist thought, the idea that at any given moment of experience there is a self beyond whatever particular bodily or mental phenomena are occurring, is equivalent to the idea that there is a permanent self which endures changelessly.'[6] This idea appears to be one which is shared by many, at least by many philosophers, in Western society. It is then argued that there is nothing in us which endures *changelessly*, and so that the idea of a persisting self is an illusion; or, at any rate, is not one which goes 'deep'. I argued, however, that there appears to be no reason to accept the idea that only what is changeless is rightly thought of as a persisting self, and suggested that that idea may rest on a failure to acknowledge that the *past* can matter to us. Be that as it may, in the absence of a demonstration that our present practices require the idea of a changeless self the connection in Buddhist thought which Collins speaks of appears to be no more than an arbitrary stipulation. For, on the face of it, we are in practice ready to accept that this is, in the important sense, 'the same person' while recognising clearly that he has changed. Is the mother's love for her developing child dependent on the thought that there is *something* in him which is unchanging? Indeed, might not the particular character of her love be crucially dependent on the fact that he is in a constant process of change?

Another argument here might appeal more directly to a claim that 'continuity of the human being' is obviously not a 'deep' connection between an individual at different stages of his life. Nor, it might be said, is there any other connection which holds between what we think of as different stages of the life of a single person which can be thought of as 'deep': there simply are no connections running through the 'life of an individual' which could justify the significance which we attach to questions concerning who this is. As I argued in Chapter 9, however, any argument of this form clearly needs to be supplemented with an account of how it is to be determined what kinds of connection are 'deep' in the relevant sense. If it is replied that it is clear, at any rate, that a merely physical or bodily continuity is not a deep connection in the sense needed we can ask: is it equally clear that the same should be said of the connection involved in being the same *human being*?

(ii) We may understand better the confidence with which it is sometimes suggested that certain connections are not deep ones by standing back a little. In my initial explanation of what the terms 'deep' and 'significant' amount to in this context I spoke of the changes in our lives called for by the claim that there is no deep sense in which it can be said that an individual at one time is the same individual as one at another time. This might seem to suggest that, on my presentation, to deny the reality of the self will simply be to make certain claims about what we ought to feel and how we ought to act. It will then be objected that this cannot be right since to deny the reality of the self is to make a metaphysical claim, a claim about what kinds of things there are in the world; any associated ethical claims, claims about how we ought to live, are *consequences* of that. Thus, Steven Collins quotes with approval Thomas Nagel's insistence that 'moral and other practical require-ments are grounded in a metaphysics of action, and finally in a metaphysics of the person',[7] adding that this is in accordance with Buddhist thinking. It is assumed, then, that we can agree in our metaphysics no matter what ethical perspective we bring to the discussion; and as a result of that agreement resolve our ethical differences.

If we approach the issue with this assumption we are likely to conclude fairly rapidly that any significant connection between an individual at different stages of his life must lie below the surface of the persisting human being: that what is deep in the ethical sense must be deep also in the sense of lying behind the observable empirical world. For it seems clear that no agreement about connections at the ordinary level of observation will *inevitably* resolve our ethical differences – will bring us into harmony no matter what ethical perspective each of us brings to the discussion. If, for example, we can imagine someone in whose life the notion of a particular individual – an individual with a particular history – plays no role, no amount of talk about 'This is the same human being as the one who . . .' seems likely, by itself, to make much difference. Thus, we will conclude that connections at some other level are what is needed; and that if they do not exist the significance which we attach to identity claims is misplaced.

We are sometimes told that it has now become clear that the thing that was needed at a deeper level does not exist.[8] We need to ask, however, how any connection at this other level would, had it existed, have done any better in meeting Nagel's requirement. The insistence that a metaphysics of the person is prior to all moral and practical demands is the insistence that it be possible to show that we are *right* to see significance in claims about who a particular individual is. Now if behind the persisting human being there lay a persisting Cartesian Ego how would that help? To the extent that it is imaginable that someone should fail to see any significance in the fact that 'This is the same human being as the one who . . .' it is, surely, equally imaginable that someone should fail to see any significance in the fact that 'Behind the human being in front of you now lies the very same Cartesian Ego as the one which . . .'. In so far as what we are after is a metaphysical grounding in this sense it is quite unclear how we move a step nearer to it in going 'behind the surface' of the human being. (That, of course, is unargued assertion. However, in the absence of a serious attempt to make what I suggest is unclear clear I am not sure what else can be done here; and I do not know of any such attempt.)

The vague picture that we had of a kind of entity that would, in the relevant sense, *justify* the ways in which we care about questions of identity over time is one that collapses under scrutiny. If, at this point, we continue to insist that our ethics must, in that sense, be grounded in metaphysics we are, then, bound to conclude that what has been shown is that our normal thought on these matters is more hopelessly adrift than we had supposed. It is not simply that there *is* no persisting self. There *could not* have been such a thing. With that, the idea of the *particular* individual, an individual with a particular history, is, we will have to conclude, revealed to be one which could not conceivably find any foothold in the world and so one which will play no role in the life of anyone who has thought the matter through clearly. A name 'is just an appellation, a form of speech, a description, a conventional usage', for the forms of concern which are linked with the use of personal names are not 'grounded in' a recognition of what is to be found in the world.

I stated dogmatically that it is unclear how 'going behind the surface' of the human being could take us any closer to finding a justification, a grounding, for the kinds of significance which we sometimes attach to the question of who this is. There is a response to this that needs to be considered. It might be said that my experience of myself, of my own identity, occupies a special position here. Thus, in my own case a concern about *who* this is is transparently in place in a way such that no justification for having that concern is needed; and so the character of my concern about who another is can be seen to be in place by reflecting on the way in which it matters to the other that she is the particular individual that she is. In this way, the first-person point of view plays a crucial part in what I have called the grounding of our ethics in metaphysics.

When explicitly stated this thought is perhaps considerably less tempting than is the parallel move in the attempt to 'ground' our reactions to the sensations of others (see Chapter 4). This is, I take it, partly because it is not particularly tempting to think that my concern about the fact that, for example, I am the one who did a certain thing is 'transparently in place' in the required sense. No doubt we might say to a philosopher troubled by a certain form of scepticism: 'Just place yourself in a situation where "you" will in a moment inevitably feel intense pain and try to doubt that the individual who will feel the pain has anything to do with *you*; and try, in practice, to doubt that it *matters* that it will be you'; but would the force of our appeal to the philosopher's personal response in a real situation be any less direct if we asked him to conduct the experiment with his child, rather than with himself? If it is replied that the latter case does not offer a route to the kind of 'metaphysical grounding' that we are seeking, since the response reflects our emotional make-up rather than an intuition of a truth, we can ask: are the reasons for speaking in those terms here any less good than they are in the case of my response to my own imminent suffering?

Nevertheless, here, as there, we do often find philosophers giving a special place to the first-person point of view; as if once we are clear about the individual's thought about his own identity his thought about the identity of others will fall into place by itself. Now I suggested that, in so far as we understand this suggestion in the case of physical sensations, 'justifications' of this form are going to result in some pretty radical criticisms of our thought about the sensations of others. In one respect at least the same point holds here. For, as I argued in Chapter 11, there is a sense in which most of us do not characteristically care who we ourselves are.

I do, of course, care that it is I who am in pain, that it will be I who am in pain tomorrow, that it was I who made that clever remark, and so on. So the more general claim that I spoke of – the claim that there is no significant sense in which people can be said to persist through time – is not likely to emerge from an approach which gives this kind of priority to the first person point of view. That it is *DC* that will be in pain or made that remark is not, however, characteristically of any importance to me. Thus, if we take the individual's thought about his own identity as the model on which his thought about others is to be based the concern about *who* this is which finds its most direct linguistic expression in certain uses of personal names will, at the very least, be dramatically truncated. Names will emerge as no more than conventional devices which serve to direct another's attention to the person we are speaking of. This line of thought, then, will lead us to the more restricted form of no-self view which I spoke of without running through the more general version of that thesis (see p. 171).

In this section I have sketched two related routes by which we might reach the conclusion that 'There exists no Individual', where this thesis is understood in the way I have outlined. Central to the first is the fact that, if we dissociate ourselves sufficiently from the ways in which we generally care about questions of personal identity and ask what features of the world provide a justification for those forms of concern, we are almost bound to conclude that nothing does or, indeed, could. The second route turns on the fact that, if we take the individual's thought about himself as the model on which his thought about others is to be built, we will find no significant place in the latter for the notion of a *particular* individual. It is not, I think, necessary for me to present my own response to these lines of thought here. Instead, I will simply note that there are strong strands in Western philosophy, at least since the time of Descartes, which *should* push one in this direction. The idea that we are only really getting at the world in so far as our picture of it is quite independent of the way in which anything matters to us – that, in this sense, metaphysics precedes ethics – has been a fairly central one. The idea that the individual's thought about himself is, in some sense, more fundamental than his thought about others has also been of crucial importance. These ideas may push us first towards the familar view that 'the self', if there is such a thing, is an unchanging core which lies behind the publicly observable human being. In so far, however, as we are pushed to this conclusion by considerations of this form the position is quite unstable. For that line of reasoning, properly applied, must carry us on to the view that our normal thought about the identity of individuals is confused in the radical sense that nothing in the world *could* have corresponded to it. Philosophers such as Hume and Parfit who defend some form of 'no-self' view have ended up in the right place given the starting point of the tradition in which they are working.[9] (Or rather, they have seen further than others. Whether *this* stopping point is a stable one is a further question.)

The two strands of Modern Western Philosophy of which I have spoken are, I think, characteristically expressions of philosophical confusion. Thus, it has been widely thought that if the notion of a person is going to get off the ground at all we will find the key to it in the first-person point of view. Much of this book has, in one way or another, been directed towards the conclusion that this is simply a mistake. I should, in conclusion, stress that I have not defended the claim that a concern for persons – in the senses I have spoken of – *must* be central to any life that we could conceivably find admirable. There may be rich traditions within which something akin to the 'impersonal' approach, which I have suggested is linked with the first-person point of view, is dominant. I have neither the knowledge nor the imagination to make any judgement on that.

13
Persons and the Personal

i) My thought about my wife or child involves an idea of her as a unique, irreplaceable individual who, in a significant sense, persists through time despite radical changes in her characteristics. This is the picture which is embodied in my responses to her. Now, how do these facts about our feelings towards and treatment of certain particular individuals connect with the general 'metaphysical' question: 'Are people creatures of that kind?' In my last chapter I suggested that if one views this relationship in a certain way one will, if one is thinking clearly, find oneself pushed towards (if not beyond) some form of the denial of the reality of the self. The alternative way of viewing this relationship which I would favour should be clear from my treatment of other dimensions of our thought about people in Parts I and II. In brief, we should not think of a 'metaphysical account of what a person is' as something which might be established prior to and independently of one's commitment to particular forms of concern for people; and thus as something which might justify that form of concern. Rather, a metaphysical picture of persons is inevitably an expression of one's commitment to a certain ideal in one's relations with others.

The other main suggestion in my last chapter was this: if one starts with the idea that the first-person point of view is the model on which all of our thought about people is to be based – if one takes that to represent the ideal for one's relations with others – then one will, or should, arrive at a position within which the notion of a particular individual has no fundamental place.

We can usefully place against the background of these two points a comparison between the injunction to 'Love thy neighbour as thyself' and that to 'Love all mankind as the mother loves her only son'.[1] Each of these injunctions presents us with a model on which our thought about all mankind is to be based. In the first, the model is my thought about myself; in the second, my thought about my child. The injunctions assume, correctly I take it, that these models are clear to us in the sense that what is appealed to in each case is a readily recognisable pattern of concern. Now, at a certain level[2] one should, I think, be struck by the fact that the model appealed to in each case is very different. The 'love', if that is the word, which most of us can be said to feel towards ourselves is utterly different in form from that which most parents can be said to feel towards their children. Various aspects of this have emerged at earlier points in this book. (See in particular Chapters 4 and 6.) In Part III, however, the contrast between the 'impersonal' character of my thought about myself and the 'personal' character of my thought about those I care for has had a central place. It is in my thought about those others with whom I have close personal relationships that the notion of a *person*, the notion of a *particular* individual, has its original home. To hold that persons are irreplaceable beings who persist through radical change is, I am suggesting, to hold that the form of concern which is central to such relationships is the model on which my attitude towards every human being is to be based. I want in this chapter to try to say something about what it might be to view all mankind as persons, as particular individuals, in this sense.

There are important obstacles to the idea that the Buddhist injunction – the injunction to 'Love all mankind as the mother loves her only son' – presents us with an attractive, or indeed coherent, ideal; and so to the idea that all of mankind should, or could, be thought of as persons in this sense. These obstacles are closely linked with two related contrasts which have a powerful impact on many philosophical discussions of ethics and of the notion of a person. The first is the contrast between egoism and altruism; the second, that between the individual's thought about himself and his thought about complete strangers. The idea that the notion of 'moral duty' must occupy a central place in any portrayal of our ethical life is connected in a pretty obvious way with these dichotomies. Now in all of this my thought about those to whom I am close tends to be set to one side; as if this can somehow be fitted into the picture later on without any significant addition to, or modification of, these basic categories. Once, for whatever reason, one has begun to view the matter in this way one may start to find further grounds for thinking that this *must* be the way to view it. For it is all too easy to view personal relationships through these eyes and so find nothing there but a corrupted altruism or a mitigated egoism. With this, the idea that we might here find a distinctive way of thinking which could provide a model for our thought about all mankind is too readily dismissed.

Consider the parent's concern about her child which I have appealed to in trying to give substance to what I have called 'the idea of this as being the particular individual that he is'. It is commonly suggested that the parent's love for her child is essentially selfish; and so while the idea of this as being the particular individual that he is may have a central place here it is not an idea which appears in an attractive light: 'In so far as the idea of the particular individual plays a role in the parent's concern it does so in the form of the thought that it is *her* child who is suffering; the relation which the child has to her is what is central to the parent's thought. Further', it will be said, 'the form which the parent's concern for her child characteristically takes involves giving a special place to her child in the sense that she attaches *more* importance to the well-being of this child than she does to the well-being of others. If, then, the parent's concern for her child is the model on which we are to understand the notion of caring *who* a particular individual is that notion is not one with which we should have much sympathy. Indeed, in so far as the suggestion is that we should extend this form of concern to all mankind we cannot even understand it. For the *exclusiveness* of the concern, the fact that this child is to be given *preferential* treatment, is precisely what makes it the form of concern that it is.'

Well, I need not respond directly to these claims about the way in which parents care for their children, nor to the assumption that these features of a parent's love are obviously objectionable. For when I appeal to this model it is not *these* features of the parent's concern that interest me. Thus, while it is obviously true that the mother does characteristically care more for the well-being of her child than for the well-being of others, this fact is not the same fact as the fact that she cares *who* is suffering when her child is suffering – at least in the sense that concerns me. This comes out in the fact that a mother with two children might have no *preference* concerning which of her children should suffer, and yet it might still matter desperately to her which of her children is suffering. If she hears news that one of her children is in severe pain there may be no room at all for the hope that it is one rather than the other who is suffering and yet it may still be of crucial importance to her to find out which one it is. The precise form which her concern about her child's suffering takes is inseparable from the thought that it is *this* individual who is suffering. Perhaps the point comes into focus most clearly if one thinks of the kind of agony that could be involved in a situation in which a parent has to choose *which* of her children is to suffer.

Closely related to that worry about the appeal to parental love as an ideal was the suggestion that the thought of this child as *my* child, a consideration of the child's relation to *me*, is central to such love. Again, without denying that a thought of that kind often plays an important role one can insist that there is no reason to believe that that is the whole story. As I suggested in Chapter 9, the significance which the child's name has on the parent's lips cannot be represented in terms of that single feature of the child's history. There will, characteristically, be many other factors which enter in a crucial way into the parent's understanding of who this is. The significance of the mother's cry of horror 'It's John!' on realising that it is he who is in great danger, or of joy on realising that he has been saved, can only be brought out by telling a detailed story of the child's past. Further, while the parent's story of her son's past will involve references to herself – memories of interactions between herself and this boy will have a central place – there will also be much that involves no such references: she has many memories of her son's past in which she does not figure in any essential way.

With these points in mind we can return to the injunction to 'Love all mankind as the mother loves her only son.' It is clear that there are certain limits on how this can be taken; certain ways of thinking which are characteristic of a mother's concern for her child must drop out. What must drop out is not only features which many might, in any case, think of as suspect. A mother has a relationship with her child: is in constant interaction with her child.[3] The precise form taken by her love for her child can hardly be separated from, for example, the joy that she finds in playing with him. Now with the vast majority of mankind I have no relationship, in that sense, at all. Further, this, I think, can hardly be thought of as a *failing* on my part since the limits on what is possible in this direction are limits of sense. Just how rapidly we reach these limits will depend on the kind of relationship we have in mind and what we think is of value in relationships of that form. There are forms of relationship between people which most, in this culture, will agree are of central importance and necessarily exclusive: in the sense that it simply would not be *that* relationship if one of those involved had a similar relationship with another. Other forms of relationship are, in that respect, much more open. However, there are, I take it, always going to be limits. (As there are not, perhaps, in the Christian's conception of God's relationship with each of us. In this way, the idea that a parent's love for her child could serve as a model for God's love for each of us – an idea which is surely quite fundamental to Christian thought – may make a kind of sense which the command that *we* should love all others in this way could never make.)

Still, even once all this has dropped out something of importance will be left. What is left is the concern about a *particular* person, about *who* this is, which is tied to the idea of this as an individual with a history. That form of concern, that understanding of others, is at least part of what is highlighted by the injunction to 'Love all mankind as the mother loves her only son.'

I can, perhaps, best indicate what I have in mind here by focusing on aspects of our thought about strangers in which this idea already has some place. Consider, for example, the horror that we may feel at the death of strangers. Now no doubt our reactions to the news that millions of lives are threatened by famine are complex. We think of the physical suffering, of the anguish of the mother whose child dies, and so on. Once everything of this kind has been said, however, there is something left over which needs to be understood. That so many are dying is, in itself, terrible. Now just how are we to say what is terrible about death? There are powerful currents in contemporary philosophy which make the thought of death as terrible extraordinarily difficult to understand. What is terrible is not, I take it, to be found in the fact that there is a shortage of people in the world, nor in the fact that the loss of a life means the loss of a certain number of net happiness units in the future.[4] Apart from anything else nothing along these lines would explain the asymmetries in our attitudes towards death and the fact that a child was not conceived when one could have been. There appears to be no room here for any way of understanding the terribleness of death except in terms of the fact that the *death* of an individual is the end of a *life*.

Of course, some think there is nothing terrible in death; and perhaps most would insist that not all deaths are terrible. For example, there is, perhaps, nothing terrible in the death of a man of 90 who has lived a rich and complete life. This need have nothing to do with the fact that death may, in this case, be a welcome relief from suffering: death may be that in the case of a teenager who is suffering terribly with an incurable disease and yet it still be the case that her death is tragic. So there is more that needs to be said here. My aim has simply been to bring out a background which is needed if there is ever to be a place for the thought that an individual's death – and not simply the effect which the death has on others – is tragic. The thought of this as a particular individual, an individual with a particular history, even though it may be a history of which I know nothing, already plays a significant role in the thought of many here.

Closely linked with this is a noteworthy feature of our response to the sufferings of people we do not know. While a clear recognition of the suffering of strangers can be horrifying that horror can take on a quite new dimension when it is brought home to us that those who are suffering are *individuals* in the sense that they are beings that have a life which is as intricate in detail as are the lives of those we know well. Once a name and a life have been given to the face that we see on television a place is created for a significantly enriched form of concern.

Beside this feature of our response to the sufferings of strangers we can place what I have spoken of as the 'impersonal' approach which is linked with the emphasis on the first-person point of view. The approach is impersonal in this sense: while the fact that there is suffering is significant, where the suffering falls – that, for example, it is John, this individual with this history, that is in pain – is of no importance. One might equally put this by saying that the importance of the information that it is John who is in pain will lie only in the way in which it tells us whom we must attend to if we are to relieve the pain. This point is connected with others which arise out of earlier chapters of this book. As pity characteristically plays no role in my thought about myself so it will, within the first-person approach, disappear from my thought about the suffering of others. Again, the kind of horror which is inextricably bound up with the sight of suffering will, at the very least, be radically truncated; as will that dimension of the pleasure I may take in another's joy which is closely tied to my observation of its expression. For the behavioural expression of my own suffering or joy plays virtually no role in the significance which these have for me. More generally, the other's bodily form and expressive behaviour may feature in my thought about her as little more than a *ground* for the judgement that I make about her. In these senses, to the extent that I take my thought about myself as the model for my thought about all mankind the idea of the *human being*, and, further, of the *particular* human being, will play no significant role in my thought.

I have spoken of our response to death and of our response to suffering, suggesting that in reactions which most of us exhibit in some measure we see a faint reflection of what it might be to fully acknowledge the particularity of others in all of one's thought about them. I want finally here to consider one other, closely related, feature of our thought. This feature is connected with an unsettling impression which may have been created by ways in which I have spoken in earlier chapters. I suggested that we can see another's pain or anger in their behaviour and expression in a way such that there is no room here for philosophical scepticism. Now this suggestion may seem to involve a failure to acknowledge an important and real sense in which the other is *not* to be seen in the 'surface' which we encounter. It may, that is, seem to involve a failure to acknowledge the role which sensitivity and imagination play in coming to understand another even when they are completely open with us. Now worries of this kind may push us towards something akin to a dualist understanding of the idea that the essential thing is hidden behind the publicly observable surface of the other; and towards the idea that identification with the other's point of view – the attempt to view their life 'from the inside' – is what is fundamental in the attempt to think of them as we should.

A preliminary response to these worries, and so to the pressure to move in this direction, would involve the insistence that we should not think of what is presented to us as simply what is taking place 'at the present moment' – whether we understand that phrase in terms of what can be captured in a photograph or rather more generously. We can add to this that it may take imagination and sensitivity to discern the significant patterns in an individual's behaviour over time. Thus, if 'the surface' is what is observable at an instant and without effort then we can acknowledge that much that is crucial 'lies behind the surface' without understanding this phrase in the ways suggested.

These points, however, may not entirely meet the worry. That there is a further sense in which what is crucial lies 'behind the surface' becomes clear when we reflect on, for example, our attitude towards the senile. In this case, it might be said, sensitivity and imagination of the kind of which I have just spoken may not reveal much in the way of rich and significant patterns; and, it might be added, even once we have done everything which there is to be done in that direction our attitude towards the senile can still fail dramatically to be what it should be. There is a further kind of imaginative work to be done: work which we might characterise in terms of remembering that this is a *person*, an individual, and not simply the current occupant of bed number 72.

Timothy Sprigge has, in discussion, presented the point in the following way:

> Nurses in hospital often have a particular way of reacting to old people, say old ladies. The old lady in a hospital evokes a particular kind of reaction, emotional reaction – one of sympathy and so on – but very often it is a slightly patronising, in a reversed sort of way a motherly approach to the dear old lady; and, as somebody said, what one should remember is that the old lady is little Maggie Smith who teased her sister or was teased by her sister in class years ago. So a human form can be so misleading. Take another kind of case. Some old person goes in who has been a great writer of some kind. The nurse may just see an old person like that and a stock set of sympathetic reactions may be evoked. All I am getting at is that the human form can be awfully misleading of what is really there inviting some kind of communication or some kind of accord and I prefer to think of it in terms of what the other person really is as being another world; and what you've got to do is not so much think about that form as think about the world that that person is experiencing.[5]

Sprigge's suggestion in his last sentence is that what is often missing in our responses to the old is sufficient reflection on what life is like for that person: the gap in our thought is to be filled by identifying with the other's point of view. Now while there is a common form of failure of imagination which could be character-ised in this way the rest of what Sprigge says appears to do nothing to support the claim that this is *the* characteristic form of failure in these circumstances. For in most of what he says the emphasis is on the idea that this person has a past – has lived a particular life. The failure of imagination of which we are often guilty is a failure to keep this fact clearly in mind. What lies below the observable surface is the individual's history. (Sprigge went on to argue that the past experience always enters into the present experience in a rich way. I suspect that we are prone to exaggeration here. We feel that what is of significance to us *must* be found in the present; and so if the past is to play a role it must be by way of some reflection of it in the present. In any case, even if there is truth in Sprigge's suggestion it does nothing to support the idea that the past itself does not have an ineliminable role to play here.)

On the face of it some kind of distinction can be made between this point about the significance of the individual's past and that concerning the patterns which are to be seen in an individual's life over time. Thus, in a particular case there may be few rich and significant patterns to be seen in the life of an old man – either because of a decline in his capacities or because he has been placed in an environment in which there is little space for the patterns which formerly characterised his life. Yet his history remains. Still, the points are clearly closely linked and perhaps there is a perspective from which they would begin to merge; for the distinction between them turns, in part, on a contrast between 'the present' and 'the past' which will gradually dissolve the 'further back' one stands.[6]

Remembering that this is a *person* is, at least in part, remembering that this individual has a past. It is, further, only in terms of this fact that we can fully articulate what it is that is, or may be, distressing about the condition of the senile. Certainly part of the distress may be tied up with, for example, a recognition of frustrations which many of those in such a condition may face. There is, however, something else here which has nothing to do with the idea that these people *mind* being in this condition. To capture this further dimension we must, I think, recognise the way in which our understanding of what is happening *now* cannot be articulated without a rich reference to the past. The thought of this as a particular individual, where that means 'an individual with a particular past', is crucial to the form which our concern here may take.

It is worth, at this point, returning briefly to death. For those, such as Sprigge and Nagel, who give *the* fundamental place to the first-person point of view the death of a human being represents a *complete* break in the history of this extended, tangible being.[7] If, however, one does not hold that the core of a recognition of another as a person lies in identifying with his point of view one may allow that there is a significant continuity between the live and dead human being. For the extended, tangible being does not lose its history through death, and our understanding of what we are confronted with when we are confronted with a corpse is, or may be, crucially conditioned by our acknowledgement of its

history. Of course, there are those who say that the attitude which
we characteristically have towards the dead body of a loved one is
simply an emotional hangover: an expression of how we, under-
standably, *feel* rather than of a *recognition* of what we are confronted with. Reason needs to be given, however, for thinking that
matters *must* be viewed in that way.

But such a use of the contrast between 'feeling' and 'recognition'
might appear in a more general worry about the ways in which I
have been speaking. The worry which has arisen at various stages
in this book concern my characterisation of the relation between
our response to certain individuals and what I have called a
'metaphysical picture of persons'. I must now turn to this.

(ii) The ways of thinking of others, the forms of concern about
others, of which I have spoken in this chapter are ones which are
seen most clearly in the context of personal relationships between
individuals. They do, perhaps, often appear in their most striking
form in the case of a parent's thought about her child. For example,
the notion of 'duty' will often have no place at all in our characterisation of the way in which the sight of her child's suffering calls
forth a response from a mother. She cannot help but respond to
what she sees; just as she does not, on the death of her child, need
to 'remind herself' that this, the corpse, is the body of a human
being. Thus, it might be said that in a parent's concern for her child
we see something which could be characterised as a pure recognition of the reality of another.[8] To accept this suggestion would be
to accept that in so far as I do not respond to another in ways such
as these I am failing to reflect properly on what I am confronted
with. It is what the parent is confronted with that draws forth the
response, say of anguish, from him. The only thing necessary on
his part is that he should appreciate what he is confronted with.
His failure to respond to, say, the suffering or death of others in
this way, and the failure of others to respond to his child in this
way, is a reflection of his, and their, failure to fully grasp what is
going on.

Now it might be argued that this way of putting the matter – in
terms, that is, of recognising something about the other – is a
serious distortion. For the distinctive ways in which I respond to
my child are not to be explained, or not to be explained exclusively,
in terms of what I *recognise* in *him*. Even if the thought of the child's
relation to *me* does not enter into my conception of the child the

fact remains that the child does stand in a special relation to me and I only feel about him as I do because of my constant contact with him. In this sense a full explanation of the special attitude which I have towards him will necessarily involve a reference to me. Thus, while I will explain my response in a particular situation by saying 'It was John', my recognition that it was that particular individual does not, in itself, render my response intelligible. For others might have recognised that it was John – the individual with that history – and yet not have been moved as I was. My recognition of a truth about the world is not, then, enough to explain my response. We must grant that something over and above this, an emotion produced by my particular relation to him, is what is ultimately responsible for my distinctive reaction.

This protest might, for some, be brought into sharper focus in the following way. The thought of this child's death is unbearable to me. Yet it is only because I happen to have been located in this relation to him that it matters to me at all. In that sense my concern could be said to turn on something which is completely arbitrary; and, at the very least, I have to concede, it seems, that the child's relation to *me* is playing a crucial role in explaining my concern. Thus, if I could stand back completely from what in my life involves both self-reference and arbitrariness that concern would disappear. This brings out that the attempt to link this form of concern, in the strong way that I have, with an understanding of what we are confronted with is seriously misconceived.

The suggestion is that it is obviously confused to suppose that we see in a parent's concern for his child a pure recognition of the reality of another. What we see is, rather, an understandable, possibly even admirable, failure to dissociate oneself from one's own limited viewpoint. Now there are, no doubt, many reasons for saying that we rarely, if ever, see in a parent's concern for his child a pure form of the recognition of the reality of another. This, however, is not one of them. Or better, the suggestion that the situation is to be described in this way is not the result of an ethically neutral observation of the facts; it does itself reflect either philosophical confusion or a commitment to another ideal.

The philosophical confusion would be seen in the objection that to speak in the way I have is to overlook something on which I myself have layed great emphasis in this book: the fact that *any* response to what we are confronted with is dependent in some way on our constitution. 'To say that the only thing necessary on the parent's part is an "appreciation" or "recognition" of what is in front of him is', so the objection goes, 'to take for granted, what cannot here be taken for granted, that he has the psychological make-up which the vast majority of parents do happen to have. It is the role played here by this contingent fact about human beings which shows that this picture of the parent as recognising a truth cannot be sustained.' We need to ask, however, why cannot what is here said to be 'taken for granted' *be* taken for granted? Of course, in certain philosophical contexts this kind of thing needs to be emphasised; but it is precisely because of the universality of the philosophical point that there is nothing wrong with the way in which I spoke of 'appreciation' or 'recognition'. *Everything* that we speak of as 'recognising a truth' operates against a background of human responses which cannot themselves be spoken of as 'recognitions of a truth'. The role played by such a background in this case can, then, hardly, in itself, show that this way of speaking is misplaced. (Unless, of course, it is suggested that our normal way of speaking in some way rests on the assumption that things are not like this. I will try to say something more about this in the Postscript.)

There was another point at which the parent's response was said to be the product of something arbitrary. His view of the situation is coloured by the particular relation which he happens to have with the child. The role played by this personal emotional involvement, so the story goes, must rule out any description of his response in terms of his 'recognition of what he is confronted with'. The point might be expressed in this way: 'Others recognise too that this is Jane, yet they do not respond as the parent does. There must, then, be something over and above his recognition of what he is confronted with – a purely emotional element deriving from his close contact with the child – which plays the crucial role in bringing about the parent's response.'

One could only think that that is the way the situation must be described if one has *already* decided that the parent's response is not an ideal to be aspired to in our thought about all mankind. For, in the absence of that moral outlook, there is no reason to accept that the parent's close involvement with the child should be described in terms of a 'colouring' of his perception rather than in terms of a 'sharpening' of it. Why should we not say that this close contact enables him to see clearly what others see dimly, if at all? Others may be aware in an abstract way that this is an individual with her own particular history. Perhaps they even know something of that history – the history which makes her that particular individual, Jane. They have not, however, had the kind of contact with her which, for most of us, proves necessary to really bring these facts home to us.[9] Now some may find this way of describing the situation absurd. Perhaps it *is* absurd; but if it is, the absurdity is not to be revealed by some form of ethically neutral philosophical reflection. It is to be revealed by exposing an absurdity of some kind in the ideal which lies behind this description of the situation.

(iii) I have linked contrasting philosophical pictures of 'the self' with a contrast between the injunction to 'Love thy neighbour as thyself' and that to 'Love all mankind as the mother loves her only son', suggesting that these injunctions appear to present us with two very different models on which our thought about all mankind is to be based. The contrast between these models, as I have represented it, is closely linked, in an obvious way, with another contrast: that between the idea that, in my thought about strangers, I should, on the one hand, imagine that it was I who was in their position and, on the other, imagine that it was my child who was. Matching the way in which the first-person point of view is often given the fundamental position in the philosophy of mind is the way in which the first of these imaginative exercises is often given the fundamental position in ethics. Now formulated in these terms my main aim in this chapter has been to give some indication of what it might be to give that place to the second of the two exercises of the imagination. If I have succeeded in doing that then I have shown that the idea that every human being is an irreplaceable individual is not obviously a foolish one: not obviously an idea which collapses under philosophical scrutiny or cool empirical reflection on what people are actually like. What makes it a significant idea which must be taken seriously is the fact that we have, in a parent's concern for her child – or, more generally, in our concern for one with whom we have a personal relationship of some form – a model of what it would be to think, in practice, of all mankind in this way. We have a model of what it would be to feel that it matters *who* this is who is suffering, a model of what it would be to think of a stranger's death as something to be grieved over, and so on.

There has, however, been a gap in my discussion which I must now attempt to fill: a gap which is closely tied up with one dominant strand in much philosophical thinking about persons. This gap in what I have said is to be seen in the fact that my thought about *myself* features in a radically different way in the two injunctions. Each insists, at least implicitly, that I am to think of myself as simply one among others; but the direction of movement is different. In the first, my thought about myself is the model and the work to be done relates exclusively to my thought about others. By contrast, the second leaves a place for the idea that part of the task facing me is that of coming to love myself – coming to think of myself as a person.[10]

Thomas Nagel writes 'But everyone who is not either mystically transformed or hopelessly lacking in self-esteem regards his life and his projects as important, and not just to him.'[11] By contrast:

> When you look at your struggles as if from a great height, in abstraction from the engagement you have with this life because it is yours – perhaps even in abstraction from your identification with the human race – you may feel a certain sympathy for the poor beggar, a pale pleasure in his triumphs and a mild concern for his disappointments. And of course given that this person exists, there is little he can do but keep going till he dies, and try to accomplish something by the standards internal to his form of life. But it wouldn't matter all that much if he failed, and it would matter perhaps even less if he didn't exist at all.

It is important to see that there is at least room for the view that in these remarks Nagel gets things diametrically the wrong way round. Is there, first, a sense in which most of us regard our life and projects as important? Well, I struggle – perhaps virtually ignoring the cost to others – to relieve my own pain or avoid my own death. I give a great deal of time and energy to writing my book, looking after my garden or raising my children; and, perhaps, I struggle hard to lead a decent life. Is that to say that I think that any of these things *matters*: that I regard my life and projects as important? Well, it is clear that despite all this I need not, and most of us do not, think that others ought to give the time and energy to my life and projects which I myself do – either in the sense of directly aiming at the same goals themselves (trying to make my garden nice) or in the sense of trying to ensure that I myself achieve the goal. In that sense the time and effort which I give to my garden, or to acting decently, coexists, with no apparent tension, with the acknowledgement that my garden, or the decency of my life, is no *more* important than that of anyone else.[12]

But the point can, perhaps, be taken further. In her 'Spiritual Autobiography'[13] Simone Weil writes: 'Until then I had not had any experience of affliction, unless we count my own, which, as it was my own, seemed to me, to have little importance.' I do not think we need to regard Simone Weil as either 'mystically transformed' or as 'hopelessly lacking in self-esteem' (unless one says this of all of us) in order to understand this remark. For, to focus again on physical pain, despite the intensity of my struggles to avoid or be rid of it there is a sense in which my concern about my own sufferings could be said to be very 'thin'. Seen in the light of the rich response to the sufferings of someone I care about my response to my own pain may appear as little more than a violent reflex; and in that sense too insubstantial to give any very significant content to the suggestion that I judge my own sufferings to have considerable importance. Thus, the horror at suffering which is closely linked with a difficulty I may find in looking at the other is, on the face of it, wholly absent from my response to my own sufferings. Absent too is the compassion which may draw me towards the sufferer and incline me to weep for her. Of course, my own pain too may bring tears to my eyes, but this is *quite* different: in this case I do not weep for the one who suffers, for, apart from anything else, to the extent that I am overwhelmed by my own suffering the *sufferer* does not feature in my thought at all. A further feature of my thought which is indicative of the sense in which I do not regard my own pain as being of much importance lies in my indifference to my own past suffering. (It is tempting to present this last point as particularly telling; to argue: 'If something is, in itself, important, its importance is not dependent on whether it lies in the past, present or future. Thus, my indifference to my own past pain reveals that my concern about my present and future pains does not involve a serious judgement of importance'. While, however, I am not sure that to present matters in this way *need* involve a mistake, there are, I think, readily available ways in which this line of thought could be resisted.)

Again, consider my thought about my own death. One way in which we might try to characterise my concern would be this: 'From my point of view the overwhelmingly significant fact here is the fact that *I* am going to die. What others are concerned about, if they are concerned about my death at all, is quite different. It is the death of DC that matters to them. Indeed, what matters to me cannot even be *articulated* by anyone other than myself.'[14] Now I am very unclear what to say about this talk of 'the overwhelmingly significant fact that *I* am going to die'. Here I want only to suggest that there may be room for the view that my fear is, as I put it before, little more than a violent reflex and, as such, too thin to give any substantial content to talk of my being struck by an 'overwhelmingly significant fact'. Placed beside my concern at the thought of my child's death my response to thoughts of my own death could, perhaps, be viewed as no more an expression of 'serious concern about my death' than is the animal's flight from danger an expression of concern about its death.

It might, then, be argued that we characteristically do not give to our own pains or death as much importance as we should. I suspect, however, that that way of putting the matter is unlikely to be too helpful; and I am, in any case, very unclear about just what claims might be defensible here. Further, the case would, I think, be considerably more difficult to make in connection with other features of our lives. What really matters to me here is probably better expressed in terms of *kinds*, rather than degrees, of importance. My point then is this. There is room for the claim that there are features of the concern which we may feel for others which we ought to feel for ourselves; for the claim that we do not value ourselves as we should in so far as we lack those forms of concern. Perhaps what is of central significance here – what is characteristically absent from the individual's thought about himself – is a concern about the *person*. Indeed, rather than say, as I did, that it is, for example, my pain that I do not think of as I should we might say that, in my absorption in my pain, I completely overlook the suffering person: me in my pain.[15]

Two central aspects of this have featured strongly at various points in this book. First, a conception of this as an extended, tangible being of the human form does not feature in my thought about myself in the way in which it features in my thought about others; and, second, a conception of who this is, a conception of this as a particular individual, plays little role in my thought about myself.

I have little to say about the first of these points. One might speak here of the way in which, in catching a glimpse of one's own physicality – say, in a sudden realisation that the person in the mirror is oneself – one may be brought to a vivid realisation of something that presents itself as a striking fact about one's own nature. Beyond this, however, there appear to be fairly narrow limits on the ways in which my physical form could enter into my thought about myself as it enters into my thought about others. There appears to be simply no room for analogues in my thought about myself for many responses of the kind I discussed in Chapter 6: responses to others, that is, which essentially involve the human form. (I do not say there is *no* room for analogues. Michael McGhee has drawn my attention here to the various ways in which one might smile at oneself in the mirror.)

It is, I think, rather clearer what might be involved in the second transformation in my thought about myself of which I spoke. Coming to regard myself in personal terms – as a particular individual – would involve a radical change in the sense in which I would care *who* this is who is suffering, who is going to suffer, who has acted in a certain way, or who is dying. As things are now I may wish that it was not me who was in pain or did that terrible thing. That the person in question is DC is, however, nothing to me. In the transformed situation the *preference* that it should not be me will disappear; but will not, as in utilitarianism, be replaced by indifference. The special place which I am inclined to give to myself will be replaced, not by a radically impersonal form of thought, but by a consistently personal form of thought. What will matter to me is not that it is *I* who am going to suffer or die, not that it was *I* who behaved so well or badly, and so on, but, rather, that the person in question is DC. This change will bring with it – better, will, in large measure, be constituted by – a change in the forms of concern for which there is a place. Essentially first-person responses such as fear and remorse will give place to, for example, pity, compassion or forgiveness. One might also express this by saying that responses to the states and activities of a person will give place to responses to the *person* whose states and activities those are. This aspect of the matter possibly emerges most clearly within the context of my thought about my own death. What, as things are now, perhaps presents itself to me as the end of perception, sensation, thought and activity will come to be viewed as the end of a *person* – the person that I am. That, I take it, will be a significant change. (Though to put the matter as I have is not to say precisely *what* change it will be. For there is room for more than one attitude which could be described as an 'attitude towards the end of a person'.)

I will say a very little about just one other aspect of the change of which I have been speaking. Consider my thought about my own actions. I already, here, recognise myself as simply one among others in the sense that I accept that others are related to my actions in the same kind of way as I am related to theirs. For example, I accept that another's hurt feelings may be quite in place in view of the way in which I have treated them. If my acceptance of that is, in one way or another, not completely wholehearted it is clear what movement, in this respect, towards the ideal would be like. In addition to this, however, there is, I think, room for other forms of displacement of the asymmetries that we now character-istically find here: there is a richer sense in which I could move towards seeing my own future actions as the actions of one person among others. Thus, consider a situation in which I am contem-plating doing something which will let a friend down in a pretty serious way. As things are now, the difficulty which I see in acting in that way is perhaps best formulated in the thought 'I can't do that to him'. Now that thought can be clearly distinguished from a thought which we might formulate in this way: 'If DC lets his friend down things will have gone considerably worse here (and not simply for his friend) than they would otherwise have done.' For one thing, the former thought involves no mention of DC. For another, as I suggested earlier, there is one clear sense in which it need involve no judgement about how much it would *matter* if I acted in this way. A movement towards seeing myself in third-personal terms – in *that* sense towards seeing myself as simply one among others – might involve a movement from thoughts of the first form to thoughts of something like the second form. Part of what that will come to will be a change in my attitude towards my own past triumphs and failings. There will also, however, be a change in my understanding of how I am to decide what I should do. My action – DC's action – will present itself to me as simply one action among others: its awfulness just one factor, on the same level as many others, which is to be placed in the scales when I am deciding what to do. My special relation to my own future actions will then lie only in the fact (in so far as it is a fact) that they are the actions over which I have the most immediate control.

This (to my slight dismay!) appears to be a shift towards consequentialist thinking. It should be stressed, however, that it is not a move towards the impersonality of utilitarianism. To the extent that the model on which I am to base my thought about my own actions is my thought about the actions of someone for whom

I care the move will be in the direction of the increasingly *personal*: *whose* action it would be, that it would be *DC's* action, will, as it does not now, present itself to me as a significant feature of the situation.

(iv) I do not, then, think it absurd to suggest that most of us fail to have towards ourselves the attitude that we should: I do not think it absurd to suggest that a central part of the task of coming to see myself as one among others is coming to see *myself* as a person; and so do not think it absurd to suggest that the Cartesian philosophical tradition – that which takes my recognition of *others* as persons to be what is fundamentally problematical – gets things precisely the wrong way round.

Having said that, however, it must immediately be added that there is, on the face of it, no reason whatsoever why it should be held that all of the movement must be in a single direction: why one of the two injunctions I have considered should be regarded as providing us with *the* ideal. I suspect, indeed, that any remotely plausible ideal of 'seeing oneself as one among others' will call for movement in both directions. My emphasis on ways of thinking which have their primary place in our thought about certain *others* has been dictated primarily by the belief that there is an imbalance which needs to be corrected in many discussions of these issues. Part of my aim has been to try to break the hold of a certain picture of the options which are available to us in our ethical thought and, with that, in 'the philosophy of mind'. The picture is clearly expressed in the following remark by Dennett: 'I declare my starting point to be the objective, materialistic, third-person world of the physical sciences'.[16] It is equally, however, to be found in the thought of philosophers whose 'starting point' is very different. Thomas Nagel, for example, endorses the suggestion that when we view ourselves from 'an objective or external standpoint' what we are confronted with is 'a world of neural impulses, chemical reactions, and bone and muscle movements'; he argues, then, that we are confronted with an opposition between, on the one hand, what he calls a 'naturalistic view' and, on the other, 'the inner view of the agent'.[17] By contrast, I have stressed that the third-person world need not be the 'materialistic world of the physical sciences'; and that if we feel that the picture of human beings presented by the physical sciences leaves out something of fundamental value in our understanding of ourselves we should not assume that it is only by turning to the first-person point of view that we will be able to restore what has been lost.

I have gone rather further than this, suggesting that if we are concerned with the notion of a 'person' it is *not* to the first-person point of view that we should turn. Thus, I have linked the notion of a 'person' with the way in which one might think about another for whom one cares. Now it might be said that in making that connection I am simply giving expression to my own view of the value of certain features of our thought about those for whom we care: the concern about the identity of the individual which is tied up with the use of personal names, or the pleasure we may find in watching another, for example. In a way, no doubt, that is right. I suspect, however, that many others view things roughly as I do; or, at least, would but for the distorting imagery which comes with the philosophical notions of 'the body', 'the materialistic', and so on. In any case, I am happy to express my point in terms of the claim that there is no obvious absurdity in the view that the notion of a person has its primary home within the context of a personal relationship.

A further point needs to be added here. This is that there may well be considerable obscurity in the way in which I have spoken of 'directions of movements'. In particular, it is far from clear, at least to me, what is to be regarded as a 'pure form of first-person thought'. This unclarity is linked with certain other worries which may have been felt at earlier stages of this book, and which I must try to say something about.

I have stressed certain asymmetries in the forms of my concern about myself and about others. I have also suggested that we should think of the meanings of terms such as 'pain', 'anger' and 'joy' as closely bound up with the forms of concern with which they are linked: in Wittgenstein's terminology, that another's pain can be given as a reason for feeling pity for him is part of the 'grammar' of the word 'pain'. Now do not these claims commit me to the familiar but implausible conclusion that, for example, the word 'pain' is ambiguous as between its first and third person uses? Further, and closely linked with this, my defence of the connection which, following Wittgenstein, I made between ascriptions of such states and the human form depended crucially on an appeal to the forms which our concern for *others* in, say, pain may take. (See Chapter 6.) Does the character of my argument, then, commit me to the claim that there is, at least, *one* case in which such ascriptions are quite independent of the form of the being to

whom the states are ascribed: namely, my own? Indeed, to take up
a theme of Chapters 11 and 12, is there anything in what I have
said which, in the case of self-ascription, touches Hume's suggestion that there need be *nothing* to which such states are ascribed?

It will, perhaps, be clear why I suggested that these worries are
linked with the unclarity about what is to be regarded as a pure
form of first-person thought. It is true that, as things are for most of
us now, there are a range of pretty fundamental asymmetries between, on the one hand, self-ascriptions together with the forms of
concern which are linked with them, and, on the other, ascriptions
to others. These two practices do not, however, simply lie side by
side – tied together by no more than, for example, the word 'pain'
and the thought of it as a bad thing. Self-ascription develops in con-
junction with ascription to others and cannot be completely separated from a recognition that just as pain is to be ascribed to others by
me so it is to be ascribed to me by others. Thus, as there develops a
place in my life for the thought of this, that I am feeling, as a pain so
there develops a place for the thought that the pain is the pain of a
person who is to be *pitied*. In that sense, as soon as I am thinking of
myself at all I am thinking of myself as one among others.

I do not believe that it is merely incidental that our thought develops in this way. That, however, is a crucial strand of Wittgenstein's treatment of these issues about which I will not try to say
anything here. I mention it only in order to note that none of what I
have said should be read in a way which conflicts with this claim. I
take it that what is correct in the claim that to think of oneself at all
is to think of oneself as one among others is clearly not in conflict
with the suggestion that there are striking asymmetries in our
normal thought about ourselves and about others.

Where does that leave the worry about ambiguity, and where
does it leave the Cartesian and Humean claims? To answer these
questions properly one would have to consider in detail the
relationship between the two claims mentioned in the last sentence
of the previous paragraph. Further, however, there is no reason to
suppose that the result of that work will be neat answers to those
questions. We will decide, no doubt, that there is no mistake in the
way that dictionaries do not give two separate definitions of the
word 'pain'. That, however, does not alter the fact that, for
example, there is not the *same* difficulty in imagining myself
'having frightful pains and turning to stone while they lasted' as
there is in imagining the same of another. (See Wittgenstein,

Philosophical Investigations, §283.) It does not alter the fact that the human form does not play the role in my thought about my own pains that it plays in my thought about the pains of others.

Where does all of this leave the notion of a 'pure form of first-person thought?' It leaves it, clearly, in a slightly ambiguous state. Is my desire that I should not be eaten when dead a pure case of first-person thought? I have very little idea how to even begin to answer that question. That I do not does not, I think, in any way blunt my criticisms of views which insist that primacy must be given to 'the first-person point of view'. The content and attraction of those views is dependent on the fact that we have a picture, however confused it may be, of what is to be included in 'the first-person point of view'. Now, to the extent that that picture *is* confused my criticisms are not the most radical ones which arise here. That, however, does nothing to weaken the force of my points. We can add that doubts about the 'purity' of the first-person point of view do not threaten the claim that there are important first/third person asymmetries. That is enough to leave some interesting content – if not the content we might have thought – to my talk of 'two possible directions of movement'.

I should close this section by noting that caution of certain forms is needed in all of this. First, there is no reason to suppose that it *must* be admirable to push the process of 'coming to see myself as one among others' as far as it can be pushed. To take it to be obvious that symmetry in our thought here is the ideal is to presuppose a conception of rationality that we do not have to accept: there is, for example, no incoherence in the suggestion that the place of forgiveness in my thought about my own actions and my thought about the actions of others should be different. A second form of caution needed here is this. There are, fairly certainly, limits of some kind to how far the process of 'coming to see myself as one among others' *can* be taken. I have mentioned possible limits on the role which the human form might play in my thought about myself. Perhaps more fundamental than this, however, is the way in which my relation to my own future actions is, in one sense, inescapably different from my relation to the future actions of others. I spoke earlier in this chapter of certain ways in which the marked asymmetries which we characteristically find here might be lessened. Now I may well, even there, have exaggerated the extent to which movement of this kind is possible. In any case, when we turn to my *knowledge* of the future actions of myself and others inescapable asymmetries are pretty readily seen. My knowledge of what another is going to do is inevitably, in part,[18] inductively grounded – grounded, for example, in knowledge of present and past features of that person – in a way in which my knowledge of what *I* am going to do is often not. Now some philosophers have, at least implicitly, played down this asymmetry: suggesting, for example, that my knowledge of what I am going to do is grounded in my knowledge of my intentions in a roughly analogous way. Others, acknowledging that first/third person asymmetries do, in practice, exist, have, in effect, suggested that they do not run deep. Thus, we are presented with images, linked with worries about determinism, of circumstances in which my knowledge of what I will do is consistently inductively grounded: grounded in knowledge of my physiology, psychology or whatever. Such images suggest that the first/third person asymmetries in our thought here are, ultimately, to be transcended. Now the point I wish to stress is simply that while I have no very clear idea about where the limits of intelligibility fall here I have little doubt that there are, here and elsewhere, such limits.

(v) There is a possible worry about the general emphasis of my approach to these issues about which I must say something before closing this chapter. It might be pointed out that the particular first/third person asymmetries which I have stressed at various points in this book are not strongly tied to asymmetries in *actions* directed towards myself and others. At least, I have not stressed such ties. Now it might be objected that it is only in virtue of such ties that the asymmetries which I have stressed have any real importance. It is, it might be said, neither here nor there whether I think of the injured man by the roadside, or, more clearly still, the starving child in Africa, in first or third personal terms if both are equally strongly linked to the one thing that matters in such a case: namely, practical help.

In response to this protest I should note first that there do seem to be important differences in the actions which will be called for by the two approaches. For example, I suggested that if we give the fundamental position to the first-person point of view then we will not attach any importance to the question of *who* is suffering; nor will we attach the importance we sometimes do to *past* suffering. These points will, I take it, have some significant bearing on the place which the idea of distributive justice has in our thought.[19]

Another immediate practical way in which the difference between the two approaches might find expression is in one's attitude towards certain ways in which charities may attempt to make an impact on us. A name, a face, and a picture of a life – factors which are central in my thought about my child's suffering but characteristically play no role in my thought about my own – can have an enormous impact on us; and this fact is often exploited in the advertising campaigns of charities. Now while someone who places the emphasis on the first-person approach may accept that such campaigns are justified on utilitarian grounds, he must think of them as appealing to something superficial or morally dubious in our nature. By contrast, one who takes my thought about my child as his model of concern for another will see such appeals as bringing us into direct contact with reality: will see what is called forth by such appeals as (at least potentially) a pure response to those who are suffering. (Of course, there are dangers here. When the press picks out Jane in Preston who needs a kidney machine enough money comes in to pay for fifty. Our response to appeals which focus on a particular individual are not always well directed; and can sometimes be characterised as 'emotional' where the use of that term involves a criticism. This criticism may, however, be based on the fact that the form that our response takes reveals a failure to properly acknowledge that Jane is just one of thousands; and *that* criticism is quite distinct from the charge that any appeal to the physical and the historical – a face and a life – is, as such, an 'emotional' one. That is the charge which will flow from a certain, natural, understanding of the injunction to 'Love thy neighbour as thyself' but be rejected by one who takes the parent's thought about her child as containing the ideal.)

I do not, then, believe that the links which the two approaches have to practical help are equally strong nor of the same kind. I must, however, also say something about the suggestion that such links are the one thing that matters.

Virtually everyone cares how, at any rate, certain other people think of them. How others think about me, and what they feel for me, is not important to me only in a secondary way: not important only in so far as it is linked with something else which can be characterised quite independently: their treatment of me. That I am liked, that I am loved, even that total strangers have towards me an attitude of goodwill rather than one of hostility or indifference is important to me. To express the point in another way, the significance which another's treatment of me has for me does not lie solely in the 'effects' which their behaviour has on me; where 'effects' are understood as states which could have been brought about in a way which did not involve another human being. The significance which another's behaviour towards me has for me lies, at the very least in some measure, in the attitude towards me which it expresses. It makes a significant difference whether another's apparent acts of kindness towards me flow from physical compulsion by a third party, a sense of duty, or something more akin to love. I suppose that to most people this kind of thing matters a great deal. They would rather undergo a substantial measure of unpleasant 'effects' than lose the affection and goodwill of others.

Now it has to be added that the force which this point has in a particular case is likely to depend on the particular circumstances of the individual. If one is starving the *attitudes* of those on the other side of the world who give something to help may seem substantially less significant than the *amount* of help that they give. However, to think that it follows *immediately* from this that one's attitude towards those in distant countries is, in itself, of very little significance is to take for granted that what is significant in my thought about another is determined exclusively by the feelings of the other; it is to give the first-person point of view the kind of priority which I have argued we do not have to give it. I grieve for my dead child, and would feel that there was something seriously wrong with me if I did not, even though it does not matter to him that I do; and, indeed, never *did* matter to him that I *would*.

Having said that, there is, perhaps, a further twist to be added here. This is that the force of the idea that the first-person point of view – the point of view of the other – is the only thing that matters increases as we consider people in increasingly desperate circumstances. Quite independently of any philosophical confusion there is a strong temptation to say that a proper attitude here will give to reflection on how it is *for* the other a more or less exclusive position; and so to say that if the other does not care what my *attitude* is, but only that help, in a purely 'practical' sense, is forthcoming, then the character of my attitude is of very little importance.[20] Thus, given the way the world actually is, one might still have serious worries – moral worries – about the attention given in this book to the character of the *attitude*, in contrast to the *behaviour*, which we exhibit towards others. (The worry is closely linked to the idea that non-utilitarian values are a luxury which we can ill afford: given the circumstances of most in the world such values are, it might be argued, a more or less serious piece of moral self-indulgence.)

This objection appeals to what is suggested to be a feature of our normal moral consciousness: the idea that a proper attitude towards those in desperate circumstances will give a more or less exclusive position to reflection on how it is *for* the other. Now if this *is* a feature of 'our normal moral consciousness', as I think it may be, it does not have to go unchallenged. Seeds of a different outlook are at least relatively widespread in normal thought. Perhaps a particularly unambiguous example is to be seen in the idea that it is important to reflect on the lives, and the sufferings, of those now dead: the idea that this is something that we, in some sense, owe to *them*. I will not, however, attempt to develop this and will restrict myself to two further observations that may help to dull the edge of the protest.

First, to hold that the attitude which we have towards strangers is important is in no way at all to sanction the kind of moral self-indulgence which would be involved in a response in which thoughts about *myself* featured in a central way: a response, that is, in which a concern about the character of my attitude towards the other stands alongside, or even displaces, a concern about the other. What I have been speaking of is the form of our response to *the other*, and in so far as my thought is focused on the other, there will simply be no room for thought about myself; and, in particular, for a concern about the character of my response. To say this is quite compatible with agreeing, as perhaps *anyone* must, that the character of my response does matter; and that, if it is rarely what it should be, I have an obligation to try to change myself in ways such that I move closer to the ideal.

The other point I will make here involves an appeal to the consequentialist considerations which lie behind the protest. I have already touched on one point that might be mentioned in this connection: the fact that the motivational force of the different attitudes I have spoken of may be very different. Love, perhaps, could move most of us to action in a way in which a sense of duty never could. My point now, however, is that certain familiar ways of insisting that our treatment of strangers is not what it should be – ways which are particularly prominent within philosophy – involve a kind of utilitarianism which may place personal relationships with particular individuals in a very dubious light. One result of this is that, however rationally compelling we may find the argument, such discussions can, for many, be little more than an abstract academic exercise. To the extent that that is so it is, even from the most purely pragmatic point of view, important to recognise a point that has been central to my discussion; namely, that giving a fundamental position to the personal is quite compatible with the insistence that our attitude towards, and treatment of, strangers is, characteristically, not at all what it should be.

Postscript:
Ethics and Metaphysics

(i) The relationship between what I have spoken of as 'ethics' and 'metaphysics' has been central to the argument of this book in two, closely related, ways. First, I have suggested that a misunderstanding of the character of that relationship may be an important source of certain widespread philosophical pictures of persons; and, with that, an important source of certain approaches to a range of fundamental ethical issues. The misunderstanding lies in the idea that our ethics must be grounded in our metaphysics. Second, having argued in opposition to this that we must think of a metaphysical picture of persons as an *expression* of an ethical outlook, I have tried to bring out the importance of the place which the notion of a human being has in our thought by setting that notion in its ethical context.

But while the ethical has been central to my argument the precise relation of what I say to particular ethical viewpoints is, at the very least, not completely clear, and I am aware of tensions in my thought which I have not completely resolved. These tensions certainly spring in part from the fact that I have not been able to totally dissociate my discussion of these questions from the value which I myself attach to certain features of our thought about each other. That, I think, is only in part a failing, however, for I believe that it would, in certain respects, be absurd to even try to do that. At any rate, it is clear that what a philosopher thinks it *worth* writing about will, in some way, reflect what he values. Further, the significance of that point will be considerably increased if one believes, as I do, that philosophical pictures can stand in the way of our recognising even the possibility of certain kinds of value.

This phenomenon is particularly marked within the philosophy of mind. Confused philosophical pictures of what a person is, or, at a more abstract level, confusions about how one must approach the question of what a person is, may focus attention away from features of our thought about each other in which some find things of value; and further, may present such features of our thought in a light such that it is very difficult to see how they *could* be valued in a clear-sighted way. Thus, the removing of philosophical confusion can be the revealing of ethical possibilities.

Now when the matter is expressed like that one might think that the relationship between philosophy and particular ethical outlooks is quite straightforward, and so that there is no excuse for the murkiness on this point into which my discussion has sometimes fallen. The contribution of philosophy, we can say, is purely negative. One is not, within philosophy, *defending* particular ethical outlooks; one is only revealing their possibility and removing certain obstacles to their acceptance. Thus, the contrast between philosophical argument and the defence of a particular ethical outlook is quite clear, and we are left with an unambiguous sense in which philosophy leaves everything as it is.

I am, however, too unclear about how to apply the distinction between 'positive' and 'negative' contributions to feel very happy with that clean way of expressing the matter. No doubt there *is* a distinction between removing an obstacle to the acceptance of a particular ethical outlook and presenting an argument for that outlook. Equally, however, I have no doubt that that distinction is context relative; and it is quite unclear to me why it should be supposed that anything legitimately to be found in a philosophy book should inevitably, and irrevocably, fall on one side of it.

Having said that, I do feel inclined to describe most of what is done in this book, in so far as it has a relation to a particular ethical outlook, in terms of 'removing obstacles to' rather than in terms of 'presenting arguments for' particular ethical views. The explanation of that may be bound up with a feeling that nothing that I say takes the ethical issues very far. For example, exposing the philosophical confusions of mind-body dualism can hardly be said to be an argument for the idea that the bodily is of fundamental ethical significance if the most important challenge to that idea comes from a religious/ethical tradition within which the 'bodily' is, quite independently of any such confusions, viewed as something to be transcended. Now I am, in fact, quite unclear to what extent that might be the case. In so far as it is, however, what I say in this book can hardly be spoken of as a *defence* of an ethical outlook which gives a central place to the extended, tangible being; and, with that, can hardly be said to undermine mind-body dualism in so far as that can be dissociated from the confused philosophical arguments with which it is sometimes defended; but perhaps that is just as it should be.

The lack of clarity at this point may, however, have another dimension too. It may be unclear to what extent the different ways of thinking that I have considered – for example, the different approaches to the identity of the individual discussed in Part III – really are different options for our ethical thought. Perhaps the ways of thinking which I have highlighted in this book are, in one way or another, inescapable features of human life; perhaps, for example, there *could not be* an ethical tradition within which a notion of *who* this is, in the sense I have discussed, has no important place. Of course, any suggestion of this kind would need a case by case defence. To the extent that there is something to it, however, it is no defect in my discussion that I do not present those attitudes to which I have given a central place as simply a possible moral outlook. Though a place will then be created for another criticism: namely, that it is seriously misleading to speak of these attitudes as a feature of our 'moral' or 'ethical' outlook.

If this last criticism is the one that has the most pervasive application to my discussion there is again, I think, *some* excuse for my failure. I suggested, in Chapter 1, that the use of the term 'attitude' within philosophy may be partially conditioned by just the range of assumptions which Wittgenstein is seeking to undermine; and in Chapter 3 I added that the same may be true of the philosophical use of terms such as 'moral', 'ethical' and 'value'. Following Wittgenstein, I have placed at the centre of the picture the range of emotions and actions which are distinctive of our relations with other human beings. The importance of highlighting these emotions and actions derives from the fact that there is a strong tradition in philosophy – the empiricist tradition – within which our primary relationship to what surrounds us is represented as being one which is untinged by any *response* on our part. Now the philosophical use of terms such as 'attitude', 'ethical', 'value' and, indeed, 'emotion' has, in large measure, been conditioned by that assumption. A central role of terms from this group has become that of signalling that what we are dealing with in a particular instance is not simply a 'passive registering' by an observer – in the sense that is fundamental in the empiricist tradition. This makes it overwhelmingly natural, within a philosophical context, to give a central place to terms from this group in any attempt to reject the assumption that such a 'passive registering' is, in a general way, our primary relationship to what surrounds us.

What makes this natural also, however, makes it hazardous. For, as I have said, this is a distinctively philosophical use of these terms; and one which derives from the tradition under attack. A more normal use of such terms is not bound up in that way with the philosophical divide between a 'passive recognition' of what one is confronted with and a 'response' to it.[1] Thus, distress at a child's hunger or death is not, as such, an 'emotional' response. My idea that another in severe pain is, other things being equal, to be helped is not a reflection of any 'moral views' or of a 'value judgement'. Similarly, my horror at the suggestion that we might eat my dead grandmother is not, I think, a reflection of the 'attitude' which I have towards her; still less is it a reflection of my 'ethical outlook'. In speaking as if it is, I am using these terms in a way which derives from the tradition which I am seeking to undermine, and so may be making my own small contribution to sustaining that tradition.

Our normal use of the terms 'ethical', 'moral', 'value', 'emotion' and 'attitude' operates against a background of human reactions – forms of concern – which generally go unremarked. To the extent that the forms of concern which I have discussed in this book are part of that background it is misleading to characterise them in these terms. Now I have suggested that it is empiricism that lies behind that way of speaking; but there is another dimension to this which I should also stress. I said that it is misleading to speak of the background as, for example, part of our 'ethical outlook'. It will, however, cease to be misleading if one wishes to present a particular feature of the background as a way of thinking whose rejection is not unthinkable.[2] Now, closely linked with the empiricist tradition – perhaps part of it – is the idea that a primary task of the philosopher is that of thinking, or at any rate presenting for serious consideration, the unthinkable. Within such a project, features of our thought – such as our refusal to eat the dead – which would never in the normal course of things be said to involve a value judgement of any kind will inevitably be presented as reflecting a particular 'moral' outlook. Similarly, responses which would never normally be described in such terms – for example, a continuing special concern for a loved one who has suffered hopeless brain damage – are characterised as 'emotional'. *Given* the project of presenting what is unthinkable as thinkable these characterisations are not wrong.

While it is in Chapter 8 that philosophical traditions of this kind have been most explicitly under discussion such traditions have perhaps, in a way, been a central concern throughout this book. To suggest that I need a special justification, such as the argument from analogy seeks to provide, for thinking of others as people is to ask me to take seriously the idea that my refusal to treat others as I treat a stone is misplaced. Analogous points arise in the discussion of identity in Part III. (Though I am not completely certain to what extent a view of the person of the kind presented by Parfit should be described as a demand that we think the 'unthinkable'.) Now my point here is, again, that it is both natural and hazardous to employ the language of 'ethics', 'emotion', and so on in combating these traditions. Natural, because the employment of a common terminology makes it easier to engage with the traditions one is criticising. Hazardous, because in employing that terminology one may appear to be taking seriously ideas which one does not think should be taken seriously.

The empiricist tradition may, then, encourage a use of the term 'ethical' or 'moral', which is such that we are speaking of the 'ethical' whenever we are speaking of what someone has reason to do or feel. This use, I have argued, is much broader, in several ways, than a normal, non-philosophical, use of that term. There are, that is, many kinds of reasons to do or feel certain things which are not 'ethical' or 'moral' reasons. An example of a particularly clear kind would be this: while I have reason to hurt this man who has hurt me, and while I accept that I do, I do not take this form of response to be something to aim at. Another, quite different, kind of case is this: while I accept that I have reason not to eat this (human flesh), and do take the avoidance of such behaviour to be something to aim at, this feature of my thinking is too basic to my life to be spoken of as a 'moral view'. Now when we return to a more normal use of the terms 'moral', 'ethical' and 'value' it may be that room will be created, at least in certain cases, for an idea which I have systematically rejected throughout this book: the idea that 'ethics' can be grounded in 'metaphysics'. The defence of what are in normal – non-philosophical – contexts spoken of as '*moral*' views will appeal to the character of the beings with which we are dealing. Thus, the fact that cows or monkeys are creatures of a kind that feel pain might be part of a common background to a dispute about the acceptability of certain features of our treatment of them. I have insisted that that common background – that agreement in our 'metaphysics' – involves an acceptance of certain kinds of considerations as reasons for doing or feeling certain things. It is only because this is so that in appealing to the metaphysics we can be offering reasons for a moral position. To share a 'metaphysics', we might say then, is to share a system of reasons for emotion and action; but that shared 'system of reasons' is not a 'moral position'. It is, rather, the stopping point in chains of justification: in defending moral positions we appeal, selectively, to considerations from within this system.

I am afraid that leaves a great deal still to be said. I will, however, make only one further point here. This is that there are a number of different ways in which one might present 'metaphysics' as fitting into this picture. One kind of option that arises here is this. I spoke in Chapter 13 of a 'metaphysical picture of persons' as being 'an expression of one's commitment to a certain ideal in one's relations with others'. Now it is possible for an individual's life to exemplify an ideal without there being room for the claim that he has *committed himself* to that ideal. One case would be that in which it is unthinkable that this man should ever abandon a loved one; yet he would not hold such behaviour up as an ideal to be aimed at since he is simply not self-conscious about his life in that way. Another case would be that in which an individual's life is dominated by patterns of thought which he himself actively *rejects*. Now we might tie the notion of a 'metaphysical picture of persons' to 'commitment to an ideal' or we might tie it to 'living a life which conforms to that ideal'. Which we do is, I think, of little importance. Since the term 'metaphysics' belongs primarily to the philosophers an eccentric use of it will carry fewer dangers than does an eccentric use of the term 'ethics' or 'emotion'. It would, of course, be argued by some that we would do better to get by without using the term at all.

(ii) I have presented various philosophical views, and in particular philosophical dualism, as being attempts to provide a form of metaphysical grounding for our thought; and have suggested, in particular in Chapter 5, that it is a confusion to think that our thought must have such a grounding. As will be clear, however, I do not believe that matters are really that simple. For one thing, it will certainly not be easy to draw any neat line between 'philosophical dualism' and ways of thinking which are untouched by this confusion. For another, it is unclear what sort of demonstration that this *is* a confusion is possible.

I have said a very little about the first of these points: about positions which are at least closely akin to, for example, 'dualism' or 'no-self views' but which are defended in ways which might be kept free of the search for 'metaphysical grounding'. I want, in this final section, to say something about the second point: about the suggestion that the search for 'grounding' involves philosophical confusion.

Nagel comments on one aspect of Wittgenstein's treatment of this issue: 'It seems to me that to accept this as the final story is to acknowledge that all thought is an illusion'.[3] He adds, 'It is as if a natural Platonism makes the attempt to view the world in any other way look phony.' Nagel's worry is closely linked with the familiar charge that Wittgenstein's philosophy involves a radical form of idealism.[4] Such charges are sometimes defended in ways which can be shown to involve what is unambiguously philosophical confusion. One such confusion would be the idea that if the kind of grounding which I have spoken of is an illusion it will not be possible to draw any distinction between truth and falsity: between getting things right and getting things wrong. When I say that this is unambiguously a muddle what I mean is that room is certainly left for *some* important distinction here. My discussion in Chapter 5 was a partial defence of that claim. I will not, however, attempt to defend the claim further here since my point how is this: it is not obvious to me that once that work has been done the distinction we will be left with is the one that, before we read Wittgenstein, we all thought we had. There may be nothing in our *practice* which requires some other form of distinction and yet it still be the case that a picture of a 'richer' distinction has a 'natural', 'pre-philosophical', hold on the thought of many. More generally, while Nagel's claim that Wittgenstein's position implies that 'all thought is an illusion' may be quite unwarranted, the suggestion that at least many of us are subject to a 'natural Platonism' may have something to it.

Wittgenstein's discussion of the role which human interests play in the development of our picture of the world *ought*, I think, to strike us initially as startling, and perhaps disturbing. Of course, that judgement is made against the background of an assumption about how most of 'us' are thinking when we first encounter Wittgenstein; and no doubt few can be said to be in a state of complete philosophical innocence when we do. To conclude, however, that we only find Wittgenstein startling or disturbing because we have been philosophically corrupted is to presuppose a distinction between the 'philosophical' and the 'pre-philosophical', or 'natural', which may prove difficult to draw with any clarity; and, while there is *something* in that distinction, what there is in it may leave Nagel's claims about a 'natural Platonism' standing. Of course, that leaves open the possibility of saying that this natural yearning for a 'metaphysical grounding' for our thought involves a confusion: that once we have fully assimilated Wittgenstein's philosophy the yearning will be undermined, or will melt away; but while I am sometimes pulled towards such claims I know of no argument that begins to look as though it fully substantiates them.

The same point can be presented in a slightly different light. I spoke of philosophical dualism as being an attempt to provide a form of metaphysical grounding for our thought. In being that it may also be an attempt to find obstacles to the degeneration of our attitude towards human beings. The prospect of a world in which our relations with each other are purely manipulative is one which fills many with horror. Equally, however, the steps towards such a world are, individually, often enormously tempting. For example, the pain involved in the recognition of another's hostile treatment of me may be considerably eased by viewing their behaviour, to the extent that I can, as simply the product of the play of natural forces. The scientific study of human beings, in its various forms, presents us with various models of how we might do this. In the purest of these the hostile treatment, and, indeed, the human being himself, will simply fall out of view (in ways touched on in Chapter 7).

Given both the temptation and the horror it is hardly surprising that a picture of persons which suggests that there is a serious obstacle along this path should have its attractions. At its simplest the idea would be this. The image of a world in which human relationships are purely manipulative is not one which *could* be realised in practice. You *cannot* treat another's behaviour as simply the product of the play of natural forces: 'cannot' in the sense that any attempt to understand human beings in scientific terms will inevitably break down at some point; and, with that, any attempt to control human behaviour as you might control the spread of a disease will inevitably fail. Between the physical input to another's body and the output in the form of physical movements of that body lies something that will never fully succumb to the manipulative approach. The development that we fear – a world in which, for example, all aggressive behaviour is 'treated' chemically – is simply not a possible development.

In so far as something along these lines represents one of the attractions of traditional dualism such a dualism is not simply a myth; it is a pernicious myth. It is suggested that the reason why we should not think of another's behaviour as simply a 'natural phenomenon', to be controlled as any other natural phenomenon is to be controlled, is that it will not work. By the time we are thinking in *that* way, however, we have *already* conceded everything of importance to the picture that we once feared. For we are thinking of the other as 'to be manipulated'. Suppose that someone suggests that I slip an anti-depressent into my wife's coffee and I protest that 'I can't help her in *that* way.' If the force of the 'can't' here is simply 'It won't work' – if this is the only notion of a 'limit' that I acknowledge in my treatment of my wife – it is, I take it, clear that our relationship is in very serious difficulties.

This very crude source of dualism must, however, be distinguished from something else. Suppose that I am contemplating the possibility of a slide towards a world in which we view each other in purely manipulative terms. How am I to formulate what is objectionable in such a slide: how am I to articulate what would be horrific in such a world? In Chapter 5 I suggested that nothing in the philosophical approach I have followed stands in the way of the claim that the most direct formulation of the objection will be in terms of the fact that 'These are people'. It needs to be added, however, that one's understanding of those words, one's acceptance that they do formulate an objection to movement in this direction, is dependent on the fact that one has not already travelled too far down this road. The protest 'But these are people!' can only serve as a *reminder*: these words are an appeal to something in the other, an attitude, which we hope he still shares, at least in a shadowy form, with us.

Now I suggested in Chapter 5 that this gives us everything that we normally want here; and that may be true in practice: we can, and do, always assume that a shadow of the attitude is left. I am not, however, completely confident that there is no desire for something that this picture does not offer; nor, that any such desire must be the product of philosophical muddle. We have a vague picture of something in the other which is a reason for not treating them in certain ways, and – and this is the crucial point – whose acknowledgement by me as being such a reason is in no way dependent on my 'attitudes' (the state of my soul): a picture of a form of 'moral' recognition which can reveal obstacles to me no matter how far the degeneration in my attitude towards other human beings has gone. We are troubled, for example, by the idea of someone who, looking at other human beings, sees nothing but the collection of entities, states and processes spoken of in the physical sciences; and we have a picture of something in the other that can be pointed out to the observer and that, no matter how deeply engulfed he may be in the scientific image, will reveal to him the incompleteness of that image: something whose significance is inescapable in a sense quite different from that in which the significance of a human face is inescapable.

Philosophical dualism is, in part, a reflection of the hold which this picture has on us. The Cartesian 'mind' is that whose significance is, in this sense, 'inescapable'. In so far as a materialist view of people flows from the conclusion that there is no such entity it is a reflection of the same fundamental drive; for it involves the thought that if the scientific image cannot, in that sense, be shown to be incomplete – if the alternative image is not, in that sense inescapable – then the scientific image is to be embraced. (Unless the scientific image is itself inescapable in that sense there is a gap here which needs to be bridged with another assumption. This was a central theme of Chapter 7.)

Our picture of what we want here collapses, I have argued, under even quite mild scrutiny. The idea that, *in this sense*, the world contains obstacles to our moral degeneration is a myth.[5] We only fail to see this, perhaps, because we slide from this picture to others. We say that what we want is that the reason I should not treat another as a mere means to my ends lies exclusively in the *other* and so does not depend on *my* state. Now we can have *that*: the reason he is not to be treated in these ways is that he is a human being; and his being that is quite independent of my attitude towards him. Yet when we read Wittgenstein we feel, with Nagel, that this was not, after all, quite all that we wanted. We feel that we are left with a crucial, and intolerable, sense in which, on this view, the obstacle to our moral degeneration lies in *ourselves*. Our grasp on this sense, and, with that, our apparent grasp on what it would be for things to be otherwise, rests, I suspect, on an appeal to the quite different notion of an 'obstacle' which I considered earlier: the sense of 'You can't treat her in that way' which goes with 'It won't work'. Of course, when this notion of an 'obstacle' is brought clearly into focus we see pretty quickly that it is not at all what we need. Kept slightly out of focus, however, it is a model which fills an important gap in our thinking.

This is speculation; and there is much in the way in which I have expressed it which is hazy. The point that primarily concerns me now, however, is simply that the picture of 'the relation between ethics and metaphysics' which has been rejected in this book may have deep roots. Certainly the desire of which it is an expression – the desire for a certain form of grounding for our thought – is often linked with philosophical confusions. Whether, however, philosophical argument on its own can remove the desire is unclear to me. It is possible that the desire has a life which is quite independent of those confusions; or that those philosophical confusions reflect deep natural tendencies in human thought which are not to be undermined by a formal exposure of errors. (With this, the notions of 'philosophical argument', 'philosophical confusion' and 'natural tendency' may be subject to strain at this point.)

Consider in this light one further example. Our commitment to particular individuals, the mother's commitment to her child for example, is dependent on certain reactions which come to us naturally and, in certain circumstances, in a powerful form. There is no such thing as showing a mother who was *wholly* lacking in this reaction that it is one which her child demands of her. I argued in Chapter 13 that we cannot conclude from this that we should not see in the mother's response a pure recognition of another's reality as a particular individual. Having said that, however, it must also be said that these points do, in principle, leave open the possibility of an unsettling view of the mother's concern. In just that sense in which nothing in the child renders the mother's concern inescapable, nothing in the mother's concern renders our normal view of it inescapable. Suppose that someone sees in that concern something that might be characterised as simply 'a biological response which has a crucial evolutionary function'. There is nothing to be pointed to in the mother's life which will, whatever his sensibilities, inevitably bring such a person round to another way of viewing the matter. Of course, there are fundamental differences from the dog's concern for its young, and still greater differences from the forms of 'concern' to be found lower down the animal scale. The similarity may, however, strike a particular individual in such a way that the differences will pale into insignificance.

Wittgenstein's philosophy does, in this sense, bring into focus the possibility of unsettling ways of viewing our relations with, and thought about, each other. Someone could be struck by this possibility in such a way that he is inclined to say that Wittgenstein has 'shown' that, for example, the mother's concern for her child is not what we normally take it to be. Now we do not have to go that way. Further, such a response will certainly sometimes reflect philosophical confusion. It has, however, yet to be shown, I think, that we cannot go this way without being confused.[6]

Notes and References

CHAPTER 1   'AN ATTITUDE TOWARDS A SOUL'

1. Ludwig Wittgenstein, *Philosophical Investigations*, §287.
2. P. F. Strawson, 'Freedom and Resentment', in P. F. Strawson (ed.), *Studies in the Philosophy of Thought and Action*, p. 75.
3. Simone Weil, 'The *Iliad*, Poem of Might', in George A. Panichas (ed.), *The Simone Weil Reader*, p. 157.
4. Expressing in the terms of an already quoted remark by Wittgenstein one aspect of a well-known discussion of 'The Look' by Sartre. See *Being and Nothingness*, pt three, ch. one, sect. IV.
5. I deliberately remain non-committal about the extent to which the ways of caring I have spoken of in this section mark our thought about other *people* off from our thought about anything else. The case of the higher non-human species is, of course, particularly pertinent here. While I will in this book say little that is explicitly addressed to this issue some of the forms of concern discussed later will have a fairly obvious bearing on it.
6. *Philosophical Investigations*, p. 178.
7. I am grateful to Lars Hertzberg for drawing my attention to the distinction and for this formulation of it. It may be worth noting that I did not have this distinction clearly in mind when developing the main lines of argument in this book. It is possible that some points would have been presented in a different, and clearer, light if I had.
8. See Derek Parfit, *Reasons and Persons*, especially Part III. The outlook which I am speaking of here is, incidentally, reflected in a more general form in much work on the theory of meaning. For an explicit formulation which links the general point directly with my concerns in this book see Michael Dummett, *Frege, Philosophy of Language*, p. 666.
9. I have given examples of particular responses which I take to be expressive of the 'characteristic' attitude. That there are wide deviations from these norms is one of the factors which re-enforces the traditional picture. I will say something about this in Chapter 3.

CHAPTER 2   SCEPTICISM, DUALISM AND ACTION

1. I will often characterise this view in terms of the idea that the crucial thing 'lies behind what I observe' or 'lies behind the surface'. I do not mean to suggest that the use of such phrases is *always* an expression of the kind of dualism I am concerned with here.
2. See, for example, Crispin Wright, 'Realism, Truth-Value Links, Other Minds and the Past', *Ratio* 22 (1980) p. 125. For some helpful expressions of astonishment at such suggestions see John Cook, 'Human Beings', in Peter Winch (ed.), *Studies in the Philosophy of Wittgenstein*.

3. For a useful discussion of some of the considerations which are relevant here see Ilham Dilman, *Love and Human Separateness*. For further important points of a rather different kind see Lars Hertzberg, 'The Indeterminacy of the Mental', *Proceedings of the Aristotelian Society*, Supplementary Volume LVII (1983).
4. H. A. Prichard, 'Acting, Willing, Desiring', in his *Moral Obligation*, p. 189.
5. This characterisation of the view comes from Peter Winch's paper 'Trying', in his *Ethics and Action*, p. 137. I have found this paper enormously helpful in a variety of ways.
6. See Prichard, op. cit., p. 189.
7. Such asymmetries are of central importance in much of Peter Winch's work on ethics. See, for example, 'Trying' and 'Moral Integrity', both in his *Ethics and Action*.
8. I am sure that this is only part of the story. Another part of it is the role played by 'chance' in everything that happens in the world of extended and tangible beings. The papers by Winch referred to in note 7 and Martha Nussbaum's *The Fragility of Goodness* are relevant here. Perhaps also relevant is the way in which our picture of 'the mental' is such as to exclude the possibility of certain forms of corruption in our thought about it. The Cartesian 'mind' is, by definition, a thing of a kind towards which it is not *possible* to feel physical lust.
9. Wittgenstein, *Philosophical Investigations*, §363.

CHAPTER 3 FACTS AND VALUES

1. P. F. Strawson, 'Freedom and Resentment', op. cit.
2. My discussion here has moved freely between ideas which I distinguished in Chapter 1 section (ii). We might distinguish different senses of the phrase 'recognising the reality of others' to match the distinctions that I made there: the distinction, for example, between reacting to others in a certain way and accepting that I have reason to react to others in this way. For my immediate purposes, however, I don't *think* too much turns on keeping such distinctions constantly in mind.
3. Do we have a firm grasp of the distinction I have drawn in this sentence? There is room for doubt. At any rate, the sense in which his talk about others could be said to be normal will be pretty thin if he does not say things at the appropriate times. Now what are the connections between that and having the relevant attitude? Well, I will not pursue this question.

CHAPTER 4 JUSTIFICATION AND THE FIRST PERSON

1. I suspect that it is very unclear what it could *be* to 'fear another's pain as I fear my own'; but I will not pursue this.
2. For a graphic development of this point see Derek Parfit, *Reasons and Persons*, sect. 69.

3. I discuss the first stage in my paper 'The Problem of the Past', *The Philosophical Quarterly*, 37 (1987). The problems involved in this proposed move from my concern about my own present pains to my concern about my own future pains are, I believe, of exactly the same form as those involved in the move from my concern about my pains to my concern about the pains of others.

4. For this reason it might be thought to be misleading to speak in terms of 'having a certain attitude' in this context. I do not believe that would affect my suggestion.

5. That, I suppose, is one of the truths behind the once much talked of 'gap between fact and value'. Though, as will be clear, I have serious reservations about both the conception of 'facts' and the conception of 'values' appealed to there.

CHAPTER 5   ARBITRARINESS

1. I will not explicitly discuss the second kind of case anywhere. The discussions in this chapter and in Chapter 6 do, however, have a direct bearing on such cases.

2. See Norman Malcolm, 'Wittgenstein's Philosophical Investigations' in his *Knowledge and Certainty*, p. 118.

3. Similarly, when Wittgenstein writes 'I am not of the opinion that he has a soul' he is not, I take it, denying that someone might be 'of the opinion' that the lump in the dark corner is a person.

4. Dewi Phillips has suggested to me that the claim that this can be said is in tension with my earlier rejection of 'metaphysical underpinning'. I believe that this is a mistake and I hope that this chapter does something to show that it is. Wittgenstein remarked 'Not empiricism and yet realism in philosophy, that is the hardest thing.' (*Remarks on the Foundations of Mathematics*, VI, §23.) This chapter could be read as a contribution to the attempt to show that it is possible; but it *is* hard.

5. See Norman Malcolm, op. cit., p. 118.

6. See David Hume, *A Treatise of Human Nature*, Book 1, Part IV, Section II (p. 187 in L. A. Selby-Bigge (ed.)).

CHAPTER 6   THE MIND AND THE BODY

1. See, for example, E. S. Haldane and G. R. T. Ross (ed. and trans.), *The Philosophical Works of Descartes*, vol. II, p. 52.

2. Others have discussed these points, and others which arise here, much better than I could. See in particular Ilham Dilman, *Love and Human Separateness*, and Lars Hertzberg, 'The Indeterminacy of the Mental', *Proceedings of the Aristotelian Society*, Supplementary Volume LVII, (1983).

3. Not, it will be replied, in the same sense as we see the pimple on his nose; but once we keep this move clearly distinct from that which I am discussing it should be easy enough to deal with.

4. I am trying with these words to characterise a familiar philosophical view: that which is linked with the argument from analogy; but I am aware that the characterisation I have offered can be taken in ways that are not philosophically muddled. The power of the philosophical muddle is, of course, in part dependent on this kind of difficulty.

5. D. M. Armstrong and Norman Malcolm, *Consciousness and Causality* p. 105.

6. I discuss certain other influences on us here in my paper 'The Mind, the Brain and the Face', *Philosophy* 60 (1985).

7. For a fuller discussion of this point, in which it is linked in some detail with our ascriptions of actions to people, see my 'The Idea of a Person as He is in Himself', *Philosophical Investigations*, 11 (1988). The central point in all of this is an analogue in spatial terms of a point about what can be said to happen at a particular *time* which is of considerable importance in Wittgenstein's discussion of meaning, intending, and expecting. See, for example, *Philosophical Investigations*, §581–4.

8. Wittgenstein, *Philosophical Investigations*, §286.

9. For some remarks about the particular significance given to the face here see my 'The Mind, the Brain and the Face', *Philosophy* 60 (1985), esp. pp. 490–1.

10. *Philosophical Investigations*, §281, my italics. Next quote Zettel §134.

11. I do not mean to rule out the possibility of arguments of a quite different form here: arguments which suggest in a way which is 'ethically neutral' that the connections here 'go deep'. Perhaps, for example, the 'alternative ethical outlooks' are not real alternatives at all.

12. I will speak of certain contemporary materialist views as forms of 'dualism'. I do not do so *simply* in order to annoy those who defend such views, for I believe that there really are important affinities here. The materialist will, of course, be struck by different affinities. So far as I can see, Wittgenstein emerges as a dualist, and a Cartesian one at that, on Davidson's system of classification! See 'Mental Events', in his *Essays on Actions and Events*, p. 213.

13. Plato, *Phaedo* 64B. As I will argue, if this were *all* that he said would be on fairly familiar ground and not at all close to what I have called 'philosophical dualism'. In fact, it is by no means all that he says; but it is the only strand in his discussion that I will consider.

14. I am assuming that we can conceive of both unbalanced and clear-sighted instances of such a colouring of an individual's thought. Not everyone will agree with that. I should, incidentally, note that the recognition that there are no sharp lines here need not lead to either of the two 'colouring' processes I have mentioned.

15. It is worth noting how this kind of thing is linked with the particular physiological make-up of the human body. My (and perhaps Wittgenstein's) stress on the human form and human behaviour might create the impression that I do not take our internal constitution to be, in itself, important in our thought about each other. This would be seriously misleading since the force of the words 'in itself'

here is quite unclear. We need to think how my relationship with another would be altered by the fact that he did not bleed when cut, never had to sit down for a meal and whose circuits would be blown by a drink of water.

16.   If not beyond it. For is not 'the mind' as vulnerable to external, contingent forces as is 'the body'? So might not the contrast we need be between *me* on the one hand and 'the mind and body', or person, on the other?

17.   I derive comfort here from the good company I am in! Related difficulties, which I will not discuss at all, arise in connection with blindness: my discussion has been dominated by the visual.

18.   It might be said that to the extent that the character of the concern is changed precise comparisons of 'degree' of concern become impossible. While that is true there will be little difficulty in making *some* kind of comparison: we can consider, for example, the urgency with which they administer the anaesthetic. It might also be argued that if my general picture is accepted the words 'physical pain' in this paragraph ought to be placed in scare quotes; for my point will have to be that in so far as certain forms of concern become impossible we can no longer think of what the other is undergoing as physical pain in just the normal sense. There is, I think, something to that; though that is not to say that there ought to be many more entries beside 'pain' in the dictionary.

CHAPTER 7   HUMAN BEINGS AND SCIENCE

1.   Daniel C. Dennett, *The Intentional Stance*, p. 5. I will, incidentally, use the terms 'science', 'physical science' and 'basic science' as if I had a secure grasp of their precise meaning. I hope, and believe, that nothing that I say is dependent on possessing more than a very rough feel of the significance of these terms as they are used by those whose work I discuss. The same point applies, perhaps, to my use of the terms 'materialism' and 'physicalism' – though it will be important to my discussion that these terms should be understood in a way such that 'the material' or 'the physical' cannot be simply equated with 'the extended and tangible'.

2.   At least I suppose it creates a place for such questions. When I do feel convinced the argument which convinces me is something like this. It is conceivable that the physical sciences should develop to a point such that they provide predictions of the movements of human bodies. Now there is such a thing as a particular prediction being inconsistent with predictions, made in the normal way, of behaviour in the normal sense. If, then, the two systems of description and explanation generally produce predictions that are consistent it must be possible to say something about why they do. (Of course, that the scientific system generally produces correct predictions of the movements of human bodies will be one of our criteria for saying that we have got our science pretty well right; but

this does not defuse the question 'Why do the two systems fit together so well?' since that is not the *only* criterion for the adequacy of our science.)

3. For an explicit formulation of this contemporary Cartesianism in a very pure form see the opening remarks of D. M. Armstrong's contribution to D. M. Armstrong and Norman Malcolm, *Consciousness and Causality*, p. 105.

4. See, for example, Thomas Nagel, *The View From Nowhere*, ch. VII, sect. 1, and Geoffrey Madell, *Mind and Materialism*, pp. 137–45.

5. 'Eliminative materialism' is most notoriously defended today by Paul Churchland. See in particular his *Scientific Materialism and the Plasticity of Mind* and 'Eliminative Materialism and the Propositional Attitudes', *The Journal of Philosophy*, LXVIII (1981). Earlier defences are to be found in Paul Feyerabend, 'Mental Events and the Brain', *The Journal of Philosophy*, LX (1963) and Richard Rorty, 'Mind-Body Identity, Privacy, and Categories', *Review of Metaphysics*, 19 (1965–66).

6. I intend the characterisations offered in these three sentences to cover the various common forms of the 'identity theory'; including those varieties which are versions of 'functionalism'. Examples can be found in works, listed in the Bibliography, by the following authors: Smart, Armstrong, Lewis, Putnam and Davidson. A very clear presentation and defence of such a position is to be found in Peter Smith and O. R. Jones, *The Philosophy of Mind* chs 11–15. The differences between the positions defended by these writers, however significant they may be from certain points of view, are of little relevance to my purposes in this chapter.

7. Versions of this suggestion, commonly characterised as 'instrumentalism', are presented by Daniel Dennett, see especially *The Intentional Stance*; and K. V. Wilkes in 'Pragmatics in Science and Theory in Common Sense', *Inquiry*, 27 (1984) and 'Nemo Psychologus nisi Physiologus', *Inquiry*, 29 (1986).

8. I believe that something very like this argument is at work in the thought of many, perhaps most, of those who defend some form of 'physicalism'. Particularly clear examples can be found in David Lewis, 'An Argument for the Identity Theory', *The Journal of Philosophy*, LXIII (1966), Peter Smith and O. R. Jones, op. cit., ch. XI, and D. M. Armstrong, *A Materialist Theory of the Mind*, pp. 78–9. It will be said, no doubt with some justice, that any such simple summary is almost bound to be unfair to those who present arguments of this general form. I can only acknowledge that, and add that it seems clear to me that the popular hold of 'materialist' views can only be explained on the assumption that an argument of this rough form is at work at some level. I will, later in the chapter, consider some slightly more sophisticated versions of the argument.

9. This point is, in effect, one of the objections made by a number of others to the idea that 'folk psychology' is an hypothesis which we have developed in order to explain human behaviour. See R. A.

Sharpe, 'The Very Idea of a Folk Psychology', *Inquiry*, 30 (1987) and John Haldane, 'Understanding Folk', *Proceedings of the Aristotelian Society*, Supplementary Volume LXII (1988).

10. K. V. Wilkes, 'Functionalism, Psychology, and the Philosophy of Mind', *Philosophical Topics*, 12 (1981), p. 150. (See also her paper in *Inquiry* (1984) pp. 353–4.)

11. Smith and Jones, op. cit., p. 252.

12. See, for example, Richard Rorty, 'Mind-Body Identity, Privacy and Categories', *Review of Metaphysics*, 19 (1965–66) pp. 29–32. It is, of course, taken for granted by authors who use this analogy that that was *the* function of talk of 'demonic possession' and so that we can say, unproblematically, that the scientific story performs the *same* function better.

13. This, I take it, is the general form of Paul Churchland's response to this kind of objection. I do not, however, intend the whole of my presentation of this move to reflect Churchland's views. For Churchland suggests that *all* normal 'observation' language is theory laden. See *Scientific Realism and the Plasticity of Mind*, ch. 2 and sect. 12.

14. See, for example, Richard Rorty, op. cit., Paul Feyerabend, 'Materialism and the Mind-Body Problem', *Review of Metaphysics*, 17 (1963–64) and Paul Churchland, *Scientific Realism and the Plasticity of Mind*, esp. chs 2 and 4.

15. By 'human terms' I will mean 'terms that presuppose the other's humanity'; not, more broadly, 'terms that reflect *the speaker's* humanity'.

16. This leaves open the possibility of indeterminism. The point is that when prediction by appeal to movements of matter is not possible reference to our normal human ontology does not help to fill the gap.

    I should note here that my use of the distinction between 'characterisations in human terms' and 'characterisations in terms of movements of matter' is very crude. For one thing there is much that simply is not covered by this dichotomy as I have used it: for example, the elegance of a building, or the melody of a piece of music. For another, I have used the term 'characterisations in terms of movements of matter' to encompass the characterisations employed in 'basic science'; and I am quite certain that such a use reflects a distinctly anachronistic view of 'basic science'. I do not believe that this crudity in the way in which I have spoken affects my basic point here.

17. Paul Churchland, 'Folk Psychology and the Explanation of Behaviour', *Proceedings of the Aristotelian Society*, Supplementary Volume LXII (1988) p. 216.

18. Daniel C. Dennett, 'True Believers', in his *The Intentional Stance*, p. 15. See also the papers by K. V Wilkes, already cited, in *Inquiry*, 1984 and 1986. I should note that despite the criticisms I will make of Dennett and Wilkes there is a great deal in what they both say which seems to me helpful and absolutely right.

19. Op. cit., *Review of Metaphysics*, 19 (1965–66) p. 26. I am not, incidentally, certain that Rorty would accept 'plays the same role in our lives'

which I offer in my next sentence as an alternative to 'serves the same purpose'; but if he would not that is another instance of the consequentialist thinking which I am suggesting is at work here.

20. The slightness of the shift that has taken place is seen clearly in those materialist writers who insist that the dispute between materialism and traditional dualism is an *empirical* one. See, for example, Armstrong's remarks on pages 157–8 of D. M. Armstrong and Norman Malcolm, *Consciousness and Causality*.

21. Though *this* claim might also be made by some, such, perhaps, as Dennett, who would not be inclined to describe our language as 'theory laden' since they take it to be obvious that our current forms of description are, by the relevant criteria, better than any possible alternative.

22. 'Materialism and the Mind-Body Problem', *Review of Metaphysics*, 17 (1963–64), p. 57.

23. There are difficulties which arise from the question: which future states are assumed to be significant? Jokes and senses of humour will be 'causally efficacious', and so will pass this test of ontology, if amused smiles are assumed to be of significance. If this test of ontology is to do real work a particular *kind* of interest in the future must be taken for granted.

24. W. V. O. Quine, *World and Object*, p. 221. Quoted in Dennett, *The Intentional Stance*, p. 342.

25. I take the first formulation from Stephen Stich, *From Folk Psychology to Cognitive Science*, p. 224. The second is from Smith and Jones, *The Philosophy of Mind*, p. 233.

26. See the papers by Dennett and Wilkes referred to in note 7. Wilkes writes 'For even though fences are not natural kinds, they are real enough – *because* we can give them secure spatio-temporal coordinates' (*Inquiry*, 29 (1986) p. 178).

27. To see the pervasiveness of this picture compare the way in which Churchland speaks of us as 'epistemic engines' in Chapter 5 of *Scientific Realism and the Plasticity of Mind* with the following remark by Thomas Nagel, a philosopher of apparently very different outlook: 'In the employment of language we are ourselves a bit like measuring instruments, able to respond consistently to certain aspects of the world, and therefore able to talk about them' (*The View From Nowhere*, p. 109).

CHAPTER 8 HUMAN BEINGS AND HOMO SAPIENS

1. See Daniel C. Dennett, 'Conditions of Personhood' in his *Brainstorms*, and Kathleen V. Wilkes, *Real People*, pp. 120–2. I should perhaps note that, so far as I can see, Dennett moves freely between the two quite different ways of understanding the role of the attitude which I am distinguishing.

2. For more on this see Peter Winch, *'Eine Einstellung zur Seele'*, in his *Trying to Make Sense*. I should, incidentally, note that in view of the

central, if ambiguous, position which Dennett gives to our attitude towards others, it is not clear that I am in any conflict with him on the present point.

3. 'Human Personality', in George A. Panichas (ed.), *The Simone Weil Reader*, p. 314.

4. This and the next quotation come from Bentham's discussion of the killing and eating of animals. See *An Introduction to the Principles of Morals and Legislation*, p. 282.

5. For a discussion of this tendency in moral philosophy, and one which contains a nice sense of the ludicrousness of much contemporary moral philosophy, see W. Gass, 'The Case of the Obliging Stranger', *Philosophical Review* 66 (1957). Gass's concerns in that paper are, indeed, very close to mine in this section.

6. Michael Tooley, 'Abortion and Infanticide', in Peter Singer (ed.), *Applied Ethics*, pp. 60–3.

7. This remark needs hedging in ways which are outlined in Chapter 5.

8. The dead are, of course, also of central relevance in this context. A proper discussion of that would, however, raise issues which I want, so far as I can, to postpone till Part III.

9. It is, incidentally, as true of the terms for primary qualities as it is of those for secondary qualities. The difference between those lies in the depth of the divergence between two who differ in their ascriptions of qualities of each of these kinds. See Jonathan Bennett, *Locke Berkeley Hume*, sect. 20. Fortunately, my point here is, I think, only very slightly compromised if this is not accepted.

10. The significance of this way of putting the matter was, in part, brought home to me by Cora Diamond's wonderful discussion of these issues in her paper 'Eating Meat and Eating People', *Philosophy*, 53 (1978). The extent of my debt to this paper will be clear to anyone who knows it. My formulation at this point, and the general direction of the argument in this chapter, also owes a great deal to work by Peter Winch: perhaps in particular to a draft of his book on Simone Weil.

11. It is a noteworthy feature of the work of a number of those philosophers whom I am criticising here that they do, explicitly, see a place for these. See, in particular, Peter Singer, *Animal Liberation*, pp. 10–15. This is connected with a way in which philosophers such as Singer take those who deny that animals feel pain far too seriously: they *argue* with them.

12. 'Conditions of Personhood', in *Brainstorms*, p. 267. Dennett speaks in this passage as if he is appealing to a notion of 'personhood' which most of us confidently employ in our daily lives. I rather hope that he is under an illusion about that. To the extent that people do speak in this way – and, in particular, as Dennett does in the final sentence – I suspect that, as with the term 'mind', popular usage has been moulded by philosophical confusion; but I will not dwell on that as it is the confusion itself that concerns me here.

13. Anthony Kenny (trans., and ed.), *Descartes: Philosophical Letters*, p. 244.
14. Jeremy Bentham, *An Introduction to the Principles of Morals and Legislation*, pp. 282–3.
15. Peter Singer (ed.), *In Defence of Animals*, p. 4. The following remarks by Regan are from the same volume, pp. 22–3.
16. Leaving herself, so far as I can see, with no way of objecting to the proposal that we should ensure that *this* foetus does *not* develop into such a being. See *Real People*, ch. 2.
17. See, for example, his 'Abortion and Infanticide', in Peter Singer (ed.), *Applied Ethics*.

CHAPTER 9   THE IDENTITY OF HUMAN BEINGS

1. John Locke, *An Essay Concerning Human Understanding*, Book Two, ch. xxvii.
2. A. Quinton, 'The Soul', *The Journal of Philosophy*, 59 (1962) p. 402. Exactly the same ways of thinking are, I believe, central to Parfit's work on personal identity; see *Reasons and Persons*, Part III, especially sect. 99. I place Quinton at the centre of my discussion since his commitment to this picture is more clearly articulated than is Parfit's.
3. It is, at this point, sometimes said that there is in practice always an underlying stability in an individual's psychological characteristics which runs right through his life. The question, however, is: how is the persistence of such characteristics related to my commitment to the individual?
4. Bernard Williams, 'Are persons bodies?', in his *Problems of the Self*, p. 81. There is a great deal in what Williams says on these issues which seems to me to be very helpful. I do, however, believe that there is something seriously wrong with his presentation here and that this confusion may reflect assumptions which he shares with those he is criticising.
5. People and, curiously, cars *have* bodies. I am not sure about cows. If there is 'some body' at the bottom of the garden it is certainly not a live human being, nor is it a fridge, that is there. If there is 'somebody' there it is, of course, very different. While I suspect that there is much, perhaps of considerable philosophical interest, to be learned from reflection on such features of our linguistic practice I will not pursue this further here.
6. I am using the terms 'same mind' and 'same body' in what I *hope* is close to the colloquial way. I am rather afraid that years of philosophical work in this area may have hopelessly corrupted my ear for normal nuance here; but, as I have stressed, I do not take my point here to turn on normal nuance.
7. See, for example, Geoffrey Madell, *The Identity of the Self*, ch. 1, sect. 3 and ch. 5, sect. 4; also, R. G. Swinburne, 'Personal Identity', *Proceedings of the Aristotelian Society*, 74 (1973–74) p. 246.

CHAPTER 10   THE IRREPLACEABILITY OF PERSONS

1. G. Vlastos, 'The Individual as an Object of Love in Plato', in his *Platonic Studies*, p. 31.
2. Martha Nussbaum, *The Fragility of Goodness*, pp. 166–7.
3. Plato, *Symposium*, 221c–d.
4. My aim here is not to defend a particular account of what *is* to be found in the *Symposium*. I should note that I found the two discussions of it to which I have referred extremely interesting and helpful.
5. Martha Nussbaum, op. cit., p. 173.
6. Josiah Royce, *The Conception of Immortality* pp. 38–9. Next quote p. 40.
7. Stephen R. L. Clark, *The Mysteries of Religion* , pp. 207–9.
8. I suspect that we do, in practice, fall into what I have called 'woolly wishful thinking' here at least in part because we feel that the special place we give to certain individuals requires that we find special characteristics in them. What I am suggesting is a philosophical confusion may, then, have close links of one kind or another with ways of thinking which, at some level, are fairly widespread.
9. I am using the term 'personality' in a way such that it makes sense to suppose that two people might have 'the same personality'. Remarks towards the end of this chapter will suggest that there is need for caution here. I develop closely related points more fully in my paper 'Commitment to Persons', in D. Z. Phillips and Peter Winch (eds), *Wittgenstein: Attention to Particulars*.
10. This may be unfair to Royce who offers a fairly detailed story at this point, cf. pp. 66–76. It is, however, far from clear, to me at any rate, just how this story is to be taken.
11. For some doubts about whether we even understand the general thesis see my paper 'The Idea of a Person as He is in Himself', *Philosophical Investigations*, 11 (1988).
12. I take it that any description which necessarily individuates involves an implicit use of indexicals. I suspect, incidentally, that this raises one of a range of worries one might have about the idea that a nonspatial object, such as an immaterial soul, could either be a possible object of love or itself love another. I will not, however, try to develop this.
13. Howard Mounce has suggested to me that the point should be put in terms of the distinction between the cause and the object of an emotion: the *person* is the object of my love, and the history is the cause. However, to say that the person is the 'object' is not yet to answer a question that we might formulate in this way: what is the characterisation of her which is significant for my love? The force of that question can, perhaps, be made clear by noting that her past does *not* simply play the role of 'cause' of my love; as we can see by considering cases in which my feelings for someone are based on a misconception about her past.

14. Paul Standish has suggested to me that what I say needs to be supplemented by a discussion of the way in which the *future* enters into my conception of this individual. As he expressed the point in one example: 'My wife is the woman I will spend my life with.' This seems to me to be interesting and important. It is not, however, a *simple* analogue of the point about the past since the change in tense brings other differences with it; and I cannot, at the moment, see how to speak about it.

15. See Peter Winch, *'Eine Einstellung zur Seele'*, in his *Trying to Make Sense*, pp. 140–53, for a good discussion of this kind of point. While I think that the way I, following Winch, have put it is clearly the right way to put it, my next sentence captures what I need in a way which does not turn on that particular formulation.

16. I say that this is clear. That is not to say that philosophers have always been clear about it; the way in which Parfit tries to do justice to the notion of a 'shared history' on page 295 of his book shows, I believe, that this is not so; but, of course, Parfit has travelled a long way before he gets to this issue. One's thinking about personal identity is almost bound to be coloured by the cases which, for whatever reason, one is inclined to place at the centre of the discussion. I assume that there are points at which, in a similar way, I have, as a result of my choice of starting point, missed what is blindingly obvious to others.

17. Dallas type solutions, that is to say ones which take the form of discovering that the other did not really die after all, are, of course, irrelevant here. I should, perhaps, also stress here that what I mean by a 'solution' is not simply 'something that enables me to carry on'. A relationship with another person might be a 'solution' in *that* sense without its being at all the case that it is just as if nothing has happened.

18. This reversal of ideas is closely linked with others which I have mentioned earlier. See Chapter 6 section (iv), Chapter 8 section (iii), and Chapter 9 section (iii). In my paper 'Commitment to Persons' I defend what may be a slightly stronger version of this suggestion: it is not that my understanding of who this is is dependent on my recognition of them as possessing certain psychological characteristics; rather, my recognition of them as possessing these characteristics is dependent on my understanding of who this is.

CHAPTER 11   PERSONAL IDENTITY AND THE FIRST PERSON

1. For a recent discussion which gives this idea a central place see Geoffrey Madell, *The Identity of the Self*. I should note that Madell would not endorse all of the suggestions I criticise in this section.

2. Madell, op. cit., p. 66. Sydney Shoemaker, 'Persons and their pasts' in his *Identity, Cause and Mind*, p. 21. As I will suggest in a moment, Shoemaker's argument for this claim sits very uneasily with the use to which Madell puts it. As a result of this, it is not clear to what

extent my objections should be read as objections to Shoemaker's views.

3. Wittgenstein, *Philosophical Investigations*, §404. The remark is within quotation marks in the text. It is clear, however, that Wittgenstein takes there to be something correct in it.

4. Is the illusion that there is some deep sense in which I cannot be mistaken about who I am tied up with this? We recognise that no discovery of further facts about this individual could transform the concern that I feel about this – my – pain: no further information about who this is could lead me, say, to care less about the pain. We take it that this must be because I already, inevitably, have all the relevant information. While that much is right as it stands, the reason that further information is irrelevant is not, as we are inclined to suppose, that I have immediate and infallible knowledge of who this is, but, rather, that I *do not care* who it is.

5. Thomas Nagel, *The View from Nowhere*, p. 224.

6. I am not completely certain exactly how this point is connected with Nagel's remark. What would Nagel say about the case in which the other feels no terror in the face of death?

CHAPTER 12   SELF AND NO-SELF

1. The *Visuddhimagga*. The next passage is from the *Cila Mara*. Both are quoted in Derek Parfit, *Reasons and Persons*, pp. 502–3.

2. David Hume, *A Treatise of Human Nature*, Book I, pt IV, sect. VI.

3. Steven Collins, 'Buddhism in Recent British Philosophy and Theology', *Religious Studies*, 21 (1985) p. 492. I am not qualified to conjecture how much what I will say has to do with Buddhism. It does, I think, have something to do with the way the anatta doctrine is understood by some in the West; and also with the form of 'no-self' view recently defended by Derek Parfit.

4. From the *Milina Panha*. Quoted in Parfit, op. cit., p. 502.

5. Derek Parfit explores ideas of this form in Part III of *Reasons and Persons*.

6. Steven Collins, *Selfless Persons*, p. 104.

7. Steven Collins, 'Buddhism in Recent British Philosophy and Theology', p. 487. See T. Nagel, *The Possibility of Altruism*, p. 18. In Nagel's book, incidentally, the search for this kind of grounding is strongly (if ambiguously) linked with giving priority to the first person and to the present tense.

8. See Derek Parfit, op. cit., p. 227–8.

9. For a limited defence of this view of Parfit's work see my critical notice of *Reasons and Persons*, *Philosophical Investigations*, 10 (1987).

CHAPTER 13   PERSONS AND THE PERSONAL

1. I am grateful to Steven Collins for drawing my attention to this popular Buddhist saying. The image is to be found, perhaps among

other places, in the *Suttanipata* and the *Karaniya Metta Sutta*. (See Nathan Katz, *Buddhist Images of Human Perfection*, p. 266.)

2. My argument has the slightly embarrassing feature of tying these injunctions to the wrong religions. This is what lies behind my assumption that if things were taken deeper the picture would be rather different.

3. The notion of a relationship in this sense has been much less central to my whole discussion than it would have been had my aim been to present a completely balanced picture. What has concerned me more, however, has been to highlight certain dimensions of our thought which I think are often overlooked or badly misunderstood.

4. But see Derek Parfit, *Reasons and Persons*, Part IV. There is much here which would suggest that Parfit would not find what I have said as obvious as I do. There are, I suspect, a number of intriguing connections between utilitarianism and optimism. For some further remarks which bear on this issue see my critical notice of Parfit's book.

5. Taken from the transcript of recordings made of discussions at the Convivium held at Mahabaleshwar in 1987.

6. In my paper 'Commitment to Persons' I stress the link between them and, among other things, try to indicate how these points might lead us to a way of understanding the idea of an 'unchanging core' to a person which is not vulnerable to the criticisms raised in this book.

7. Unless, of course, as commonly happens, the extended, tangible being is viewed as never having been anything other than, so to speak, an animated corpse.

8. I should note that the phrase 'parent's concern' as I use it here must also cover the less attractive aspects of our thought about, and treatment of, those we are close to. There are, for example, forms of meanness which we reserve for those we care for. I do not rule out the possibility of a way of thinking about these issues which would tie talk of 'recognition' to forms of response to others which we find admirable. Thus, Simone Weil writes 'Belief in the existence of other human beings is *love*' (*Gravity and Grace*, p. 56); but nothing that I have said could justify that link.

   The relationship between love, on the one hand, and altruism, or acting from a sense of duty, on the other, is of central importance in all of this in a way which I have not managed to make completely clear. My recognition of the importance of this theme is largely due to unpublished work by Michael McGhee.

9. Michael McGhee has suggested to me the following way of putting the point: in terms of the Buddhist injunction, it happens that I am only able to have this care under special conditions; and the injunction suggests that I can bring it about that concern does not depend upon such special conditions and can be consequently widened.

10. Simone Weil writes: 'To love a stranger as oneself implies the reverse: to love oneself as a stranger' (*Gravity and Grace*, p. 55). It,

perhaps, hardly needs saying that there is plenty of scope for misunderstanding of a self-indulgent form here. Still, I think it is worth saying since ideas can be too readily discarded when not kept clearly distinct from possible corruptions which they may undergo.

11. Thomas Nagel, *The View From Nowhere*, p. 217. Next quote p. 216.

12. Parfit's defence of the claim that what he calls 'common sense morality' is self-defeating rests on a failure to grasp this point; at least, so I argue in my critical notice of his book. See *Reasons and Persons*, ch. 4.

13. Simone Weil, *Waiting on God*, p. 33.

14. I take it the last sentence of this is correct. Nagel writes of his own coming into existence: 'In the objective flow of the cosmos this subjectively (to me!) stupendous event produces hardly a ripple' (op. cit., p. 55). Given that he is speaking of '*My* coming into existence' rather than 'TN's coming into existence' the 'hardly' is clearly wrong.

15. I owe this last phrase, which seems to me very helpful here, to Michael McGhee.

16. Daniel C. Dennett, *The Intentional Stance*, p. 5.

17. *The View From Nowhere*, pp. 110–11.

18. I say 'in part' since in so far as I have a relationship with another I will think it in place to *reason* with her about some aspects of her future behaviour. To that extent my relationship to her future behaviour takes on the form which my relationship to my own future behaviour characteristically has. While this point is very relevant to my discussion in this paragraph it does not incline me to qualify the main suggestion I am making here.

19. Part III of Parfit's *Reasons and Persons*, is, in part, an attempt to think through the implications of the impersonal approach.

20. I find it difficult to keep a clear hold on the issues here as the discussion has moved up one level. We are concerned, not directly with the other's 'first level' needs, but with his feelings about my response to those needs. The question is: what role should those feelings play in determining the character of my response?

POSTSCRIPT: ETHICS AND METAPHYSICS

1. My use of the terms 'passive recognition' and 'response' in this sentence are, I suspect, themselves a reflection of the empiricist tradition in exactly the same way.

2. I am concerned here with the idea of what is, for want of a better phrase, '*morally* unthinkable'. To hold that something is 'morally unthinkable' is not, I take it, to hold that there could not be a society in which it is thought; but there are difficulties here which I do not want to go into.

3. *The View From Nowhere*, p. 107. Nagel is speaking here of the suggestion that, as he puts it, '*nothing* in my mind determines the infinite application of any of my concepts'. I think it is clear, how-

ever, that he would say the same of that dimension of Wittgenstein's thought which has been central to my discussion.

4. See, for example, Bernard Williams, 'Wittgenstein and Idealism', in his *Moral Luck*. For a clear demonstration of straightforward mistakes in Williams' discussion see Peter Winch, '*Im Anfang war die Tat*' in his *Trying to Make Sense*.

5. Nagel would object to my confidence here. I am happy, then, to express my point by saying that I am aware of no attempt to fill out the picture which looks as though it might succeed.

6. Thus, I am very unsure to what extent we should say that Hume, who saw so much so clearly here, was philosophically confused in drawing the conclusions that he did. I am thinking here primarily of his treatment, in Book I of the *Treatise*, of causal inference and the continued and distinct existence of bodies.

Bibliography

Armstrong, D. M., *A Materialist Theory of the Mind* (London: Routledge & Kegan Paul, 1968).

Armstrong, D. M., and Norman Malcolm, *Consciousness and Causality* (Oxford: Blackwell, 1984).

Bennett, Jonathan, *Locke Berkeley Hume: Central Themes* (Oxford: Clarendon Press, 1971).

Bentham, Jeremy, *An Introduction to the Principles of Morals and Legislation* (London: The Athlone Press, 1970).

Churchland, P. M., *Scientific Materialism and the Plasticity of Mind* (Cambridge: Cambridge University Press, 1979).

Churchland, P. M., 'Eliminative Materialism and the Propositional Attitudes', *The Journal of Philosophy*, LXXVIII (1981) 67–90.

Churchland, P. M., *Matter and Consciousness* (Cambridge, Mass.: MIT Press, 1984).

Churchland, P. M., 'Folk Psychology and the Explanation of Human Behaviour', *Proceedings of the Aristotelian Society*, Supplementary Volume LXII (1988) 209–21.

Clark, Stephen R. L., *The Mysteries of Religion* (Oxford: Blackwell, 1986).

Cockburn, David, 'The Mind, the Brain and the Face', *Philosophy*, 60 (1985) 477–93.

Cockburn, David, 'The Problem of the Past', *The Philosophical Quarterly*, 37 (1987) 54–77.

Cockburn, David, Critical Notice of Derek Parfit *Reasons and Persons*, *Philosophical Investigations*, 10 (1987) 54–72.

Cockburn, David, 'The Idea of a Person as He is in Himself', *Philosophical Investigations*, 11 (1988) 13–27.

Cockburn, David, 'Commitment to Persons', in D.Z. Phillips and Peter Winch (eds), *Wittgenstein: Attention to Particulars* (Macmillan, 1989).

Collins, Steven, *Selfless Persons* (Cambridge University Press, 1982).

Collins, Steven, 'Buddhism in Recent British Philosophy and Theology', *Religious Studies*, 21 (1985) 475–93.

Cook, John, 'Human Beings' in Peter Winch (ed.), *Studies in the Philosophy of Wittgenstein* (London: Routledge & Kegan Paul, 1989).

Davidson, Donald, *Essays on Actions and Events* (Oxford: Clarendon Press, 1980).

Dennett, Daniel C., *Brainstorms* (Montgomery, Vermont: Bradford Books, 1978).

Dennett, Daniel C., *The Intentional Stance* (Cambridge, Mass.: MIT Press, 1987).

Descartes, René, *Descartes: Philosophical Letters*, trans. and ed. Anthony Kenny (Oxford: Clarendon Press, 1970).

Descartes, René, *Philosophical Works*, trans. and ed. E.S. Haldane and G.R.T. Ross (Cambridge University Press, 1967).

Diamond, Cora, 'Eating Meat and Eating People', *Philosophy*, 53 (1978) 465–79.

Diamond, Cora, 'Anything But Argument', *Philosophical Investigations*, 5 (1982) 23–41.

Dilman, Ilham, *Love and Human Separateness* (Oxford: Blackwell, 1987).

Dummett, Michael, *Frege, Philosophy of Language* (London: Duckworth, 1973).

Feyerabend, Paul, 'Materialism and the Mind-Body Problem', *Review of Metaphysics* 17 (1963–64) 49–66.

Feyerabend, Paul, 'Mental Events and the Brain', *Journal of Philosophy*, LX (1963) 295–6.

Fodor, Jerry A., *Representations* (Cambridge, Mass.: MIT Press, 1987).

Fodor, Jerry, A., *Psychosemantics* (Cambridge, Mass.: MIT Press, 1981).

Gass, William H., 'The Case of the Obliging Stranger', *Philosophical Review*, 66 (1957) 193–204.

Haldane, John, 'Understanding Folk', *Proceedings of the Aristotelian Society*, Supplementary Volume LXII (1988) 223–54.

Hertzberg, Lars, 'The Indeterminacy of the Mental', *Proceedings of the Aristotelian Society*, Supplementary Volume LVII (1983) 91–109.

Hume, David, *A Treatise of Human Nature* (1739), ed. L.A. Selby-Bigge (Oxford: Clarendon Press, 1978).

Katz, Nathan, *Buddhist Images of Human Perfection* (Delhi: Molital Banarsidass, 1982).

Lewis, David, 'An Argument for the Identity Theory', *Journal of Philosophy*, LXIII (1966) 17–25.

Lewis, David, 'Psychophysical and Theoretical Identifications', *Australasian Journal of Philosophy*, 50 (1972) 249–58.

Locke, John, *An Essay Concerning Human Understanding*, ed. A. C. Fraser (London: Constable, 1959).

Madell, Geoffrey, *The Identity of the Self* (Edinburgh University Press, 1981).

Madell, Geoffrey, *Mind and Materialism* (Edinburgh University Press, 1988).

Malcolm, Norman, *Knowledge and Certainty* (Cornell University Press, 1963).

McGhee, Michael, 'In Praise of Mindfulness', *Religious Studies*, 24 (1988) 65–89.

Nagel, Thomas, *The Possibility of Altruism* (Princeton University Press, 1970).

Nagel, Thomas, *The View From Nowhere* (Oxford University Press, 1986).

Nussbaum, Martha C., *The Fragility of Goodness* (Cambridge University Press, 1986).

Parfit, Derek, *Reasons and Persons* (Oxford: Clarendon Press, 1984).

Phillips, D. Z., 'My Neighbour and My Neighbours', *Philosophical Investigations*, 12 (1989) 112–33.

Plato, *Phaedo*, in *The Last Days of Socrates* (Penguin Classics, 1969).

Plato, *Symposium* (Penguin Classics, 1952).

Prichard, H. A., *Moral Obligation* (Oxford: Clarendon Press, 1949).

Putnam, Hilary, *Mind, Language and Reality* (Cambridge University Press, 1975).

Quinton, Anthony, 'The Soul', *The Journal of Philosophy*, LIX (1962) 363–409.

Quine, W. V. O., *Word and Object* (Cambridge, Mass.: MIT Press, 1960).

Rorty, Richard, 'Mind-Body Identity, Privacy, and Categories', *Review of Metaphysics*, 19 (1965–66) 24–54.

Royce, Josiah, *The Conception of Immortality* (London: Constable, 1906).

Sartre, Jean-Paul, *Being and Nothingness*, trans. Hazel E. Barnes (London: Methuen, 1969).

Sharpe, R. A., 'The Very Idea of a Folk Psychology', *Inquiry*, 30 (1987) 381–93.

Shoemaker, Sydney, 'Persons and their pasts', in his *Identity, Cause, and Mind* (Cambridge University Press, 1984).

Singer, Peter, *Animal Liberation* (New York: Avon, 1978).

Singer, Peter, (ed.), *In Defence of Animals* (Oxford: Blackwell, 1985).

Singer, Peter, (ed.), *Applied Ethics* (Oxford University Press, 1986).

Smart, J. J. C., 'Sensations and Brain Processes', *Philosophical Review*, 68 (1959) 141–56.

Smith, Peter, and O. R. Jones, *The Philosophy of Mind* (Cambridge University Press, 1986).

Stevenson, Ian, *Twenty Cases Suggestive of Reincarnation* (Charlottesville: University Press of Virginia, 1974).

Stich, Stephen, *From Folk Psychology to Cognitive Science* (Cambridge, Mass.: MIT Press, 1983).

Strawson, P. F., 'Freedom and Resentment' in P.F. Strawson (ed.), *Studies in the Philosophy of Thought and Action* (Oxford University Press, 1968).

Swinburne, R. G., 'Personal Identity', *Proceedings of the Aristotelian Society*, LXXV (1974–75) 231–47.

Tooley, Michael, 'Abortion and Infanticide', in Peter Singer (ed.), *Applied Ethics* (Oxford University Press, 1986).

Vlastos, G. 'The Individual as an Object of Love in Plato', in his *Platonic Studies* (Princeton University Press, 1981).

Weil, Simone, *Waiting on God*, trans. Emma Craufurd (London: Routledge & Kegan Paul, 1951).

Weil, Simone, *Gravity and Grace*, trans. Emma Craufurd (London: Routledge & Kegan Paul, 1963).

Weil, Simone, *The Simone Weil Reader*, ed. George A. Panichas (New York: Moyer Bell, 1977).

Wilkes, K. V., 'Functionalism, Psychology, and the Philosophy of Mind', *Philosophical Topics*, 12 (1981) 147–67.

Wilkes, K. V., 'Pragmatics in Science and Theory in Common Sense', *Inquiry*, 27 (1984) 339–61.

Wilkes, K. V., 'Nemo Psychologus nisi Physiologus', *Inquiry*, 29 (1986) 169–85.

Wilkes, Kathleen V., *Real People* (Oxford: Clarendon Press, 1988).

Williams, Bernard, *Problems of the Self* (Cambridge University Press, 1973).

Williams, Bernard, *Moral Luck* (Cambridge University Press, 1981).

Winch, Peter, *Ethics and Action* (London: Routledge & Kegan Paul, 1972).

Winch, Peter, *Trying to Make Sense* (Oxford: Blackwell, 1987).

Winch, Peter, *Simone Weil* (Cambridge University Press, 1989).

Wittgenstein, Ludwig, *Philosophical Investigations*, eds G.E.M. Anscombe and R. Rhees, trans. G.E.M. Anscombe (Oxford: Blackwell, 1968).

Wittgenstein, Ludwig, *Remarks on the Foundations of Mathematics*, eds G. H. von Wright, R. Rhees and G. E. M. Anscombe, trans. G. E. M. Anscombe (Oxford: Blackwell, 1978).

Wittgenstein, Ludwig, *Zettel*, eds G. E. M. Anscombe and G. H. von Wright, trans. G. E. M. Anscombe (Oxford: Blackwell 1967).

Wright, Crispin, 'Realism, Truth-Value Links, Other Minds and the Past', *Ratio* 22 (1980) 112–32.

Index